*Libre Acceso*

SUNY series in Latin American and Iberian Thought and Culture

---

Jorge J. E. Gracia and Rosemary Geisdorfer Feal, editors

# *Libre Acceso*

## Latin American Literature and Film through Disability Studies

Edited by

Susan Antebi and Beth E. Jörgensen

SUNY PRESS

Published by State University of New York Press, Albany



Printed in the United States of America



For information, contact State University of New York Press, Albany, NY
www.sunypress.edu

Production, Diane Ganeles
Marketing, Anne M. Valentine

**Library of Congress Cataloging-in-Publication Data**

*Libre acceso* : Latin American literature and film through disability studies / edited by Susan Antebi and Beth E. Jörgensen.
pages cm. — (SUNY series in Latin American and Iberian thought and culture)
Includes bibliographical references and index.
ISBN 978-1-4384-5967-7 (hc : alk. paper)—978-1-4384-5968-4 (pb : alk. paper)
ISBN 978-1-4384-5969-1 (e-book)
1. Spanish American literature—History and criticism. 2. People with disabilities in literature. 3. Motion pictures—Latin America. 4. People with disabilities in motion pictures. 5. Human body in literature. I. Antebi, Susan, editor. II. Jörgensen, Beth Ellen, editor.

PQ7081.L456 2016
860.9'98—dc23 2015011059

10 9 8 7 6 5 4 3 2 1

# Contents

## Part IV
## Imagining Other Worlds

# Illustrations

# Acknowledgments

This book is the result of a collaborative project sustained over several years, through dialogues between the editors, contributors, and other scholars and activists from Latin America, Canada, and the United States. The idea for *Libre Acceso*, as a volume that would feature recent scholarship on Latin American literature and film informed by disability studies perspectives, stemmed from our awareness of the current lack of work of this kind. Given the recent increase in disability studies scholarship on Anglo-American literature and film, and the growing disability awareness, activism, and scholarship in many Latin American countries, the need to facilitate and highlight the roles of disability and disability studies in Latin American literary and filmic production seemed particularly urgent.

We are grateful to our many interlocutors who have engaged with us throughout this project, including Benjamin Mayer Foulkes and Beatriz Miranda, of the 17 Instituto de Estudios Críticos, in Mexico City, as well as Patricia Brogna and many other participants at the Institute's 2013 disability studies colloquium. Federico Fleischmann, Carlos Ríos Espinosa, Karla Calcáneo, and Ernesto Rosas Barrientos were generous in granting interviews to Beth Jörgensen in June 2011, and Elena Poniatowska was instrumental in making those interviews possible. We also wish to thank our colleagues and students at the University of Toronto and the University of Rochester, including Tanya Titchkosky, Rod Michalko, Anne Mcguire, Eliza Chandler, and the members of the Disability Studies Cluster at the University of Rochester.

Support for some parts of the project was provided by the University of Toronto Jackman Humanities Institute, the Connaught Fund, and the Office of the Deans of the College at the University of Rochester. We also wish to thank our editor Beth Bouloukos and assisting staff at the State University of New York Press for helping to bring our work to fruition, and to the careful and generous readings of our two external reviewers.

# Introduction

## *A Latin American Context for Disability Studies*

Susan Antebi
Beth E. Jörgensen

"Let's achieve a miracle" (Logremos un milagro) was the slogan of the first Telethon in Chile, a charity fund-raiser for the rehabilitation of children with disabilities. "La Teletón," founded by Mario Kreutzberger[1] in 1978, was so successful that its name and structure have been replicated through an umbrella organization operating in twelve different Latin American countries.[2] Images of children equipped with state-of-the-art rehabilitation devices for learning how to walk thus came to appear regularly on television screens throughout the region, accompanied by slogans of hope for the future, love, and solidarity, along with pleas for donations by media celebrities. As in the case of similar televised fund-raisers in the United States and elsewhere, Teletón's use of children with disabilities to evoke the public's compassion—and to open its wallets—exploits the children in question, legitimates the activity of staring at them, and equates disability with a tragedy to be erased or overcome.[3] Latin American disability rights activists and scholars have similarly criticized the Teletón model, advocating for human rights and social justice rather than voyeurism and charity, particularly in the wake of the 2006 United Nations' Convention on the Rights of Persons with Disabilities, which has been signed by most Latin American countries.

Yet the specificity of the Latin American Teletón's beginnings and its slogan of miracle making also suggest something further about the role of disability representation in contemporary Latin American societies. The

1978 reference to the "miracle" of fund-raising and rehabilitation echoes Milton Friedman's description of Chile's "economic miracle," in the era of Pinochet. In the years following the 1973 military coup, a period during which the Pinochet regime murdered thousands of political dissidents, the privatization of state-run industries and the massive reduction of public spending would come to define Chile's economy in a global context, through increased opportunities for foreign investors and a widening gap between the wealthiest and the poorest population sectors. For proponents of neoliberal economics the metaphor of a miracle defined Chile as a potentially exportable model of economic success in the region. Similarly, Chile's Teletón miracle became the basis for the disability charity enterprise throughout Latin America. Most criticism of Teletón in Mexico, Chile, and other Latin American countries has tended to focus on the issue of economic exploitation, as privately run television stations are said to benefit from the tax write-offs made possible by public charitable giving, while transnational corporations reap the rewards of Teletón advertising spots, creating a positive association between their products and compassion for disabled children. In Mexico, the very substantial channeling of public funds by the federal and state governments into the private Teletón enterprise has also been the target of criticism.[4] In a contemporary global and Latin American cultural scene increasingly defined by visual media and the rapid circulation of literal and symbolic capital, the miracle metaphor falls flat for many consumers, and yet for large sectors continues to generate interest, affect, and economic participation.

Disability and its representations in Latin America are thus increasingly marked by public critique of socioeconomic inequality, uneasy boundaries between public and private sectors, and by profoundly contradictory messages. Market-driven initiatives such as Teletón have increased the visibility of disabled people[5]—albeit in troubling ways—while growing national and international engagement with disability as a human rights issue has contributed to public awareness regarding disability rights in a more positive sense. Yet it is nonetheless true that stigma and exclusion continue to define the status of many disabled people in the region, in contrast to both Teletón's promise of a miracle, and recent legislation that purports to eliminate discrimination on the basis of disability.

We begin *Libre Acceso: Latin American Literature and Film through Disability Studies* with the miracle metaphor of the Chilean economy and of Teletón as a means to underscore the complex conditions impacting the politics and representation of disability in Latin American contexts. Teletón's use of disability tends to reinforce the familiar stigma of physical disability as a personal tragedy to be overcome. Yet the overarching metaphoric role of the miracle also reveals disability and its extended web of meanings as central to the broader notions of neoliberal economics, national transformation, and the politics of inequality. Although this particular cultural scene is just one of many possible, varied examples with which one might choose to illustrate disability representation in the region, it effectively points to a tension we wish to highlight in this volume, between disability defined through individual experience, and through a more biopolitically oriented emphasis on populations or collectives.

In this book, we focus on selected Latin American literary and filmic representations of disability, grounding our approaches at meeting points between the fields of disability studies and Latin American literary and cultural studies. The broader context for the volume includes the social, legal, and cultural changes around disability that have been occurring in Latin America over the course of the past fifteen to twenty years, as documented in disability studies scholarship by Latin American academics. The changing constructions and roles of disability make a regionally informed disability studies not only relevant but urgently needed in order for research in the humanities to keep pace with a shifting ideological landscape. Disabled people in Latin America have traditionally been drastically marginalized, remaining isolated and hidden from view in the family home or less often relegated to institutions,[6] or publicly visible only in the activity of begging on the streets.[7] In the context of late twentieth and early twenty-first century disability activism and reevaluation of the meanings of disability, acquiescence to these long-standing discriminatory practices is being vigorously challenged.

Evidence of a growing paradigm shift can be seen in Mexico's initiative in proposing the drafting of the United Nations Convention on the Rights of Persons with Disabilities in 2007, and the impressive number of Latin American nations who are now signatories of the Convention.[8] Disability rights activism assumes different forms in different national contexts, but it is on the rise throughout the region. According to the prominent Mexican activist Federico Fleischmann, in 2011 Mexico had more than one hundred and sixty organizations that were active in the movement, and many of them were created by and for people with disabilities. The disability rights activist and author James Charlton points to the specific case of Nicaragua, where the Organization of Disabled Revolutionaries was formed in the early 1980s as a result of the imperative to respond to the needs of those who were disabled by war injuries during Nicaragua's lengthy civil conflict (142–143).[9] In Chile, which ratified the U.N. Convention in 2008, the February 27, 2010, earthquake and tsunami cast a harsh light on the inadequacy of stipulated preparations to assist those with physical disabilities during natural disasters and it prompted criticism of the government's response by such groups as Rehabilitation International and the U.N. Committee on the Rights of Persons with Disabilities.[10]

## Disability Studies in the Latin American Context

As an academic discipline, disability studies in Latin America can trace its origins to sources including local activism, legislation and policy analysis, and international dialogue in the fields of education and psychology among others. In addition, disability studies scholarship in the region has developed in relation to academic and activist models from the United Kingdom, the United States and Canada, as well as Spain.[11] Such models, which together have produced the interdisciplinary field of disability studies now increasingly present in universities in the Global North, may in turn be traced to the rise of disability rights movements in several locales in the 1970s and 1980s, with developments in the United Kingdom often leading the way.[12] As disabled people saw civil rights activism for racial equality in the United States and women's movements in many nations gain strength, they soon perceived the transformative potential of speaking and acting on their own behalf against stigmatization and discrimination, and for equal rights, access and full inclusion in society. In a manner parallel to the emergence of African American or Africana studies and women's and gender studies, disability studies in the academy developed from an activist base, and it retains an important ethical and social justice dimension as well as a commitment to interdisciplinarity. Apropos of this book, the study of literature and film was transformed for many scholars, particularly in the United States and the United Kingdom, by the questions that the new disability studies theories raised for understanding our cultural representations of disability, illness, and debility, and new ways of reading both canonical and emerging texts soon made their appearance.

In our research experience in Latin America to date, disability studies and related scholarship tends to appear in the social sciences, more than in the demonstrably rich field of literary discourse. The recent work of such Latin American scholars as Patricia Brogna, Miguel Ángel Vite Pérez, Manuel Aramayo Zamora, Carolina Ferrante, and many others working in a variety of disciplines and in countries throughout the region demonstrates growing interest in disability studies and related issues, particularly in the context of debates on human rights, social justice and economic inequality. Aramayo Zamora's 2010 edited volume *Hablemos de la discapacidad en la diversidad* (Let's talk about disability in diversity), highlights the Venezuelan context, addresses inclusion in education, and proposes a uniquely Venezuelan adaptation of the social model aimed toward the challenge of social transformation in a framework of social diversity (85). Recent work by Miguel Ángel Vite Pérez and Carolina Ferrante, on Mexico and Argentina, respectively, emphasizes the socioeconomic vulnerability of disabled people in relation to the neoliberal marketplace, as well as the roles of the state and of the informal sector in this dynamic.[13]

Patricia Brogna's 2009 edited volume, *Visiones y revisiones de la discapacidad*, offers a range of scholarly approaches to disability and disability studies from Latin American, Spanish, U.S.-based and British authors, and encompassing disciplines such as history, psychoanalysis, anthropology, legal theory, literature, law, sociology, and political science, as well as areas typically viewed as part of the "medical model" of disability studies, such as rehabilitation, psychiatry, and medicine. In bringing together this geographical diversity of scholars from widely varied disciplines, Brogna creates an important dialogue between distinct approaches to the field, and implicitly proposes a disability studies that is at once Latin American and global. The volume makes evident some of the trajectories of disability studies scholarship and activism in Latin America that may not have been previously familiar to humanities-based Latin Americanists (including scholars of literature). As Brogna notes, while disability studies in the Anglo-American context has historically focused more on the question of individual rights, in Latin America, emphasis has tended toward analysis of the macrosocial ("Introducción," 16). This observation suggests, as we have also noted here, that those who seek evidence of disability studies, or what they consider to be disability studies, in the Global South may have to adjust their expectations, critical tools, and avenues of research. In addition, Brogna's comment reflects the overall framework we propose for the present book, in which we explicitly juxtapose individual and collective models of disability studies, though here, unlike Brogna, we are especially interested in reading disability through literary and filmic discourse.[14]

The framework for this volume, though oriented toward the study of literature and film, nonetheless must incorporate possibilities for dialogue with those in fields whose disability lexicon and foundational concepts may be different from the prevailing theories in humanistic research. In this sense, the interdisciplinary model we propose for a Latin Americanist disability studies means the foreclosure of a finalized definition of "the field" and an opening to expanded contexts for analysis. We note, too, that there is an immediate risk inherent in disciplinary "encounters" across geopolitical spaces, especially in the context of Latin American studies, in which the South too often serves as raw material for imported theoretical processing and export, and in which "encounter" often works as a thinly coded term for violent conquest. Yet disability and disability studies, as we have shown here, are already present and active features of Latin American academics, activism and cultural production, in some cases in dialogue with Anglo-American intellectual traditions, and at times in ways more attuned to the specificity of local circumstance and disciplinarity. Our initial task is to better understand the terms and risks of this interdisciplinary, international engagement. In this regard, we offer as examples one publication and a recent international colloquium that further demonstrate how disability and disability studies have achieved relevance in Latin Americanist and transnational approaches to cultural production and social theory.

In the introduction to his book, *Nothing About Us Without Us*, James Charlton describes that he first came across his title phrase in 1993, as used by leaders of the group "Disabled People South Africa" (3). Yet he didn't begin to use the phrase as his working title until two years later, when he saw a picture in the Mexican newspaper, *La Jornada*, of peasants marching with the banner, "Nunca Más Sin Nosotros" [Never Again Without Us] (16). This anecdote effectively captures the way in which disability oppression and resistance acquire a particular inflection in regions that Charlton—writing nearly two decades ago—called "underdeveloped," and that we term the Global South. Disability cannot be defined exclusively by global, racialized structures of inequality or lack of access to resources. Yet such patterns parallel disability oppression, compound it, and frequently create it. In other words, Charlton's work highlights an inextricable link between disability and what Aníbal Quijano has defined as the coloniality of power.[15]

In January of 2013, the editors were invited by Benjamín Mayer Foulkes and Beatriz Miranda to speak at a colloquium at the 17 Instituto de Estudios Críticos in Mexico City, with the title "De cómo la Discapacidad entrecomilla a la normalidad" [On How Disability Puts Normality in Quotation Marks]. The event brought together more than twenty scholars of disability studies and related fields, as well as artists, writers and activists, with a high level of public attendance. That such an event took place, and included Mexican, Latin American, and a few Anglo-American disability studies scholars, attests to the internationalization of the field, and to a growing interest in disability studies in Mexico.[16] Though the public included a large percentage of graduate students from the 17 Instituto, focused in areas such as psychoanalysis and critical theory, many in attendance were not academics, or in some cases expressed interest in the question of disability as divorced from discipline-specific academic pursuits. The space of the colloquium allowed for a questioning of the parameters of what constitutes "disability" and "disability studies" and required participants to continually shift disciplinary languages in order to engage in effective dialogue with one another. This event thus demonstrated how focus on disability means working both within and beyond the confines of the academic sphere, in ways specific to day-to-day embodied experience and physical space.

## Disability Studies and Latin American Studies: A Transdisciplinary Approach

This volume stages an encounter between two complex and vigorously debated disciplines: Latin American literary, film, and cultural studies, and disability studies. In a variety of important ways, scholars of Latin American literary and cultural production have been "doing" disability studies for some time—that is, they have been articulating debates in which some of the concerns of disability studies implicitly emerge. However, disability studies per se is not yet highly visible in Latin American studies as practiced in the U.S. academy or as demonstrated, for example, in the research presented by international scholars at the annual congress of the Latin American Studies Association.[17] Latin American studies worldwide has not engaged extensively with disability studies in the humanities. To cite evidence from one essential source for research on literature and film, the bibliography of the Modern Language Association (MLA) in mid-2013 listed 579 entries under the rubric of "disability studies," of which roughly a dozen were immediately identifiable as pertaining to Latin American topics. While factors such as the determination of search terms perhaps figure into the underrepresentation in the bibliography, it is nevertheless clear that disability studies has not taken hold in our field to the same extent as in Anglo-American theory and criticism.[18] In the experience of the editors and the contributors to this volume, there are relatively few venues for presenting our research, and our work in disability studies is often received with expressions of surprise, which can be either welcoming or dismissive. Considering that Latin American studies frequently engages with issues relevant to contemporary disability studies, such as political oppression and resistance, the delimitation and exploration of minority identities, the affective politics of the multitude, and theorizations of the subject, the body and the collective, the lack of engagement with disability itself seems worthy of critical attention.

The high stakes of lived, embodied, and unpredictable corporeality and its representations, as well as the practices and consequences of discrimination based on bodily and cognitive difference make a well-grounded engagement with disability studies a crucial project for scholarship on Latin American literature and film for a variety of reasons: the pervasive presence of cultural representations of disability in the region; the changing social, political and human rights status of disabled people; the increase in the production of art by disabled people, some of which represents disability from an "inside" perspective; and the ethical imperative to interrogate and overturn histories of stigmatization and oppression—histories that often overlap with those of other marginalized communities—and to recover instances of resistance to that oppression, among many others. In such circumstances, we read disability and disability identity as more than just another "other" to be added to the list of minority identities.[19]

In response to these pressing demands on our attention, *Libre Acceso: Latin American Literature and Film through Disability Studies* brings together essays on multiple genres of literature and film from seven countries of Latin America, produced in the twentieth and twenty-first centuries. Works from Argentina, Brazil, Chile, Colombia, Cuba, Mexico, and Peru are examined, thereby spanning highly diverse societies of North America, the Caribbean and South America. The diversity of genres is equally wide: narrative fiction (novels and short stories), poetry, autobiography, essay, children's literature, the colonial codex and colonial medical reports as intertexts, and narrative and documentary film. Our incorporation of both literature and film in the volume is based on a notion of cultural production that is inclusive of diverse media and genres, and attentive to the ways in which a variety of works—in this case, films and written texts—may speak to one another. We do not attempt to offer a fully representative spectrum of works from each medium, but rather to consider the presence and complexity of disability in Latin American cultural production, and hence the relevance of disability studies-informed approaches to these works. Readers will undoubtedly also find many of these approaches useful to works not considered here. In the essays, corporeal, sensory, and psychosocial conditions come into play in analyses that question their status as commonly perceived deficiencies. Disability also intersects with factors of class, race, and gender to prompt critical reflection on the complexities of the social and cultural construction of disability as well as the human being's inescapably embodied experience of the world.[20]

In what follows of the introduction, we first review several foundational concepts and debates for the history of contemporary disability studies in order to contextualize the recourse to Anglo-American theory in many of our analyses of Latin American literature and film. Readers who are not already well-versed in the field will find ample references to prior studies to prompt further exploration. Then we discuss the specificity of conducting humanities-based disability studies research in Latin American contexts, and we conclude with an overview of the organization of the volume and the thirteen individual chapters.

## Concepts in Disability Studies

The development of the social model of disability and the interrogation of the concept of normalcy are two highly significant achievements of the 1980s and 1990s, which led to a series of ever more radical challenges to the status quo around issues of disability. The articulation of disability as socially constructed and not inherent in certain bodies marks a foundational moment, one that is repeatedly invoked in Anglo-American disability studies scholarship. As Tom Shakespeare has described, the "social model" of disability arose in the 1970s in Great Britain through the activities and ideology of UPIAS or Union of Physically Impaired Against Segregation ("Social Model" 214–215). It represented a radical alternative to the prevailing medical model, which posited that disability inheres in the individual body or mind, and that anomalous human conditions ("impairments") should be subjected to treatment and rehabilitation to cure the individual (216). UPIAS defined disability as: "the disadvantage or restriction of activity caused by a contemporary social organization which takes little or no account of people who have physical impairments and thus excludes them from participation in the mainstream of social activities" (quoted in Shakespeare 215). Impairment was defined as "lacking part of or all of a limb, or having a defective limb, organism or mechanism of the body" (Oliver 11). This definition of disability has achieved slogan-like status in many disability studies programs, and in some cases effectively removes disability from the individual body, relocating it almost exclusively in social structures and physical environments. The distinction between disability and impairment has historical significance in the evolution of disability studies, because it has allowed for emphasis on topics such as accessible education, work, and living environments for disabled people, and social and cultural representations of disability, rather than on disability as a problem belonging to individual sufferers in need of a medical solution. Strict adherence to the social model has subsequently been questioned by many contemporary disability studies scholars. Shakespeare (cited earlier) notes limitations to the model, including the fact that it de-emphasizes the material, bodily effects of impairment, such as the sensation of pain, it ignores the social aspects of impairment, and it presupposes the possibility of removing all barriers to access in the world (218–220). It has also been noted that it was developed by men with spinal cord injuries and responded primarily to their conditions and needs, and has much less to say about neurodiversity, cognitive disability, or those who have more complex physical impairments. The emphasis in Oliver's definition on missing or defective limbs illustrates this observation.

In another significant move, disability studies scholars challenged the nearly universal privileging of normative ability and "health," an ideology captured by the term "ableism." Lennard J. Davis's book *Enforcing Normalcy* (1995) made an early and enduring contribution to disability studies by tracing the history of "normalcy" to its origins in the Industrial Revolution and the requirements of industrial labor, and demonstrating its deleterious impact on people with anomalous bodies and minds.[21] The rise of nationalism, as David Mitchell and Sharon Snyder show more recently in their article, "The Eugenic Atlantic," also contributed to the privileging of the normal, as the strength of the nation was seen to depend on the fitness of its citizens.

Disabled people have been termed the world's largest minority group, and as some disability studies scholars have noted, disability is the only minority identity that crosses the lines traced by other identity markers, such as gender, age, race, ethnicity, nationality, and sexual orientation. It is estimated that 10 percent to 15 percent of the population worldwide lives with a disability, and it is the one significant identity category that any one of us can enter at any time, and that most of us, as we age, eventually will.[22] Nevertheless, the great diversity of physical, cognitive, and psychosocial conditions that are categorized as disabilities and the inherent instability of any person's status as "able" have prompted a rich debate over the meaning of disability as a minority identity and the coherence of the category itself. The work of Lennard Davis and Tobin Siebers represents important yet divergent positions in this debate. Davis, in his book *Bending Over Backwards* (2002), advocates for conceiving of disability as an inherently unstable identity category and for extending its application broadly across society against the background of the exhaustion of identity politics and contemporary science's dismantling of the biological bases for many longstanding identity categories. (23–26).[23] Siebers in *Disability Theory* (2008) leaves the category of disability more or less in place, but argues for claiming disability as a valid and valuable form of human diversity, rather than a personal defect or misfortune (3). He posits that one of the strengths of persons with minority status, including the disabled, is that they are able to critique aspects of hegemonic ideologies from their position outside or marginal to the privileges that these ideologies grant (26).

Although the debate illustrated by Davis's and Siebers's positions is crucial to the evolution of disability studies, and relevant to Latin American contexts, it is complicated by scholarship on disability as a global phenomenon. As Robert McRuer's discussion of global bodies underscores, the idea that "everyone will be disabled if they live long enough" shifts its function in the face of a display of coffins nailed to a wall near the Tijuana airport, representing the number of Mexicans who die each year in attempts to cross the border, those who "didn't live long enough" (200–201). And as Michael Davidson notes, "While it is true that many individuals will become disabled, it is just as certain that those who become disabled earlier in life (. . .) are poor and live in an underdeveloped country" (172). In his reading of globalized disability, Davidson further emphasizes that attention to community contexts necessarily undermines the model of disability based on individual rights (173). Reading disability in Latin American cultural production thus requires becoming attuned to diverse and sometimes conflicting models of disability identity, community, and the politics of inequality.

## Literary and Cultural Disability Studies, Latin Americanist Readings

Tanya Titchkosky and Rod Michalko's statement that "studying disability" is not the same as disability studies has relevance for the project that this volume takes up (*Rethinking* 5). Their observation clarifies the critical split between a health sciences or medical model of disability and disability studies as a critical mode of inquiry in the humanities. That is, a disability studies approach to cultural production does not seek to diagnose disabled characters in literature and film, or to project desires for the characters' greater adherence to normalcy, but rather to examine the narrative function and the cultural valence of the representation of disability. For this reason, narratives in which disabled characters "overcome limitations," provide inspiration to readers and viewers, or serve to further the redemption of morally flawed but otherwise "normal" characters are frequently critiqued as problematic from a disability studies perspective. Such literary representation sustains the view that disability is a problem in need of a solution or is primarily valuable as an instrument of another's salvation.[24] Instead, disability studies reads disability either as socially and politically constructed, or somewhere at the juncture or melding of the social and the corporeal as proposed by Siebers's concept of "complex embodiment" (*Disability Theory* 23–25). Disability studies approaches to the humanities concur in viewing disability as a significant and valuable aspect of human experience, interaction and diversity as we have outlined.

Influential contributions to the study of literature from a disability studies perspective include David Mitchell and Sharon Snyder's groundbreaking work, *Narrative Prosthesis* (2000) and Ato Quayson's *Aesthetic Nervousness* (2007). Mitchell and Snyder advance the theory that literary fiction often depends on the representation of disability, like a crutch or prosthetic limb, in order to tell its story, and to offer the illusion of tangible materiality to the text. A frequently cited term from this work is "metaphorical opportunism," by which the literary work takes advantage of the seemingly evocative and meaning-laden qualities of the disabled body, in order to advance its own symbolic agenda. In reference to Mitchell and Snyder's model, one might note that the recognized canon of Latin American literature is replete with characters who "suffer" from disability or disabling illness, and whose discursive presence and literary destiny primarily serve to jumpstart the narrative and further the development of the "able-bodied" protagonists of the texts. María, of Jorge Isaacs's eponymous novel, is both epileptic and "biologically Jewish" (although professing the Christian faith), and her death from tuberculosis conveniently removes her as an obstacle to her criollo lover's assumption of his destiny in Colombia's "national romance."[25] Robustiana, Don Zoilo's "consumptive" daughter in Florencio Sánchez's play *Barranca abajo*, acts as a foil to her morally inferior kinswomen, and her death contributes to her honest, but ineffectual father's decision to commit suicide rather than continue to live in a state of humiliation and powerlessness. In *Santa*, Federico Gamboa's bestselling 1903 novel about a beautiful Mexican prostitute, the blindness of the piano player who falls in love with her is a convenient pretext for the detailed narration of her physical attributes, visible only to the musician's young assistant. Thanks, too, to the man's blindness, he remains a faithful lover despite the effects of age and the venereal disease that eventually kill Santa.[26] Similar instances of the prosthetic function of literary disability are legion, but have gone largely unexamined from a disability studies perspective.

Ato Quayson effectively adapts elements of Mitchell and Snyder's theory to his analysis of disability in postcolonial literature. For Quayson, however, "this prostheticizing function is bound to fail" (210), meaning that the representation of disability ultimately unsettles its ostensibly categorical function. In many of the most familiar works of twentieth-century Latin American literature, too, the unstable function of the narrative prosthesis is apparent. This is strikingly so in major works of the Boom, such as Gabriel García Márquez's *One Hundred Years of Solitude*, or José Donoso's *The Obscene Bird of the Night*, novels in which the anomalous features of characters' bodies seem to bring the stories to life, even as the narratives themselves center on the dizzying, otherwise ungraspable circularity of a repeating and frustrated project. In García Márquez's text, national history becomes a seemingly endless procession of names, battles, and family generations that point not to a productive future but rather to a vortex of predetermined self-destruction. The novel's conclusion illustrates national and familial history as this fulfilled prophesy of destruction, through the figure of a human infant with a pig's tail, the last of his lineage, who is ultimately devoured by ants. Here Quayson's notion of aesthetic nervousness, or the unmoored prosthesis, is useful in pointing to the ways in which disability underscores the continuous, self-reflexive unraveling of the narrative project.

The study of literature and film has an undeniable importance for disability studies, just as disability studies brings necessary new insights to our reading of literary and filmic texts. As individuals and as communities, we create our sense of self and other and our collective identities in large part through our absorption and processing of the stories that come to us through time and those that are continually produced in the present. Paul Ricoeur speaks of our "narrative identity" to capture the sense that human action and subjectivity are "entangled in the stories" and informed by the "intrigues we received from our culture" ("Life" 131). A historically and culturally situated disability studies is a critical tool for interpreting the stories that shape our lives and for enlarging the "narrative identity that constitutes us" ("Life" 131) in ways that are more inclusive and just.

The essays collected in *Libre Acceso*, with their focus on the roles and representations of disability in Latin American cultural contexts, necessarily highlight phenomena of stigmatized identity and radical social inequality that are inextricably bound to specific economic and politico-historical processes. These include racialized colonialist violence, instances of entrenched authoritarianism, and the material effects of contemporary global capitalism. Such conditions, it is worth noting, translate into higher percentages of disabled people in Latin America and in the Global South overall.[27] Indeed, recent scholarship on disability as a global phenomenon, whether from a social sciences perspective, or read through the lens of postcolonial discourse, often notes the socioeconomic disparities that produce unequal distributions of disability, and points to the need for disability studies approaches that would account for such global inequalities, while transcending dominant Anglo-American frameworks.

Shaun Grech has emphasized the need for a decolonization of disability analysis in the contexts of the Global South, pointing out the danger of what he calls "academic neo-colonialism" (Alatas, 601; quoted in Grech, "Disability and the Majority World" 59). He also notes the pervasive intertwining of neocolonial globalization and the oppression of disabled people, borrowing here from the work of key Latin Americanist thinkers such as Fernando Coronil and Aníbal Quijano. Along similar lines, Stuart Murray and Clare Barker address disability studies in the context of postcolonialism, contending that, "the history of colonialism . . . is indeed a history of mass disablement" (230). They contend that the common disability studies practice of criticizing associations between disability and trauma or loss becomes problematic in contexts where, "the *acquisition* of disability may be tied into wider patterns of dispossession—the loss of family, home, land, community, employment" (230). The challenge for a global disability studies and for this volume is to maintain awareness of the situated contexts in which disability or disablement take place, as well as strategic responses to these contexts, while at once allowing for openness to more unpredictable meanings and valuations of disability, not necessarily limited by a logic of prescripted causality.

Reading disability and the construction of otherness in Latin American literary contexts also requires attention to traditions in which cannibalism, monstrosity, and racial difference frequently operate as mutually referencing figures and in which resistance to oppression may often stem from this dynamic. The ways in which disability sometimes emerges as a metaphor in Latin American literature is thus partially determined by elements derived from a colonialist tropology of otherness.[28] Although this discursive tradition is inseparable from the political and economic histories of the region, it is important to note that the literary discourses participating in the configuration of otherness and national or individual selfhood do not map directly onto an overarching reading of global capitalism and geopolitics, but instead add greater complexity to the representations and experiences of disability that this book examines.

## Libre Acceso

In the present volume our aim is to open an interdisciplinary and transregional dialogue on disability studies, so as to expand our analysis toward what disability might mean and might allow in its future Latin Americanist configurations, as well as in the interdisciplinary humanities more generally. To this end we employ a critical framework and chapter organization that highlight the tension between a Latin American lettered tradition that tends to emphasize what we call the cultural production of the self, and a focus on communities and populations through which the body becomes a feature of collective experience, practice, and representation. Paying attention to overlaps and points of contact between these seemingly divergent modes of reading Latin American cultural production allows us to consider the shifting characteristics of the field, and to locate disability as central to a dynamic through which collectives and selves might encounter, contest, or engage one another.

We have organized the thirteen chapters into four sections according to shared thematics and discourses. The sections themselves trace an overarching movement from a consideration of disability in the construction of individual identity and consciousness as expressed in autobiographical discourse; to an emphasis on collective phenomena and human rights in literary and filmic works of fiction and nonfiction; to an examination of the intersection of race and social marginality with disability; and concluding with two texts that create alternative worlds through the exercise of the imagination and authorial experimentation as modes of questioning typical categories of normative and anomalous embodiment and neurological function and of literary form. The question of disability in the analyses that comprise the book continues to define a tightrope walk between self and community and between localized, embodied, or represented experience, and the more globalized biopolitical readings that inevitably inform contemporary approaches to both Latin American cultural studies and theories of the body.

The three chapters that comprise Part I, "Disability Life Writing and Constructions of the Self," represent divergent literary genres and writing styles around the common project of a writer's exploring and inscribing his or her own identity as a person with a disability. The specific conditions of blindness and the physical limitations due to cerebral palsy inform the poetry, interviews, essays, short stories, and autobiography that are treated here. The opening chapter by the acclaimed Chilean novelist Lina Meruane stands apart from the other chapters of the book, as it is a literary essay with a significant autobiographical dimension and not a research study per se, and yet it also provides a disability-centered reflection on practices of reading and writing. In "Blind Spot: (Notes on Reading Blindness)" Meruane enacts a reading journey through the literature of blindness and traces the process of writing her most recent novel *Sangre en el ojo* (Seeing red), winner of the 2012 Sor Juana Inés de la Cruz Prize. To a greater degree than her other works, *Sangre en el ojo* represents a literary transformation of the writer's own experience, that of temporary vision loss.

Meruane weaves several thematic threads drawn from texts by Jorge Luis Borges into her essay, and these are picked up and reworked in the following chapter on the famed Argentinian writer. The idea of disability as an advantage or a gift for the writer, the need for the blind person to "see" through the prosthesis of others' eyes, and the "secret power" attributed to the blind in Western culture are concepts that reappear in Kevin Goldstein's study of Borges's poetry. In "La cara que me mira: Demythologizing Blindness in Borges's Disability Life Writing," Goldstein examines the resistance in Borges's late work toward positioning the figure of the blind seer in isolation, and an expressed interest in the banality of the blind body. This demythologizing tendency coincides with a growing shift in Borges's work toward life writing: personal essays and lectures and, at times, nearly confessional lyric poems.

The final chapter of Part I "Negotiating the Geographies of Exclusion and Access: Life Writing by Gabriela Brimmer and Ekiwah Adler-Beléndez," serves as a bridge from the autobiographical reflections highlighted thus far to the concern with collective identities and human rights in Part II of the volume. Beth Jörgensen's chapter examines life writing by two Mexican poets and activists with cerebral palsy. This reading of *Gaby Brimmer* by Elena Poniatowska and Gabriela Brimmer and of poetry by Ekiwah Adler-Beléndez draws on theories of disability life writing, and incorporates Tobin Siebers's theory of complex embodiment in an analysis that attends in part to sexuality and access to the spaces of pleasure as a particularly stubborn taboo for people with disabilities

Part II, "Global Bodies and the Coloniality of Disability" includes four chapters focused on dilemmas specific to the geopolitical locations of disability in Latin American cultural contexts. In the films and novel under consideration, disability representation appears as intrinsic to tensions between local and global economies, and to the individual and collective bodies through which such economies operate. The notion of collective bodies is crucial here, and illustrates a partial contrast with the mode of disability representation centered on the characteristics, experiences, and rights of the individual body as subject, as emphasized in the chapters of Part I. Emphasis on biopolitics and collective corporeality also contextualizes these essays in relation to contemporary debates in Latin American literary and cultural studies on the multitude and on theories of affect.[29]

Ryan Prout's essay "Otras competencias: Ethnobotany, the *Badianus codex*, and Metaphors of Mexican Memory Loss and Disability in *Las buenas hierbas* (2010)" offers a reading of María Novaro's film focused on the interplay between the pre-Columbian pharmacopeia as depicted in the *Badianus codex* and the global phenomenon of dementia diagnosed as Alzheimer's disease. As Prout suggests, the film centers on a female ethnobotanist with Alzheimer's, and incorporates visual material from a sixteenth-century indigenous herbal almanac, so as to move between the global and the local, and to offer an implicit critique of contemporary globalized biomedicine.

Following Prout's essay and also treating film, "Cripping the Camera: Disability and Filmic Interval in Carlos Reygadas's *Japón*" by Susan Antebi examines the role of cinematographic technique in contributing to an intercorporeal mode of disability as both representation and embodied identification. The technique is manifested when the viewer follows the uneven "limping" perspective of the camera and then sees in a subsequent frame that the protagonist limps and uses a cane. The essay argues that Reygadas's film creates a unique landscape through which diverse bodies and objects may become interchangeable, questioning the boundaries of individual bodies, and creating an unpredictable, at times collective mode of disability.

Victoria Dickman-Burnett takes up a related theme in her chapter, "Bodily Integrity, Abjection, and the Politics of Gender and Place in Roberto Bolaño's *2666*," by juxtaposing the role of the visual artist, Edwin Johns, who cuts off his own hand in order to increase the value of his paintings, with that of the violated and murdered bodies of the hundreds of young women of Santa Teresa, a fictionalized version of Ciudad Juárez. As this chapter shows, *2666* interrogates the dilemma of differently valued, exchanged, or commodified bodies in the borderlands between global North and South, space of a violent global marketplace through which bodies circulate and may become mutilated or disappear.

Part II concludes with Victoria L. Garrett's essay, "Violence, Injury, and Disability in Recent Latin American Film," focusing on Francisco Vargas's *The Violin* (2005) and Claudio Llosa's *The Milk of Sorrow* (2009). Garrett argues that the disabilities of the protagonists of both films intersect with their racial, social, aged, gendered, and/or political alterity to indict social injustice in their respective societies. In considering how recent Latin American cinema treats the injury that results from structural violence and violent states, the chapter takes up one of the key challenges of engaging disability in postcolonial contexts. Specifically, Garrett negotiates both the potential and the pitfalls of disability representation as an ethical intervention in the globalization of inequality.

The four essays of Part III, "Embodied Frameworks: Disability, Race, Marginality" continue the thematics of Part II by paying attention to disability in the representation of communities and populations, and as inseparable from the impact of global capitalism. More specifically, these essays highlight the complex roles of disability, race, and social marginality as metaphorical or at times literal cross-references of one another. The connected themes of fixed versus porous identity categories and intersectionality have become central to debates in disability studies, and link the field to gender and queer studies and critical race theory. As Patricia Hill Collins describes: "[a]s opposed to examining gender, race, class, and nation as separate systems of oppression, intersectionality explores how these systems mutually construct one another . . ." (63; quoted in Erevelles and Minear, "Unspeakable Offenses" 130).[30] As identities open toward the referencing or construction of one another, their boundaries may be called into question, returning us to the debate surrounding disability as a stable versus unstable category.

In "Sô Candelário's Inheritance: Leprosy as a Marker of Racial Identity in João Guimarães Rosa's *Grande Sertão: Veredas* (1956)" Valéria Souza focuses on the portrayal of leprosy in this sprawling novel, set in the nineteenth century but in dialogue with ancient, medieval, and modern notions of disease and race, including frequent convergences between these categories. In Souza's analysis of the encounter between two leprous characters, one figured as white and the other as Afro-Brazilian, leprosy threatens to emerge as lighter marks on darker skin, confounding the division between the hereditary and the contagious, and intertwining anxieties of racial difference and illness. Melissa E. Schindler's chapter "*A solidão da escuridão*: On Visual Impairment and the Visibility of Race" also treats the intersecting categories of race and disability, but through emphasis on (primarily) Brazilian literary encounters between blindness and blackness, and on the related dilemma of "seeing" race.

Following these chapters on disability and race, are two essays that treat representations of mental illness. Nicola Gavioli's "Mythicizing Disability: The Life and Opinions of (what is left of) *Estamira*," similarly focuses on a Brazilian cultural context, but in this case emphasizing the construction and representation of psychosocial disability in documentary film. Gavioli examines the ethics of disability representation through an analysis that combines perspectives from disability studies with theories of testimonial literature, documentary filmmaking and trauma, in order to consider the intertwined dilemmas of authenticity, aesthetics and the representation and construction of marginality.

" 'En ninguna parte': Narrative Performances of Mental Illness in *El portero* by Reinaldo Arenas and *Corazón de skitalietz* by Antonio José Ponte," closes Part III of the volume. Laura Kanost reads the two Cuban narratives in the context of national mental health policies of the 1980s and 1990s, under which many formerly institutionalized patients came to occupy a transitional placelessness, at times inextricable from the liminality of the socially marginalized. In Kanost's chapter, as in Schindler's, Souza's and Gavioli's, the characters' experiences of corporeal or cognitive differences complicate the historically and discursively determined categories they appear to occupy.

Part IV, "Imagining Other Worlds" concludes the volume with two chapters that examine the production of a disability aesthetic in works of experimental fiction that privilege the imagination as a way of resisting conventional categories of disability. Here we circle back to a focus on individual writers, and on the representation of individual disabled people, as in Part I, but without returning to the autobiographical mode. The chapter by Emily Hind, "The Disability Twist in Stranger Novels by Mario Bellatin and Carmen Boullosa" considers the dilemma of inclusivity and its limits in narrative fiction, through her analysis of experimental works by the two

Mexican writers. Hind suggests that alternatives to the traditional narrative arc that tends to diagnose and cure its characters allow us to reflect on the relationship between disability and novelistic fiction, even if such literary experiments do not ultimately transcend what Lennard Davis has referred to as the realist average that is central to the novel as genre.

Juan Manuel Espinosa reads Gabriel García Márquez's iconic *One Hundred Years of Solitude* alongside recent popular culture uses of characters with Asperger's syndrome in the book's final chapter. In "The Blur of Imagination: Asperger's Syndrome and *Cien años de soledad*," an understanding of the faculty of imagination based on Kant's definition provides an unexpected connection between the experience of reading the novel and that of misreading Asperger's. Ultimately, Espinosa's chapter argues against the ways in which a condition of apparent "otherness" like Asperger's has been medicalized, suggesting that the reading of *One Hundred Years of Solitude* can have a role in promoting an expanded, ethically sound response to the diversity of experiences and thought processes that constitute human life.

The research and writing of this volume has taken place at a time in which the field of disability studies, as well as that of Latin American literary, film, and cultural studies, have continued to undergo processes of self-questioning and critical redefinition. In disability studies, an increasing diversity of approaches, as well as attention to interdisciplinary models and to the paradigm of globalization have led some to express concerns that the field may be co-opted and diluted in its political efficacy. Latin American cultural studies, in the meantime, can no longer be primarily defined in terms of its alliances with the subaltern or with other political subjects, but instead represents multiple angles on the question of what might constitute a politically and culturally relevant Latin Americanist project, including approaches in which no identifiable subject of alliance is posited.[31] In both cases, the dilemma of the discipline's future hinges not simply on who or what is the specific subject with whom one communicates, identifies, or expresses solidarity. In tracing the movement between disability as articulation of the self, and as that of the collective, or more amorphous multitude, we have sought to underscore this critically productive tension as a focus through which to bring disability studies and Latin American literary, film, and cultural studies into dialogue. In addition, if disability in the contexts of Latin American cultural production demands long-overdue critical attention, it is equally true that Latin Americanism as academic discipline might benefit from turning to disability, not only as a key element of human subjective experience, but also as a social process that itself demands ongoing redefinition.

## Notes

1. Kreutzberger, or "don Francisco" is also the host of the popular television show, *Sábado Gigante*.

2. Brazil, Chile, Colombia, Costa Rica, El Salvador, Guatemala, Honduras, Mexico, Panama, Paraguay, Peru, and Uruguay. Teletón was modeled on the work of Jerry Lewis in the United States.

3. See Paul Longmore for a critical analysis of the use of disability in telethons in the United States.

4. Rafael Cabrera's 2012 article in the journal *emeequis* offers ample evidence that in Mexico one of every three pesos donated to Teletón is from public funds, which go to supporting the organization's privately built and run rehabilitation centers. He quotes Clara Judisman, a former secretary of Desarrollo Social in Mexico City as saying that Teletón has become a monopoly, to the detriment of other organizations and governmental services to disabled children.

5. Some disability studies scholars prefer the "people-first language" term of "people with disabilities." Others favor the term "disabled people" as a way to emphasize that disability can be a central and celebratory element of human identity, rather than an incidental, secondary characteristic, or a motive for shame. As Tanya Titchkosky suggests, people-first language posits that disability is a problem to which this same language offers the solution; its goal is to "dismember disability from the self" ("A Rose By Any Other Name" 134). However, we note the frequent usage of "personas con discapacidad" (literally, "persons with disability") in Spanish-speaking disability studies contexts, and we recognize that the appropriacy of terminology depends on a variety of contextual factors. For this reason, both terms appear at different points in the book.

6. Disability Rights International has conducted research on the abusive conditions in institutions for disabled people, particularly in psychiatric facilities, in Mexico, Argentina, Peru and Paraguay. See www.disabilityrightsintl.org.

7. See Carolina Ferrante on this topic.

8. Latin American nations that are signatories to the Convention are Argentina, Belize, Bolivia, Brazil, Chile, Colombia, Costa Rica, Cuba, Dominican Republic, Ecuador, El Salvador, Guatemala, Haiti, Honduras, Jamaica, Mexico, Nicaragua, Panama, Paraguay, Peru, and Uruguay.

9. James Charlton's book *Nothing About Us Without Us* showcases the work of disability activists in Latin America and other world regions, primarily through interviews, in combination with a Marxist analysis informed by the British social model of disability. As scholars of Latin American studies will recognize, this title and the dynamic it invokes suggests close ties to the genre of *testimonio*, and to the highly politicized debates surrounding its role as literary and political discourse and as tool of education and resistance.

10. The U.N. report was covered in an April 15, 2010 article posted in the online version of the *Santiago Times*.

11. Ana Rosato and María Alfonsina Angelino's edited volume offers extensive examples of transnational dialogue and influence at work in Latin American disability studies. Many authors in the volume make reference to works by disability studies scholars such as Tom Shakespeare and Michael Oliver, and citations of a 1998 Spanish translation of Len Barton's *Disability and Society* (from a Madrid-based publisher) are frequent. Examples of disability studies scholarship from Spain include work by Miguel Ángel Verdugo Alonso and Xabier Etxeberria.

12. Two articles that offer a useful overview of the history of disability studies are David Pfeiffer's "Philosophical Foundations of Disability Studies" (2002), and Helen Meekosha's "Drifting Down the Gulf Stream: Navigating the Cultures of Disability Studies" (2004).

13. Also see Stuart Schrader and Facundo Chavez Penilla's article in relation to this topic.

14. Brogna's more recent work includes her 2013 doctoral dissertation, her 2014 book *Adultez, trabajo y discapacidad*, and a 2014 comprehensive study of disability issues, accessibility and scholarship at the Universidad Nacional Autónoma de México (UNAM).

15. For further discussion of Quijano's concept of the coloniality of power, see Susan Antebi's chapter in this volume.

16. We do not wish to imply that this is the only conference of its kind. We note here the increasingly international quality of the U.S.-based Society for Disability Studies Conferences, as well as events such as the 2013 International Disability Studies Conference in the Netherlands, featuring the work of Ecuadorian scholar Beatriz Miranda, among many others, and a 2008 conference in Buenos Aires on the body and disability from a critical sociological perspective. In addition, it is perhaps surprising that, according to Simi Linton ("Re: [DS-HUM]") the first conference on disability studies in the humanities was held at the University of Puerto Rico at Mayagüez in 1993, and featured local academics as well as names that have since become familiar to disability studies scholars in the Anglo-American context.

17. A notable and recent exception to this tendency is a special section on disability studies in Hispanic literature, edited by Encarnación Juárez-Almendros, in the *Arizona Journal of Hispanic Cultural Studies*. In addition, Benjamin Fraser and Mathew Marr's recently published books on Spanish literary and cultural production are the first monographs in English to employ disability studies approaches to this area of scholarship.

18. Rosemarie Garland-Thomson illustrates the role of search terms in revealing or obscuring relevant scholarship in a recent conference presentation, "converting crippled saints." Here she describes how the MLA bibliography at one point omitted the term "crippled" as it was deemed insulting to disabled people, meaning that an article on a "crippled saint" could only be accessed via the search term "saint."

19. This phrase is borrowed from Catherine Kudlick's article "Disability History: Why We Need Another 'Other.' "

20. Leprosy, blindness, Asperger's Syndrome, cerebral palsy, Alzheimer's disease, loss of limbs through injury and amputation, schizophrenia and self-mutilation are represented in the texts under study.

21. Henri-Jacques Stiker's *History of Disability* also represents an important source on the construction of disability as an evolving and historically specific phenomenon. A version of Stiker's book first appeared in French in 1982. It was published in English in 1999. Another important work on disability representation and history is Rosemarie Garland-Thomson's *Extraordinary Bodies* (1997). All of these texts depend on Foucauldian analyses of the concept of normalcy. For a more recent treatment of this topic, see Shelley Tremain's volume, *Foucault and the Government of Disability* (2005).

22. The United Nations "Factsheet on Persons with Disability" gives the 10 percent figure, while the World Health Organization puts the figure at 15 percent. As Michael Davidson notes, "A common refrain in disability studies is that disability is the one identity category that, if we live long enough, everyone will inhabit (cf. Berubé, "I should live")." Davidson further refers to disability's "crossing of racial, sexual, and gendered categories" (172).

23. A concise treatment of Davis's argument can be found in his essay "The End of Identity Politics."

24. In *Aesthetic Nervousness*, Ato Quayson offers a thematic typology of disabled literary characters, among which he includes those who act as the ethical background to the actions of other characters (36). Charles Dickens's *A Christmas Carol* can be seen as an example of this last tendency, in that Scrooge is redeemed by his contemplation of the goodness and innocence of Tiny Tim.

25. See chapter 6, "*María*'s Disease: A National Novel (Con)Founded" in Doris Sommer's book *Foundational Fictions.*

26. See Antebi, "Blindness and Freakishness."

27. As Shaun Grech notes, "The World Health Organisation estimates that around 600 million people or 10% of the world's population is disabled, with more than 80% concentrated in the global South." ("Recolonising" 87).

28. For a more complete treatment of this concept, see Antebi, *Carnal Inscriptions.*

29. We refer, for example, to the impact of the work of Hardt and Negri and their notion of the multitude on Latin Americanist scholarship. Also see Mitchell and Snyder's article on disability and the multitude. Recent interest in the politics of affect is exemplified in the volume co-edited by Mabel Moraña and Ignacio Sánchez Prado, and in a frequently cited article by Diedra Rieber on the Mexican film, *Amores Perros.*

30. Disability studies scholarship offers multiple angles to the topic of intersectionality. See, for example, Rosemarie Garland-Thomson's *Extraordinary Bodies* as an approach to disability and feminist theory, as well as disability and race, and Robert McRuer's *Crip Theory,* on heterosexuality and able-bodiedness. Nirmala Erevelles studies the historically specific mutual constructions of race and disability in her *Disability and Difference in Global Contexts*, while Christopher Bell's edited volume, *Blackness and Disability* provides an additional range of approaches.

31. On this point see for example Alberto Moreiras's article, "¿Puedo madrugarme a un narco?"

## Works Cited

Alatas, Syed Farid. "Academic Dependency and the Global Division of Labour in the Social Sciences." *Current Sociology* 51 (2003): 599–633. Sage. Web. August 23, 2013.

Antebi, Susan. "Blindness and Freakishness." *Literal. Latin American Voices* 16 (2009): 27–28.

———. *Carnal Inscriptions: Spanish American Narratives of Corporeal Difference and Disability*. New York: Palgrave Macmillan, 2009.

Aramayo Zamora, Manuel, comp. *Hablemos de la discapacidad en la diversidad. Investigaciones venezolanas sobre las personas con discapacidad.* Caracas: Universidad Monteávila, 2010.

Barker, Clare, and Stuart Murray. "Disabling Postcolonialism: Global Disability Cultures and Democratic Criticism." *Journal of Literary and Cultural Disability Studies* 4.3 (2010): 219–236. *Project Muse.* Web. August 12, 2013.

Barton, Len, comp. *Discapacidad y sociedad.* Madrid: Morata-Fundación Pandeia, 1998.

Bell, Christopher M., ed. *Blackness and Disability: Critical Examinations and Cultural Interventions.* East Lansing: Michigan State UP, 2011.

Berubé, Michael. "Afterword: If I Should Live So Long." Brueggeman, Snyder and Garland-Thomson, 337–343.

Brogna, Patricia. *Adultez, trabajo y discapacidad. El trabajo de crecer.* Mexico City: Trillas, 2014.

———, ed. *Visiones y revisiones de la discapacidad.* Mexico City: Fondo de Cultura Económica, 2009.

———. "Introducción." *Visiones y revisiones de la discapacidad.* 15–20.

———, and Damián Rosales Manjarrez. *Diagnóstico sobre el estado que guarda la atención a la temática de la discapacidad en la Universidad Nacional Autónoma de México desde la perspectiva de los derechos humanos.* Mexico City: UNAM, 2014.

Brueggeman, Brenda Jo, Sharon L. Snyder, and Rosemarie Garland-Thomson, eds. *Disability Studies: Enabling the Humanities.* New York: Modern Language Association, 2002.

Cabrera, Rafael. "Teletón: El monopolio de la atención a la discapacidad." *emeequis* 295 (December 2, 2012): 36–43. Web. July 2, 2014.

Charlton, James. *Nothing About Us Without Us: Disability Oppression and Empowerment.* Berkeley: U of California P, 2000.

Chen, Mel. *Animacies: Biopolitics, Racial Mattering, and Queer Affect.* Durham: Duke UP, 2012.

Coronil, Fernando. "Elephants in the Americas? Latin American Postcolonial Studies and Global Decolonization." *Coloniality at Large: Latin America and the*

*Postcolonial Debate*. Edited by Mabel Moraña, Enrique Dussel, and Carlos Jáuregui. Durham: Duke UP, 2008, 396–416.

Davidson, Michael. *Concerto For the Left Hand: Disability and the Defamiliar Body.* Ann Arbor: U of Michigan P, 2008.

Davis, Lennard J. *Enforcing Normalcy: Disability, Deafness, and the Body*. London: Verso, 1995.

———. *Bending over Backwards: Disability, Dismodernism and Other Difficult Positions*. New York: New York UP, 2002.

———. "Constructing Normalcy." *The Disability Studies Reader.* Edited by Lennard J. Davis. 1st ed. New York: Routledge, 2013, 9–28.

———. "The End of Identity Politics: On Disability as an Unstable Category." *Disability Studies Reader.* Edited by Lennard J. Davis. 4th ed. New York: Routledge, 2013, 263–277.

———. "Introduction: Disability, Normality, and Power." *Disability Studies Reader.* Edited by Lennard J. Davis. 4th ed. New York: Routledge, 2013, 1–14.

Erevelles, Nirmala. *Disability and Difference in Global Contexts: Enabling a Transformative Body Politic*. New York: Palgrave Macmillan, 2011.

———, and Andrea Minear. "Unspeakable Offenses: Untangling Race and Disability in Discourses of Intersectionality." *Journal of Literary and Cultural Disability Studies* 4.2 (2010): 127–145. *Project Muse*. Web. November 19, 2012.

Etxeberria, Xabier. *La condición de ciudadanía de las personas con discapacidad intelectual.* Bilbao: Universidad de Deusto, 2008.

Ferrante, Carolina. "Mendicidad y discapacidad en la ciudad de Buenos Aires: un síntoma de nuevas formas de vulnerabilidad social." *Disability and the Global South* 1.1 (2014): 85–106. Web. July 15, 2014.

Fraser, Benjamin. *Disability Studies and Spanish Culture: Films, Novels, the Comic and the Public Exhibition*. Liverpool: Liverpool UP, 2013.

Garland-Thomson, Rosemarie. *Extraordinary Bodies: Figuring Physical Disability in American Culture and Literature.* New York: Columbia UP, 1997.

———. "Converting Crippled Saints: How the MLA Came to Recognize Disability." Avenues of Access. The State of Disability Studies. MLA Annual Convention. Boston. Jan. 5, 2012. Conference Presentation.

Grech, Shaun. "Disability and the Majority World: A Neocolonial Approach." *Disability and Social Theory*. Edited by Dan Goodley, Bill Hughes, and Lennard Davis. New York: Palgrave, 2012, 52–69.

———. "Recolonising Debates or Perpetuated Coloniality? Decentring the Spaces of Disability, Development and Community in the Global South." *International Journal of Inclusive Education.* 15.1 (2011): 87–100. Taylor & Francis. Web. August 23, 2013.

Hardt, Michael, and Antonio Negri. *Multitude: War and Democracy in the Age of Empire.* New York: Penguin, 2004.

Hill Collins, Patricia. "It's All in the Family: Intersections of Gender, Race, and Nation." *Hypatia* 13.3 (1998): 276–291. ProQuest. Web. August 23, 2013.

Juárez-Almendros, Encarnación, ed. "Special Section: Disability Studies in the Hispanic World: Proposals and Methodologies." *Arizona Journal of Hispanic Cultural Studies* 17 (2013): 151–261.

Kudlick, Catherine. "Disability History: Why We Need Another 'Other.' "*American Historical Review* 108 (2003): 763–793.

Linton, Simi. "Re: [DS-HUM] Article of Potential Interest." Message to DS-HUM@LISTSERV.UMD.EDU. August 14, 2013. Email.

———. "What Is Disability Studies?" *PMLA* 120.2 (2005): 518–22. *JSTOR*. Web. August 23, 2013.

Longmore, Paul. "The Cultural Framing of Disability: Telethons as a Case Study." *PMLA*. 120.2 (2005): 502–508. Web. *JSTOR*. November 21, 2012.

Marr, Mathew J. *The Politics of Age and Disability in Contemporary Spanish Film: Plus Ultra Pluralism*. New York: Routledge, 2013.

McRuer, Robert. *Crip Theory: Cultural Signs of Queerness and Disability*. New York: New York UP, 2006.

Meekosha, Helen. "Drifting Down the Gulf Stream: Navigating the Cultures of Disability Studies." *Disability and Society* 19.7 (2004): 721–733. Taylor & Francis. Web. August 23, 2013.

Mitchell, David T., and Sharon L. Snyder. *Narrative Prosthesis: Disability and the Dependencies of Discourse*. Ann Arbor: U of Michigan P, 2001.

———."Disability as Multitude: Reworking Non-Productive Labor Power." *Journal of Literary and Cultural Disability Studies*. 4.2 (2010): 179–194. Project Muse. Web. June 29, 2011.

———. "The Eugenic Atlantic: Race, Disability and the Making of an International Eugenic Science, 1800–1945." *Disability and Society* 18.7 (2003): 843–864. Taylor & Francis. Web. October 9, 2011.

Moraña, Mabel, and Ignacio Sánchez Prado, eds. *El lenguaje de las emociones: Afecto y cultura en América Latina*. Madrid: Iberoamericana, 2012.

Moreiras, Alberto. "¿Puedo madrugarme a un narco? Posiciones críticas en la Asociación de Estudios Latinoamericanos." *Fronterad. Revista Digital*. June 27, 2012. Web. September 4, 2013.

Oliver, Michael. *The Politics of Disablement*. New York: St. Martin's, 1990.

Pfeiffer, David. "Philosophical Foundations of Disability Studies" *Disability Studies Quarterly* 22.2 (2002): 3–23. Web. September 15, 2011.

Quayson, Ato. *Aesthetic Nervousness: Disability and the Crisis of Representation*. New York: Columbia UP, 2007.

Quijano, Aníbal. "Coloniality of Power, Eurocentrism and Latin America." *Nepantla: Views from the South* 1.3. (2000): 533–580. Project Muse. Web. December 15, 2011.

Reber, Dierdra. "Love as Politics: *Amores Perros* and the Emotional Aesthetics of Neoliberalism." *Journal of Latin American Cultural Studies*. 19.3 (2010): 279–298. Taylor & Francis. Web. August 23, 2013.

Ricoeur, Paul. "Life: A Story in Search of a Narrator." Translated by J.N. Kraay and A.J. Scholten. In *A Ricoeur Reader: Reflection and Imagination*. Edited by Mario Valdés. Toronto: U of Toronto P, 1991, 425–437.

Rosato, Ana, and María Alfonsina Angelino, Coords. *Discapacidad e ideología de la normalidad. Desnaturalizar el deficit*. Buenos Aires: Noveduc, 2009.
Schrader, Stuart, and Facundo Chavez Penilla, "Crisis, Class and Disability in Argentina: Red por los Derechos de las Personas con Discapacidad." *Disability Studies Quarterly*. 33.2 (2012). Web. July 14, 2014.
Shakespeare, Tom. "The Social Model of Disability." *Disability Studies Reader*. Edited by Lennard J. Davis. 4th ed. New York: Routledge, 2013, 214–221.
Siebers, Tobin. *Disability Theory*. Ann Arbor: U of Michigan P, 2008.
Sommer, Doris. *Foundational Fictions: The National Romances of Latin America*. Berkeley: U of California P, 1991.
Stiker, Henri-Jacques. *A History of Disability*. Translated by William Sayers. Ann Arbor: U of Michigan P, 1990.
Titchkosky, Tanya. "Disability: A Rose By Any Other Name? 'People-First Language in Canadian Society.' " *Canadian Review of Sociology and Anthropology* 38.2 (2001): 125–140. ProQuest. Web. August 23, 2013.
———, and Rod Michalko, eds. *Rethinking Normalcy: A Disability Studies Reader*. Toronto: Canadian Scholars' Press, 2009.
Tremain, Shelley, ed. *Foucault and the Government of Disability*. Ann Arbor, U of Michigan P, 2005.
United Nations. "Factsheet on Persons with Disabilities." n.p. Web. July 31, 2013.
"UN Seeks Protection and Assistance for Chile's Disabled Post earthquake." *Santiago Times*, April 16, 2010.
Verdugo Alonso, Miguel Ángel, dir. *Personas con discapacidad*. Madrid: Siglo XXI, 1998.
Vite Pérez, Miguel Ángel. "La discapacidad en México desde la vulnerabilidad social." *Polis: Investigación y Análisis Sociopolítico y Psicosocial* 8.2 (2012): 153–173. Web. June 1, 2014.
World Health Organization. "Disability and Health." n.p. Web. July 31, 2013.

# Part I

# Disability Life Writing and Constructions of the Self

Chapter 1

# Blind Spot

## *(Notes on Reading Blindness)*

Lina Meruane

Translated by Beth E. Jörgensen

> Para la tarea del arte, la ceguera no es del todo una desdicha: puede ser un instrumento. (For the making of art, blindness is not an absolute misfortune: it can be a tool.)
>
> —Jorge Luis Borges

### brief retelling of a loss

*Sangre en el ojo* (Seeing Red) is the account of a medical emergency. The story of an ocular hemorrhage. The chronicle of blindness foretold. After such a unique event (unique but perhaps repeatable) writing poses a question. Could the absence of one of our senses diminish the legitimacy—the moral, bodily, and textual legitimacy—of a character who signs her books (or used to sign, before her blindness) under the name of Lina Meruane? Could sightlessness, against all expectations, confer some advantage over those who see? The novel examines how the experience progressively transforms her, the newly blind woman, as much as the other characters: her new boyfriend, her elderly mother. The novel sets its sight on her treating physician, on the ethical but limited vision of medicine and on the viewpoints of the multiple secondary characters. Loss appears like a sticking point around which all conduct changes and at times collapses. Because blindness, I think or thought, while I was writing this novel, threatens all of our assumptions, all the habits that anchor each of us safely in our work. In the urgency of the present moment, each character confronts the questions detonated by blindness. Lucina (that is her real name, that sudden blind woman) must resolve how to inhabit, among the seeing, an invisible present. How to avoid turning into a passive victim of circumstance. How to turn the situation to her benefit. To the benefit, as well, of a writing that accounts for this moment of hers. But to place on the page what is no longer seen is of necessity an exercise aided by the tricks of memory and by the spoken (but always questionable) visual truth apported by others. She will have to make use of eyes on loan, seeing eyes that impose their own reading of reality. The novel is organized, then, around this dilemma. The blind woman's subordination in the very act of perceiving and apprehending (or reapprehending) the world. The manipulations that we carry out on the real. The choice of point of view. Disputed authorship and authority over a shared tale. Sometimes writing will require other eyes, but then this question arises: Where does the other's gaze leave off and one's own begin; where does Ignacio's body end and that of his blind woman begin?

## a loss foretold

A few more words so as not to lose sight of a decisive fact: the writing of *Sangre en el ojo* was triggered by my own experience of temporary blindness. A loss, as I said, foretold; an event of unknown dimensions for which I had prepared myself as well as possible. It wasn't always easy to follow the strict medical orders that demanded complete rest. Impossible to refrain from sudden movements, bending over, lifting heavy or bulky objects that could make the malformed veins of the eyes burst. In the months before the hemorrhage, I saw those malignant veins creeping across the retina like slow-growing roots. If I shook my head a little, they also moved, rhythmically, supported by the jelly-like vitreous humor. Their relentless growth assured that my quietude would only delay what was destined to happen, what began to occur one day, while I was bending over to pick up a piece of trash stuck to the carpet. The first drop of blood appeared suddenly, like a dark light burning between the back of my eye and the wall. It was a pinpoint stain that began to spread right away, turning the world into a blur that lasted for hours. The blurry days recurred with increasing frequency, and I finally accepted that soon it wouldn't be one or two drops. My eyes would fill with blood.

## closing my eyes

"Uno tiene muchos ojos dentro del cerebro, como un atadijo de estrellas. Por eso hay que cerrar los ojos corporales, macizo, aunque venga la anochecida, aunque no sea de día, para poder ver detrás" (Poniatowska, *Hasta* 12). (We all have many eyes inside our brain, like a string of stars. To be able to see clearly, you have to keep your eyes closed tight, even at night when there's no daylight" [Poniatowska, *Here's to You* 6].) It's as if Jesusa Palancares were whispering these words in my ears, words first spoken to Poniatowska, and later read by me.

## the singular experience

Seeing again little by little after three months was a singular experience that I knew nothing about. A story never told in literature. There were blind people narrated by the sighted, and the permanently blind—very few—who told or bore witness to their condition. But the account of sight regained had not been written. It was a unique experience, potential writing matter. Not to downplay the value of literature: any everyday experience can become *unique* if the writer gives it a personal stamp, if memory transforms it (Tabucchi 23). But Roberto Calasso cautions and even says specifically that there are experiences that have a different status. Experiences that are "more exceptional than others" and produce strange or "unique" books, even considering the prior work of their writer. (The loss of a physical ability is one of those instances, the loss of a loved one is another.)[1] Calasso designates these rare documents as unclassifiable and heterogeneous, as tales in which one acknowledges "que al autor le ha sucedido algo y que ese algo ha terminado por depositarlo en su escrito" (qtd. by Rabassa). (something has happened to the author and that something has been put into his work for safekeeping.) Perhaps because of their particular origin, these "unique books" (that might never have been written) shouldn't be judged only for their literary value but also for the courage of the author in facing up to that critical moment without looking away. Without waiting for mediating others, for false translators. Without avoiding the first person or the proper name.

## wretched stuff

Working with the stuff of suffering, however, is delicate work and it stays the hand. A dilemma arises: one expects the sick person to make a direct and detailed confession of their suffering, in that event writing could go straight downhill. Josefina Vicens, like Borges, lost her sight. Sunk into a deep depression, she considered the possibility of undertaking a final book—a book that could have been "unique" if it had been written. Vicens said: "Después de *Los años falsos* [su novela segunda y final] se me ocurrió escribir una novela acerca del problema de mi ceguera, pero muy pronto me dije 'yo no escribo nada de eso, va a salir una cosa lastimera' " (González Dueñas 10). (After "The False Years" [her second and final novel] it occurred to me to write a novel about the problem of my blindness, but soon I told myself 'don't write about that, it's going to turn out to be a wretched thing.' ") Perhaps that is why Borges also abstained from this kind of writing and limited himself to referring to the matter only in a speech or a literary essay from 1977. Blindness runs through Borges's poetry, it is part of his poetics of blind mirrors, ocular labyrinths, praise for the shadows (Borges's blindness was not night but twilight). His poetry makes reference to venerable blind men, Milton and, of course, Joyce, but he does not devote his short stories to plotting blindness.

In the same fashion, James Joyce would only write about his afflicted vision and his successive surgeries in epistolary form. Like Borges, Joyce suffered from an eye condition since childhood. He consulted different doctors, got different diagnoses (iritis, conjunctivitis, glaucoma, episcleritis, cataracts), went through several surgeries and spent long periods of his adulthood in near blindness. It was no secret: Joyce was already a well-known author when he posed in Paris for Berenice Abbott with his eye covered after surgery. (Anecdotally, his only daughter, born when Joyce was 25 years old, was named Lucia, after the patron saint of the blind.) His visual impairment would not prevent Joyce from writing his masterpieces: it is well documented that his collective composition practice was derived from such impairment. (Interesting to note, too, is that Samuel Beckett collaborated with Joyce and Beckett's own work is filled with blind characters). Other than in passing—as in the brief episode in *Ulysses* when Bloom assists the blind boy to cross a street—blindness is not a central theme in Joyce's work. However, visual affliction is referenced in a profusion of word games in both *Ulysses* and *Finnegans Wake*.

It is as if a fear of also losing the pulse of the imagination loomed over the crisis. A fear of turning to stereotyped and superficial images of suffering. Revealing, perhaps, that excessively wretched stuff that could irreversibly damage writing or existence, sully the name of the author.

## naming an I

During the time that I was engaged with *Sangre en el ojo* I asked myself if it would be wise to reveal the novel's basis in biography, if it would be pertinent or inadequate to unveil the intimate origin of the tale. I debated with myself over including or not my own name, and I finally decided to do so. It was necessary in order to produce an illusion, let's say an optical illusion, in the reader: that Lucina would sign her novel as Lina made her name a fiction. An indispensable device, I thought, for constructing a falsified truth, tossing in the real name in order to destabilize it and deny it toward the end of the novel. "A false I" (I don't know who said this before): "I wish to say I, but each time I say it, I self-destruct."

## losing an eye that never abandons you

It would be easy to think that *Sangre en el ojo* began to take shape afterward. Or that its writing was contemplated during the dark months of blindness. It wasn't like that, however. This story began to take shape long before the event. It sent out its slow roots across many years, across many separate stories. One of those tentative texts was finished in the months that passed between the diagnosis and the hemorrhage; it was a strange, fragmentary story about a woman who was losing her sight, confined to a house full of shedding cats; in this story there is also a man, a neighbor who can see, an elusive adulterous redhead, who visits that soon-to-be blind woman from time to time. I remember the appearances of the ever more fiery-haired lover (as she grows more blind, his hair is the only thing she can make out), and I remember that the loss is triggered in her by a strange allergy that the shedding cats caused; nothing more. This story is now as lost to my old computer's memory as it is to my own. But that wasn't my first fiction about the loss of sight. Reading backward in time I have found that this theme already appeared in a 1995 story that ended up in *Las infantas*. The plot goes like this: a doll who is in love with her doll maker tears out an eye out of jealousy for her flesh-and-blood sister (or stepsister). The doll blinds herself when she comprehends that her cloth body is the insurmountable limit to her human aspirations; her body, she grasps once she meets the stepsister (of whom she, the doll, is an exact copy), isn't what she thought and so she destroys it, or better put, she tears it apart, starting with her eye. That scene, nevertheless, wasn't new either; I realized it later, when I found a forgotten writing exercise dated 1990 in a drawer. On those two sheets I found, to my astonishment, another doll who lost her sight in an fit of hatred. Now, as I retrieve these stories, I understand that a line once scribbled in a notebook full of random sentences that I kept during my months-long blindness, illegible and written at an angle, had come true: a sentence like so many others, tossed blindly on the page, that worked like a command. Like a theory.

Like a premonition. "You can abandon a text—I decipher in my twisted calligraphy—but the text never abandons you."

## the corporality of the world

Writing about illness was something that I had spent years mulling over. Years putting off. I still find quotes sprinkled on scraps of paper and I don't recognize the handwriting, although I know it's mine: the pointy handwriting I used to have. Other notes found their place in a file started two decades ago. At random I choose one among dozens. Andrés Sánchez Robayna writes: "Es preciso que el cuerpo perciba la carnalidad del mundo para poder inscribirse en él" (5). (The body needs to perceive the corporality of the world in order to inscribe itself in it.) This time memory serves. I know that I stole this verse in the Canary Islands, in the reading that I did while proofreading my first novel. It wasn't my book. A poet who would later make a quick cameo appearance in *Sangre en el ojo* must have lent it to me.

## attempting a memory

In some indeterminable moment I know that I considered writing a memoir. I had in mind two "unique books": *Darkness Visible*, a suitable title for my topic, although it is the account of William Styron's deep depression, a memoir that had captivated me when I was in my twenties. There was also *The Bell Jar*, the suicide autobiography of Sylvia Plath, who had her first depressive episode when she arrived in New York. I recall being stretched out on a bed listening to the anguished narrative on a huge tape recorder. I recall the voice on the double cassette tapes that the library for the blind sent to me. "I was supposed to be having the time of my life." No need to jot down that line: it would have served to describe my own New York crisis. This line became the epigraph of the memoir that I later threw away. I failed in my attempt. I never found the right register. I couldn't stick to the facts. The act of imagining what is not seen took precedence, getting the better of me.

## oblivion's certitude

Writing about that episode has distanced it, made it so diffuse as to erase it from my memory. Its only certain existence is found in the fictional reconstruction. Writing is its only reality. Lina Meruane.

## involuntary trilogy

I began the manuscript of *Sangre en el ojo* against my expectations. I didn't have a conscious plan—although there was a document with odd memories about the episode that hadn't found a place in the novel. I had neither the intention nor the time. When I got the invitation to contribute a text to the anthology *Excesos del cuerpo* (2009) (Bodily Excess), I had just started to draft my PhD dissertation on the impact of AIDS in Latin American literature. (That book would be called *Viajes virales* [Viral Voyages].) Nor was I enthusiastic about returning literarily to illness following the recent publication of *Fruta podrida* (2007) (Rotten Fruit), a novel governed by the degenerative logic of diabetes. Only due to the editors' insistence (I didn't have a plan, I said; I didn't have time, I insisted; it wasn't going to work, but I never told them this), I set out to write just a short story that, against my will, began to drift into a long one: the beginning of a novel that would conclude my "involuntary trilogy" (Mario Levrero *dixit*) on illness. I call it "involuntary," but above all, I call it strange or bizarre, because each one of these books (an essay, two novels) published over the course of a decade, interrogate in heterogeneous ways, in dissimilar registers, using different styles and different genres, they all interrogate, I repeat, the death drive, the political resistance of bodies that deviate from the norm, the survival instinct that accompanies the existence of the invalid. A trilogy that points to, without foreclosing on it, the diverse experiences of loss of validity, of in-validity, brought about by bodily decay.

## blood: sweet or fresh

I'll set aside the trilogy's essay in order to focus on the two diabetic novels and their protagonists. Now I think (hindsight allows me this conjecture) that the two of them, suspended between Chile and New York, present conflicting, even opposite positions, when faced with the same ideological context: the social utopia of corporeal perfection (which physical disability invalidates) and the dream of immortality (hindered and even negated by the irrevocable fact of decay). Faced with the same degenerative illness and its various trajectories—gangrene in the 2007 novel, blindness in 2012—the protagonists set out on divergent paths. The girl with sweet blood, native of Ojo Seco, a blind alley in the middle of Chile's industrial fruit belt, chooses to travel and die in front of a foreign hospital, in a performance of critical resistance against a system that discarded her as useless. Her decision lays claim to the natural strength of imperfection, the expected horizon of the unhealthy, the organic cycle of life and death, as opposed to the capitalist system of incessant production.[2] The woman in *Sangre en el ojo* appropriates this same unscrupulous medical insistence on health present in *Fruta podrida* and carries it to its final consequences. She takes advantage of her disabled status, however, to save herself. Contrary to the death wish of the girl from Ojo Seco, this other woman, blinded by a cruel instinct for life, looks for a fresh eye. But perhaps, I now think, following these disorganized notes, the differences between the two novels aren't so extreme. Perhaps they can be read as opposite sides of a single, complex situation—the ethics of the body in our society—that forces us to take sides. To find our place on shifting ground. In my view this is what the novels accomplish: they carry the question of life and death to almost unbearable extremes against one single biopolitical background. Only extreme situations, I believe, lend true perspective on a problem.

## drafting blindness

Looking at both books with a critical eye (and not with my author's cross-eyed squint), I see that the newer novel returns to the scene of the loss. It starts there, as if to pick up something that remained open or hanging in the prior text. *Fruta podrida* concludes with the discovery that the infected foot has disappeared or exploded (as the prose also explodes at the end of the novel). *Sangre en el ojo* begins with another explosion, one in which what is lost is sight and not life, however. In the time elapsed between one novel and the next (time during which I managed to finish *Viajes virales*) I asked myself somewhat anxiously if the death of a character, besides being understood as a sign of political resistance in extreme situations—as with a suicide bomber—might signify a capitulation, a loss of that obstinate energy that defines the political. Exemplary or model suicides whether in literature or real life are always pyrrhic victories. That's what I thought or could have thought, not entirely convinced that those deaths could make possible a social transformation. Halfway, limited victories, unsustainable triumphs, I told myself, and then perhaps I asked: Victories run-through with the paradox of failure? Could the resistance posed by a sick body influence the workings of the body politic? Maybe it would be necessary (more creative, more defiant) to imagine the polar opposite. Write another scene: not the scene of the self-elimination of the novelistic imaginary, but the imposition of bodily illness or loss on others. That is, instead of marginalizing the sick from the scene, place her in the center, disseminate that bodily experience, impose it on others. Cut the distance between the healthy and the sick, between the sighted and the blind, between the valid and the invalid. Do this in the new novel, certainly, but also in a wider sense, add pathology to the social imaginary of the normal: destabilize the certainty that a border exists, depose health as the norm. Turn the mirror on the healthy and make them face their own illness.

## prior fermentations

This morning, in the final revision of this essay, I get the idea to open the file of my first novel, *Póstuma* (2000) (Posthumous). It occurs to me to search for the words "fruit" and "rotten" in the text. The following sentence appears, after the encounter between the protagonist and her dying, diabetic grandmother. "Me acerqué, respirando por la boca para no sentir el intenso olor a fruta podrida. Era ella, la vieja, como cosecha en fermento" (32). (I approached her breathing through my mouth so as not to smell the intense aroma of rotten fruit. It was her, the old woman, like fermenting wine.) I narrow the search to "fruit." I find this: "En la morgue, tal vez, [. . .] ahí debía estar mi abuela, su cuerpo extrañamente frío y rígido, un cuerpo ya empezando a volverse blando otra vez, otra vez suave, pulposo como una fruta madura" (12). (In the morgue, maybe, that was where my grandmother must be, her body strangely cold and stiff, a body starting to turn soft again, smooth again, fleshy like a piece of ripe fruit.) I think again that illness has not wanted to abandon me.

## women in love

I only remembered this one line by the writer Agata Gligo. I met her before I had read her work, when she was already ill. She still had a bright gaze. She wore a turban that highlighted her green eyes, now darkened. She smiled mysteriously. In her posthumous diary she reveals that she had "fallen in love with her own illness." (Agata, I think, calling her to mind, I wonder if I have also fallen in love with mine?)

## groping in the dark

A setback in this essay: getting off track. What was supposed to be a reflection on writing disability, on the creation of disabled characters, has become something else: a text that cannot complete its task. A disabled, fragmentary text. I begin to circle the room (as I have circled this essay). I trace desperate, determined circles around the discovery that I have never stopped to consider this theme before. More circling. Perhaps I should sit down and rethink my omission. Perhaps, I conclude (my breathing agitated by so much circling, so much groping in the dark) I simply haven't thought about loss in the terms that were suggested. Invalidism. Inability. Disability. A person with reduced talents. This jargon is alien to me. I find myself reflecting on the alternative abilities of the supposedly disabled. On the need to invest loss with gain, physical limitation with the development of new muscles. At least in fiction. I feel trapped, looking through my window at the wall of the house next door, when the inspiring logic of the Oulipo comes to me by free association: the imposition of limits is an indispensable requirement of the creative process. Limit as resource, obstacles as a way of carrying language and literary form to a higher imaginative level. Thinking about the Oulipian technique, I return to the limited body. To the physical restrictions that could lead to the formulation of a poetics and an ethics of the possible. But my disquisition doesn't end here. I am assailed by doubts about opposing the disdain that originates in the sense of superiority and condescending, paternalistic pity with an equally perverse move: that of making disability into a virtue.

## the curious monster

I talk about reading, but it's just a turn of speech. What I did in those months was to listen to books. Dozens. All listed in a document titled "Books on Tape," which perhaps ought to be called "Books to Keep You from Going Crazy." Now in my notebook on blindness I find this reference to *Pale Horse, Pale Rider* by Katherine Anne Porter, taken down after I had recuperated while I was still on the path to reading with my own eyes again. "The body is a curious monster"—the narrator speaks to me with her seductive voice, and I rewind the tape to listen again—"The body is a curious monster, no place to live in. How could anyone feel at home there. Is it possible that I will ever accustom myself to this place, she asked." I find other lines jotted down following these. It is an accidental dialogue between two very different authors. Severo Sarduy answers Porter: "Antes disfrutaba de una ilusión persistente: ser uno. Ahora somos dos, inseparables, idénticos: la enfermedad y yo" (Sarduy 111). (Before, I enjoyed a persistent illusion: that I was one. Now we are two, inseparable and identical: illness and I.) For Porter the body is an uninhabitable house, a monstrous prison. For Sarduy, the sick body is the inescapable double. I don't find any hint of virtue in either one. Maybe virtue is written here in invisible ink.

## terror's superior form

Some "élan vital" must have emanated from the readings undertaken for *Viajes virales*. From Emil Cioran's funereal but existential breviaries. From Sarduy's plague diaries. From Reinaldo Arenas's challenging novels of terminal illness. From the necrophiliac urge in Bellatin's writing. From all that literature touched by the magic wand of tuberculosis. From the metaphorical rigors of cancer in the essays of Susan Sontag. In all of them, the captivating, rebellious optic of Virginia Woolf's early reflections on illness is visible. Texts that think about illness, that turn over the idea of loss, that ask how to invert the logic of illness as death or as an elimination round. Readings filled with clues that subvert the terminal narrative. Those are the tracks that *Sangre en el ojo* was ultimately following: during the prolonged reading period, the need arose to overturn the tragic course of *Fruta podrida*. Search for empowering instances of the figure of the blind woman. Think about loss as a lucid or illuminating or hallucinating force in the context of which health is "an insignificant state of perfection" (Cioran 125). Because health, Cioran tells us, sedates us, makes us inattentive to reality. And a full life demands the consciousness (a political consciousness, I would add) of being alive, and the body grants us that knowledge precisely when it is in pain, when everything begins to come apart. The experience of terror granted by illness or disability is a dramatic revelation about being alive, a superior form of consciousness that is associated with vitality and where "the apostacy of the organs" (Cioran 126) comes to fruition. Because in its beginning stages, consciousness (to paraphrase from Cioran) is consciousness of the internal organs.

## suspicions

"A rule of conduct: mistrust the sickly" (129). Cioran again. He warns us that illness is understood as an exceptional state governed by an I who is unbound by the norms of social harmony, even free to practice cruelty. I fine-tune his rule: don't trust the blind and their intelligent dead eyes.

## ocular intelligence

But where does the intelligence of a sightless eye come from and what does it mean? What power does blindness grant? Lucina says about the hemorrhage:

"estar así, en esta bruma, es como estar dormida y a la vez despierta. Es como estar un poco sorda" (Meruane, *Sangre* 39). (to be that way, in that fog, is like being asleep and awake at the same time. It's like being slightly deaf.) It is a demoralized statement, but only apparently so, because what comes out of that fog is an unexpected wisdom that allows her to reorganize everything that she knows in that unfavorable setting. Rather than a shaky start to the story, I think of that moment in the novel as an opportunity above all (in dream, in deafness) to turn within. Blindness confers an introspective, secret power (which others lack and as a result fear). Borges, one of Derrida's "blind ancestors" of the literary canon,[3] refers to this knowing relationship that the blind establishes with himself in an affirmative way, but through a rhetorical question: "[W]ho lives more with themselves? Who can explore themselves more? [. . .] According to the Socratic phrase, who can know himself more than the blind man?" (106). One doesn't only turn within, but rather soon one begins to disregard the coercive or pitying gaze that others' eyes flaunt, and then hierarchy suffers a subtle but meaningful transformation. If we accept what blind writing proposes, then the lost or wandering or indefinable gaze of those who do not see is disturbing to those who do. It raises suspicion about what the blind man or woman perceives. The clouded eye seems to reawaken obscure anxieties about a reality that goes beyond the natural. At least that seems to be the discovery that the Lange sisters make in *Cuadernos de infancia* [Childhood Notebooks], as they tell it: "Habíamos creído que [el hombre] tenía una vista sobrenatural. En realidad, estaba casi ciego" (184). (We had thought that [the man] had supernatural vision. In reality, he was almost blind.) The same mistake repels and attracts Ana in a disturbing story by Clarice Lispector, when she observes a blind man at a bus stop chewing gum, "sin sufrimiento, con los ojos abiertos" (Lispector 23). (without suffering, with his eyes open.) These blank but defiant eyes take hold of the protagonist's imagination like a tortured but obsessive love, and they accompany her to the house where her husband and children are waiting for her. There are episodes in which the empty gaze provokes panoptical epiphanies: blind men posted on city streets tapping their tin cups to attract attention, wearing large dark glasses like thugs of the dictatorship (in a travel chronicle by Maruja Torres); or standing in line like security guards in a supermarket (in a short story by Mayra Luna). In "Valium" (one of Nicolás Poblete's short stories), a similar anxiety arises when the protagonist convinces herself that she is being spied on and pursued by a woman who turns out to be blind. These impossible gazes disturb the security of those who think they are being observed (all of them young, fragile women). The blind eye holds an unspeakable power that enthralls them.

## anx-eye-eties

Or perhaps they fear blind contagion. I thought about this a great deal later, after publishing *Sangre en el ojo*, when I was struck by the infinite accounts of the eye conditions suffered by the novel's readers. Hemorrhages caused by blows, small strokes in the optical nerve, severe myopia, the threat of glaucoma, macular degeneration, retinal flashes or floaters like insects caught in the eye. It didn't surprise me that Lucina's blindness let loose an identity crisis. I had seen it before in my own notes: "Es automático. [El personaje v]e a un ciego y se imagina ciego" (Zambra 20).[4] (It's automatic. The character sees a blind person and imagines himself to be blind.) Some pages on he adds that "no temía propiamente a la oscuridad sino a la posibilidad de quedarse ciego. Una noche despertó sin resquicios de luz a que acudir: primero tuvo la impresión de que alguien había *cerrado* la pieza, y luego la pavorosa convicción de que había quedado ciego" (55). (he didn't exactly fear darkness but rather the possibility of going blind. One night he woke up in the pitch dark: first he thought someone had closed the door to the room, and then he had the terrifying conviction that he had gone blind.)

## a blindness that cannot be seen

José Lezama Lima introduces this odd philosophical affirmation in *Paradiso*: "No es bueno que el *hombre* no vea nada, no es bueno tampoco que vea lo suficiente para conocer lo que ha perdido. Es bueno ver y no ver: esto es precisamente el estado de la naturaleza (Pascal)" (33, emphasis added). (It's not good for *man* to see nothing, nor is it good for him to see well enough to know what he has lost. It is good to see and not see: that is precisely the natural state [Pascal].)

## victims, the vision-less, visionaries

I return to my notes in search of clues to help me understand this rejection and, in the process, to examine the ways in which the eye appears in the texts of our tradition. I confirm that since long ago its vigilant presence has insured the social order. The abrogation of the gaze that safeguards order is terrifying. The eye is god or king: that is the form it takes. It is the highest authority: knowledge (or *sa-voir*, Derrida declares) that emanates from the watchful eye. It is the law of the father; for that reason the drama of blindness is of the order of the masculine. Jacques Derrida affirms (I merely paraphrase him) that in our culture there are only great blind men. They are all renowned. What the philosopher does not also explain is that blindness hangs over that gender because power is culturally their territory. (In the symbolic realm, a blind woman does not have the same semantic weight nor does she generate the same fear: a woman cannot lose what she has never owned.)[5] The classical imagination produced two masculine embodiments of power centered on that organ, two emblematic characters simultaneously opposite and complementary. The failure of power, the mutilated eye of the seeing king (Oedipus) who, after solving an intellectual riddle blinded himself to the reality before his very eyes (his crime consisted of not perceiving the familial hierarchy clearly: killing his father, committing incest with his mother). Oedipus is not capable of sustaining the legitimacy of power that has been conferred on him nor of confirming his visual knowledge, that is, that he sees and therefore he knows (*insight*, Derrida notes, implies comprehension). He is a fallen, disgraced, and distracted king who punishes his lack of vision (his not knowing, his not having the power he thought he had) by making it literal. He thus tears out his eyes to make his earlier blindness public but also to show that the truth had finally been revealed to him. In this ancient work, power goes in the end to the blind visionary, Tiresias, who supplements the lack of eyesight with a superior ability that allows him to know things in advance. His blindness is a sign of divine omniscience, the embodiment of a total power and an absolute knowledge that can do without the organ of sight. A superhuman ability.

## blind love

A woman tears out her eyes for love in a story by Clemente Palma titled "Los ojos de Lina" (Lina's Eyes). (A Peruvian writer commented on it, noticing the shared name.) Palma, I thought upon rereading the story a decade later, didn't repeat the Oedipus myth, but rather, perhaps, St. Lucy's, who before becoming a saint served her eyes on a tray to her betrothed. That terrifying scene provided me with another clue as I moved ahead with the writing. (I copied two of Palma's lines for a potential epigraph, which eventually made it into the novel.) I also wrote down that a woman who makes a gift of her eyes before the wedding—to spare her betrothed the anxiety that her diabolical gaze produced in him—carries out the social imperative of surrender. A macabre fulfillment of the marriage vow in which she renounces her subversive sexuality (the diabolical gaze) and voluntarily complies with the expectation of the married women's submission (the command, expression of a hegemonic power, functions without needing an expressed order). The loss of sight completes the idea that feminine love is (and must be) blind. Turning the metaphor into reality made visible the violence of that renunciation.

## upside down promises

The rhetoric of love governs the evolution of *Sangre en el ojo*. It is, nevertheless, a mixed up rhetoric: the proof is demanded of him, not her; she asks him for unconditional support. What would you be willing to do for love. What would you sacrifice for me. Are you able to take my place. Do you dare to become my eyes. Will you lend them to me. Make them mine. Be part of this distorting mirror. Would you dare to be my equal. Lucina doesn't put it that way, I don't know if she even thinks of it in these words. But these are the questions that are turning over and over in the novel. These questions and this certainty: that every love relationship is also an asymetrical one that tries to even itself out in the other's body.

## hell

Again, Cioran: "[T]he only equality which matters to us, also the only one of which we are capable, is an equality in hell" (130).

## dependence

More notes about dependence. 1. An unworkable model for living together long term. 2. Production of complicated mechanisms for accepting and rejecting dependence. 3. Abuse of power, usually but not uniquely masculine. Power relations can be reversed. 4. Subordination as a consequence of the need for the other. 5. Insubordination as a first step to achieving autonomy. 6. Warning: dependence engenders its own monsters.

## never stop

"La escritura corre—dice Botho Strauss—ya no hay escapatoria" (25). (Writing starts now—says Botho Strauss—there is no escape.)

## the mind's eye

Maybe I already said this. That I was obliged to improvise the world, which has disappeared for Lina, or Lucina. My memory of blindness was so opaque that light couldn't shine through it. There were gray or blurry moments (not the blues, greens, and washed-out yellows that Borges describes). The novel wasn't going to be anything but literally black, dark like my blindness. It would devote itself, then, to a synergistic exploration of my remaining senses. It would be, above all, an oral novel (following the message that I had left for myself years before in yet another note). In effect: I found Lucina's voice and I worked on my four senses, but the account was run through, even dominated, by images that infiltrated the plot and refused to abandon it. I understood then that in the work of constructing the past, memory lent an unexpected aid. It filled the gaps of blindness with exact details of scenes previously or later viewed, or vividly imagined. The memory of the newly blind woman continued to belong to the visual realm, it was an *imaginative* memory. The things her eyes didn't see, the mind's eye captured ("the mind's eye" means the ability to visualize, remember or imagine in images). I understood that you don't see *with* the eye, but rather *through* it, with the brain, from memory. Even in the dark, reality is stored as an image. And from that mental image, the whole story is told. The one who sits down in front of the blank page re-creates scenes without seeing them, or foretells them in total uncertainty. One writes, one has always written, in a state of stunning blindness.

## fresh eye

In blindness, then, arises the possibility of fiction: a hazy and unlikely zone. Reality's facts become fiction's facts. You don't know when the reality principle fails, when we start to be witnesses of a fictitious memory. When the limit experiences that the novel explores and exploits demand a fresh eye from us.

## what is irretrievable

". . . y cuando nada de nada, absolutamente nada de atroz ni de irreparable te ocurre, es que estás muerto" Carlos Droguett (6). (. . . and when not a single thing, absolutely nothing terrible or irreparable happens to you, it means you're dead.)

## Notes

1. In this Calasso agrees with Gian-Paolo Biasin, who affirms that illness always "triggers a personal poetics, a unique vision of the world."

2. The novel is also part of this system of production. Looking to interrogate that system of market production, in search of a certain internal coherence with what this novel is confronting, I included poems written by the protagonist in her *(De)Composition Notebook* (poetry as alien to the commercial concept of writing); in addition I wrote a chaotic and possibly absurd (in the existential sense) ending, which falls outside of the register of the three earlier parts.

3. In his genealogy of blind ancestors Derrida includes Homer, Milton, Joyce, and Nietzsche.

4. I register the strength of the terror toward blindness in an episode, surprising to me, that occurred outside of the fiction but in a literary setting. After receiving a positive reading of *Sangre en el ojo*, one international editor decided not to publish it (and there was a certain vehemence to that rejection). The reason: a widespread rumor that the translator of José Saramago's novel *Blindness* had lost his sight after finishing it. (Discretion prevents me from citing the source or naming those involved.)

5. It's not that there haven't been blind women, Derrida explains, it's just that they are few and little known. Saint Lucy is one, and there are two versions of her story: one says that her suitors blinded her but she continued seeing (like Tiresias), the other is that she tore out her eyes (like Oedipus?) in order to present them to her betrothed on a tray. Be that as it may, she is the martyr of the blind and the patron saint of opticians. Another saint, Odilia, was born blind and was threatened by her father with death, but God restored her sight when she was baptized.

## Works Cited

Arenas, Reinaldo. *El color del verano, o, Nuevo "Jardín de las delicias."* Barcelona: Tusquets, 1999.

Biasin, Gian-Paolo. *Literary Diseases. Theme and Metaphor in the Italian Novel.* Austin: U of Texas P, 1975.

Borges, Jorge Luis. "Blindness." *Everything and Nothing.* Translated by Donald A. Yates et al. New York: New Directions Books, 1999, 94–108.

Cioran, E.M. "On Sickness." *The Fall into Time.* Translated by Richard Howard. Chicago: Quadrangle Books, 1970, 125–139.

Derrida, Jacques. *Memoirs of the Blind. The Self-Portrait and Other Ruins.* Translated by Pascale-Anne Brault and Michael Naas. Illinois: U of Chicago P, 1993.

Droguett, Carlos. *La señorita Lara.* Santiago, Chile: LOM Ediciones, 2001.

Ellman, Maud. "Drawing the Blind: Gide, Joyce, Larsen and the Short Story." *Oxford Literary Review,* 26. 1 (2004): 31–61.

Ferré, Rosario. "La muñeca menor." *Papeles de Pandora.* New York: Vintage, 2000, 1–9.

Gligo, Ágata. *Diario de una pasajera*. Mexico City: Alfaguara, 1997.
González Dueñas, Daniel, and Alejandro Toledo. *Josefina Vicens: la inminencia de la palabra*. Mexico City: Ediciones Sin Nombre. 2009.
Guerrero, Javier, and Nathalie Bouzaglo, eds. *Excesos del cuerpo. Ficciones de contagio y enfermedad en América Latina*. Buenos Aires: Eterna Cadencia, 2009.
Joyce, James. *Ulysses*. New York: Vintage International, 1990.
Lange, Norah. *Cuadernos de infancia*. Buenos Aires: Losada, 1957.
Lispector, Clarice. "Amor." In *Lazos de familia*. Translated by Cristina Peri Rossi. Barcelona: Montesinos, 1998, 20–32.
Luna, Mayra. "Me miran." *Lo peor de ambos mundos: relatos anfibios*. Mexico City: CONACULTA, 2006. 62–69.
Meruane, Lina. *Póstuma*. Santiago, Chile: Planeta, 2000.
———. *Fruta podrida*. Santiago, Chile: Fondo de Cultura Económica, 2007.
———. *Sangre en el ojo*. Santiago, Chile: Mondadori, 2012.
———. *Seeing Red*. Translated by Megan McDowell. Dallas: Deep Vellum, 2016.
———. *Viajes virales. La crisis del contagio global en la escritura del sida*. Santiago, Chile: Fondo de Cultura Económica, 2012.
Navarro, Elvira. *La ciudad en invierno*. Madrid: Caballo de Troya, 2007.
Palma, Clemente. "Los ojos de Lina." In *Narrativa completa I*. Edited by Ricardo Sumalavia. Lima: Pontificia Universidad Católica, 2006, 217–225.
Poblete, Nicolás. "Valium." *Frivolidades*. Santiago, Chile: RIL Editores, 2008, 83–91.
Poniatowska, Elena. *Hasta no verte Jesús mío*. 1969. Mexico City: Era, 1969.
———. *Here's to You, Jesusa!* Translated by Deanna Heikkinen. New York: Farrar, Straus and Giroux, 2001.
Plath, Sylvia. *The Bell Jar*. 1967. New York: Harper Perennial, 1999.
Rabasa, Eduardo. "El libro único." *Milenio*, 12/14/2008. n.p. May 1, 2013. www.milenio.com/cdb/doc/impreso/8508940
Sánchez Robayna, Andrés. "Prólogo." In *Presencia de Manuel González Sosa*. Las Palmas de Gran Canaria, Spain: Ediciones del Cabildo Insular de Gran Canaria, 1998, 3–7.
Sarduy, Severo. *Pájaros de la playa*. Barcelona: Tusquets, 1993.
Strauss, Botho. *La dedicatoria*. Translated by Genoveva Dieterich. Madrid: Alfaguara, 1985.
Styron, William. *Darkness Visible: A Memoir of Madness*. New York: Random House, 1990.
Tabucchi, Antonio. *Autobiografías ajenas. Poéticas a posteriori*. Translated by Carlos Gumpert. Barcelona: Anagrama, 2006.
Torres, Maruja. *Amor América: un viaje sentimental por América Latina*. Madrid: El País/Aguilar, 1993.
Zambra, Alejandro. *La vida privada de los árboles*. Barcelona: Anagrama, 2007.

Chapter 2

# "La cara que me mira"

## Demythologizing Blindness in Borges's Disability Life Writing

Kevin Goldstein

Disquiet accompanied the birth of Jorge Luis Borges in August of 1899. After searching the eyes of his newborn son for a sign of the vision problems that had affected five generations of his family, a relieved Guillermo Borges declared to his wife: "está salvado, tiene ojos claros, heredó tus ojos" (Bioy Casares 114). (He's saved, he has light-colored eyes, he inherited your eyes [my translation].) This diagnosis would prove mistaken.

The young Borges indeed displayed signs of the progressive vision loss, which would persist throughout his life. At the age of eight, his mother asked him to read the label on a container of Crosse & Blackwell sweets, to which the child responded: "no dice nada. Es un papel blanco" (Bioy Casares 114). (it doesn't say anything. It's blank. [my translation].) An ophthalmologist, one Molard, diagnosed him with incipient cataracts. Later, he would be diagnosed with pathological myopia. Evidence suggests that, even as early as the 1920s, the author periodically struggled to read the page before him. In 1927, he underwent the first of eight cataract operations that would span the next thirty years.

Finally, in late 1955, while vacationing in Mar del Plata, Borges experienced a retinal detachment, which resulted in the loss of what he called his "reader's and writer's sight" (Weinberger 475). Of necessity, the author returned to poetry, a form he had largely abandoned in favor of prose a quarter-century prior; though now, instead of writing free verse poems exclusively, he experimented with sonnets and other rhymed verse, which he could revise mentally before dictating them to an amanuensis. Alluding to the incident in a seminal 1977 lecture in Buenos Aires, Borges downplays the significance of 1955 in his visual life: "Para los propósitos de esta conferencia debo buscar un momento patético. Digamos, aquel en que supe que ya había perdido mi vista, mi vista de lector y de escritor. Por qué no fijar la fecha, tan digna de recordación, de 1955. No me refiero a las épicas lluvias de septiembre; me refiero a una circunstancia personal" (EC II 41).[1] (For the purposes of this lecture I must look for a pathetic moment. Let's say that moment in which I knew that I'd lost my sight, my reader's and writer's sight. Why not settle on the date, so worthy of remembrance, of 1955. I'm not referring to the epic September rains, but to a personal situation [my translation].) Careful to distinguish between this very personal event and the concurrent Revolución Libertadora,[2] he invokes that conflict in part to throw the insignificance of his blindness into sharp relief: "My case is not especially dramatic . . . that slow nightfall, that slow loss of sight, began when I began to see. It has continued since 1899 without dramatic moments, a slow nightfall that has lasted more than three quarters of a century" (Weinberger 475).

With studied reluctance, Borges grants 1955 as "un momento patético" in order to tell his audience a coherent story, yet he adamantly refuses to assume the role of tragic hero, offering the audience little pathos and no awe. Blindness represents yet another mode of being in the world: "Blindness has not been for me a total misfortune; it should not be seen in a pathetic way. It should be seen as a way of life: one of the styles of living" (Weinberger 478). He later avers: "[Blindness] is one more instrument among the many—all of them strange—that fate or chance provide" (Weinberger 483). Blindness is not a gift per se, but simply an instrument among many that destiny or chance offer the poet, and indeed, everyone. This decisive statement belies the complex, ambivalent treatment of blindness in Borges's late work, which alternates between the vindication of the figure of the blind seer—that is, blindness as a precondition for gnosis—and an interest in the banality of the blind body. This essay probes that ambivalence. Time and again, the writer returns to the reality of his frail, limited body, thus subverting the trope of triumphal inner vision and, in turn, creating a space for bitterness, vexation, and tedium in his performance of blindness. Psyche must contend with soma.

It is worth considering Borges's self-representation in light of the social model of disability, which distinguishes between impairment (the physical condition) and disability (the social consequences of that impairment).[3] According to this model, disability is caused by the choices a society makes in organizing itself. Progress means removing the barriers in society that continually produce disability. This model critiques our notions of normativity and creates a space in which we might recognize blindness not as a problem in need of a solution but as a mode of being and, indeed, a vibrant culture. By not conceiving of blindness purely as deficit, but as a mode of being in the world, Borges forces us to consider the value of disability as difference. Blindness has things to teach us.

Endeavoring to articulate the qualia associated with this "modesta ceguera personal," he proclaims a world of vague, luminous shapes; blue, green, gray, and yellow, all volatile colors that have the power to elicit rich, complex memories. Borges's phenomenology of blindness, so rich in color, runs counter to common knowledge: "People generally imagine the blind as enclosed in a black world. There is, for example, Shakespeares's line: 'looking on darkness, which the blind do see.' If we understand 'darkness' as 'blackness,' then Shakespeare is wrong" (Weinberger 474). With a simple account of blind color perception, Borges puts the lie to the poetic convention that equates blindness and darkness, undercutting thousands of years of Western literature, yet as the reader will find below, he exhibits no compunctions about employing it frequently in his own work. Regardless of his personal experience, he is immersed in the rhetoric of blindness. As Rod Michalko writes: "[M]any of us live disabilities. Our lives are influenced by the ways our culture represents disability. We are living examples of those representations" (*Difference* 13). This dissonance between personal experience and poetic representation in Borges's aesthetic—in short, its nonmimetic character—parallels the divide disabled men and women experience between lived experience and social interpellation. Stephen Kuusisto echoes Borges when he writes: "I am driven by the vagaries of poetry and the imagery in my prose is entirely unreliable though it feels clear for all that. I do not write about what I see, I write about what I do not see with words that feel good to the ear. When I write about the morning skin of ice on a birch tree I'm saying it because it feels right, not because I watched it" ("Digressions" 198–199).

This complicated relationship between reality and art, or truth and language, destabilizes the category of life writing as it concerns Borges. The Argentine believed that words constitute symbols for shared experiences, but all experience is idiosyncratic. To a great extent, we experience the world through language, but language cannot accurately represent that experience. This is the paradox that animates all of Borges's work. With this in mind, I extend the category of life writing to include not merely autobiographical lectures, essays, and interviews, but fiction and poetry as well.[4] Essentially, the Borges who inhabits the poems is no more or less a fiction than the man answering a reporter's questions with mischievous inventions.

One can trace a relation, if a somewhat perverse one, between Borges's playful, postmodern interest in identity and the memoir boom of the past half-century. Commenting on this phenomenon, G. Thomas Couser writes: "the contemporary moment is particularly amenable not only to life writing but also to disability life writing. Disability has been a staple of cultural production for centuries, indeed millennia, but only in the recent past has it generated such a large body of self-representation in the form of personal testimony" (230). Thus the content of Borges's late poetry often inclines toward the personal, particularly the subject of life with low vision, if indeed transmuted by poetic convention.

A number of Borges's works poeticize the fraught moment in which the nearly blind poetic subject encounters a mirror. Able to discern little save the ashen gray and gold of his hair, his image becomes alien, incomprehensible. Perpetuating the ocularcentrism that is his cultural inheritance, Borges locates identity and self-understanding in a body both present and elusive: "Soy la carne y la cara que no veo" (OC III 226). (I am the flesh and the face that I don't see [my translation].) The face, reflected but obscured, constitutes a device for probing blindness in relation to the self. Within the always unreachable, unseen, or vaguely luminous face, the poet imagines a center, an archetype, a source of gnosis. Yet the resolution the face offers proves elusive; it is a continually deferred object, or better, something that never quite becomes an object. Borges highlights this process both positively and negatively, envisioning imminent self-discovery variously with exultant optimism, resigned skepticism, and horror. In charting the face as device, we can begin to identify the contours of Borges's disability life writing.

Equally important is the social impulse in Borges's treatment of blindness. As the reader will note below, much of Borges's late work reifies the cultural script of the blind subject in isolation, confronting only his half-seen visage in the mirror; nevertheless, other pieces seek affiliation and identification with various blind figures. In order to constitute himself as a blind man and as a blind poet, Borges invokes both his paternal line and what Derrida calls a genealogy of blind ancestors (32), Homer, Milton, and Joyce, while simultaneously registering his failure to live up to these heroic forebears, these strong poets. This has important implications for disability studies. Margaret Torrell calls for "an examination of life-writing texts which feature stories of disabled people and groups, thereby challenging notions about the singular, isolated voice often associated with autobiography" (323). As Paul Celan asserts in the Meridian speech: "The poem intends another, needs this other, needs an opposite. It goes toward it, bespeaks it . . . the poem becomes conversation—often desperate conversation" (49–50). In key moments, Borges's work engages in such a conversation.

The titular poem from Borges's 1969 volume, *Elogio de la sombra* ("In Praise of Darkness"), frames late-onset blindness in mythical terms, as the triumph of the mind over an aging body:

> La vejez (tal es el nombre que los otros le dan)
> puede ser el tiempo de nuestra dicha.
> El animal ha muerto o casi ha muerto.
> Quedan el hombre y su alma. (1–4)
> Old age (the name that others give it)
> can be the time of our greatest bliss.
> The animal has died or almost died.
> The man and his spirit remain. (Merwin 299)

The poetic subject articulates a world of dissipating images: "Vivo entre formas luminosas y vagas / que no son aún la tiniebla . . . mis amigos no tienen cara, / las mujeres son lo que fueron hace ya tantos años . . . no hay letras en las páginas de los libros." ("I live among vague, luminous shapes/ that are not darkness yet. . . . my friends have no faces/ women are what they were so many years ago . . . there are no letters on the pages of books"; 5–6, 20–21, 24; Merwin 299.) Rather than frightening him, he finds it "una dulzura, un regreso" ("a sweetness, a return"; 25; Merwin 299). Unlike Democritus, who tore out his eyes in order to think, he declares: "el tiempo ha sido mi Demócrito" ("time has been my Democritus"; 16, Merwin 299). In a 1985 interview, Borges muses: "In a certain way there is purification in blindness. It purifies one of visual circumstances" (Burgin 243). "Elogio de la sombra" perhaps best illustrates this sentiment: visible forms, indeed, flesh itself, give way to a few precious memories, a handful of books the poetic subject keeps "leyendo en la memoria, leyendo y transformando" ("reading in my memory, / reading and transforming"; 28–29; Merwin 299). Blindness promises the substitution of imminent gnosis, or pure logos, for the visible world. The poem ends with the promise of anagnorisis; now able to forget the visual world, the poetic subject arrives at his center: "a mi álgebra y mi clave / a mi espejo. / Pronto sabré quién soy." ("my algebra and my key, / my mirror. / Soon I will know who I am"; 43–46; Merwin 301.) This mirror has the potential to spark a moment of self-recognition, a secret center where Borges may encounter not a sensual but an ideal reflection.

In his seminal lecture on blindness, Borges recites a stanza of Fray Luis de León: "I want to live with myself/ I want to enjoy the good that I owe heaven/ alone, without witnesses" (Weinberger 482). Interpreting the lines in light of his condition, he concludes: "if we accept that in the good of heaven there can also be darkness, then who lives more with themselves?

Who can explore themselves more? Who can know more of themselves? According to the Socratic phrase, who can know himself more than the blind man?" (Weinberger 482). Blindness entails introspection: "El tiempo minucioso, que en la memoria es breve, / me fue hurtando las formas visibles de este mundo." ("frittering time, so brief in memory, / kept taking from me the visible forms of this world"; 17–18; Reid 311). Given this sustained period of loss, the poet accepts blindness as a gift, "un don": it is his duty as a poet to conceive of blindness as an instrument of his art. One recalls the stanza from "Arte poética" ("Ars Poetica"):

> A veces en las tardes una cara
> Nos mira desde el fondo de un espejo
> El arte debe ser como ese espejo
> Que nos revela nuestra propia cara. (17–20)
> At times in the evenings a face
> Looks at us out of the depths of a mirror;
> Art should be like that mirror
> Which reveals to us our own face. (Merwin 137)

By transforming a disappearing, disintegrating world into art, Borges imagines he can arrest this process. Mimetic art offers the promise of chaos framed, stabilized. A dissolving face, he hopes, will suddenly appear intact, an image in his poem. And yet, and yet, the body continually puts metaphorical blindness in check.

Borges often registers a bittersweet melancholy and a resistance to blindness as vision. The metaphor of inner vision breaks down, blindness becomes nothing more than the unseen face in the unseen mirror. "Un sábado" displays a remarkably quotidian, unguarded depiction of visual impairment. It locates the blind poetic subject "en una casa hueca" ("in a hollow house"; 1; McHenry 409). He wanders the halls, touches the walls, the smooth glass of the interior doors, the bindings of the books he cannot read, the family silver, the spigots, moldings, coins, and a key. Without intending to, he lies upon his bed, sensing himself a piece in a game conducted by an enigmatic god. He recites "fragmentos de los clásicos y ensaya / Variaciones de verbos y epítetos / Y bien o mal escribe este poema." ("some fragments from the classics and rehearses / variations of verbs and epithets / and, good or bad, at last he writes this poem"; 19–21; McHenry 409.) Published in the 1977 volume *Historia de la noche* the poem conveys the sense of a routine both solitary and painfully tedious. Here, the writing of poetry materializes from the recitation of remembered fragments, and for better or worse, their reconfiguration. The house itself is empty, hollow, never perceived in one piece. One recalls Borges's identification with Milton's line, "in this dark world and wide" (EC II 421). The poet renders the serial perception of the apartment on Maipú street formally through a succession of conjunctions, "y . . . y . . . y," while we follow the poetic subject's course, defined almost exclusively by haptic perception. Solitude and introspection do not bring anagnorisis; Borges composes a poem, uncertain of its literary merit, nor even of his purpose in doing so.

In another sonnet from *La rosa profunda*, titled "Un ciego" ("A Blind Man"), Borges expresses a sentiment wholly counter to the triumph of inner vision found in "Elogio de la sombra": "No sé cuál es la cara que me mira / cuando miro la cara del espejo." ("I do not know what face is looking back / whenever I look at the face in the mirror"; 1–2; Reid 357.) His hands explore the unseen face, and a flash of light reveals hair of ash, or perhaps gold. He invokes Milton:

> Repito que he perdido solamente
> la vana superficie de las cosas.
> El consuelo es de Milton y es valiente,
> Pero pienso en las letras y en las rosas.
> Pienso que si pudiera ver mi cara
> sabría quién soy en esta tarde rara. (9–14)
> I say again that I have lost no more
> than the inconsequential skin of things.
> These wise words come from Milton, and are noble,
> but then I think of letters and of roses.
> I think, too, that if I could see my features,
> I would know who I am, this precious afternoon. (Reid 357)

While Milton's words—echoing Borges's own blind father—offer the poetic subject a measure of solace, they do not entirely ring true. By 1975, Borges had been unable to read from the printed page, or write, except by dictation, for roughly twenty years. He dictated "Un ciego" at roughly the same time as he underwent an operation that briefly restored part of his vision, only reawakening a sense of loss. Able to discern the ashen gray and gold—two of the few colors left to him—of his hair, the poet's mirror image becomes even more mysterious. Unlike the poet of "Elogio de la sombra," glorying in the loss of sensual vision and the impending encounter with his archetypal visage, here the poet slowly caresses his face, searching its contours in vain for self-understanding. "Soy la carne y la cara que no veo" (OC III 226). (I am the flesh and the face that I don't see; 42; [my translation].) For a moment, the compensation afforded by inner vision does not suffice; the consolation offered by Milton's words are ineffective. Borges longs for forms visible, not ideal. Self-understanding is the face in the mirror.

The Argentine sums up the 1975 surgery with a humor both characteristic and revealing: "A los setenta y seis años recuperé parte de mi vista y volví a contemplar el rostro de una hermosa amiga de mi juventud. Comprendí que eran preferibles las tinieblas" (Mejia and Molachino 95). (At seventy-six I partly regained my sight and once again saw the face of a beautiful female friend from my youth. I realized that blindness was preferable [my translation].) Better to depend on a receding visual memory, he decides, than to witness the past so transformed by the aging process. The face of the old friend becomes the site of a cognitive dissonance between what is seen, if minimally, and what is remembered, no doubt minimally as well. "Los días y las noches limaron los perfiles / de las letras humanas y los rostros amados" ("Both days and nights wore away the profiles / of human letters and of well-loved faces") writes Borges in "El ciego" (19–20; Reid 311). The poem ends with lines equally anguished and candid: "El espejo que miro / es una cosa gris . . . Ahora sólo perduran las formas amarillas / y sólo puedo ver para ver pesadillas." ("The mirror I look into is gray . . . only shades of yellow stay with me / and I can see only to look on nightmares"; 24–28; Reid 311.) "El ciego" radically critiques the notion of inner vision by striving to impress upon the reader not the condition of total blindness but of low vision. With progressive vision loss, faces ossify, fade, and finally disappear. Borges inhabits a cognitive terrain in which the face has not totally vanished. As a consequence, the poet's reflected face dissolves into an amorphous gray. Vague, luminous shapes rest just out of reach. Rather than substitute inner for sensual vision, Borges articulates sight slowly abandoned by the phenomenal world.

In these poems, impairment, not disability, is the subject. In Florence Yudin's words: "In his poignant expression of such a terminal mode, Borges voices an unremitting dialectics of disease" (104). Unlike the mirror of "Elogio de la sombra," this mirror offers little save nightmares. Indeed, throughout his life, Borges claimed a fear of mirrors and masks. In a 1985 interview with Amelia Barili, a year before his death, the writer describes a recurrent nightmare: "I dream of a mirror. I see myself with a mask, or I see in the mirror somebody who is me but whom I do not recognize as myself" (Burgin 240). "El espejo" ("The Mirror"), published in the 1977 volume *La historia de la noche*, poeticizes this nightmare:

> Yo temo ahora que el espejo encierre
> El verdadero rostro de mi alma
> Lastimada de sombras y de culpas

El que Dios ve y acaso ven los hombres. (11–14)
Now I fear the mirror may disclose
the true face of my soul,
bruised by shadows and guilt,
the face that God sees, that men perhaps see too. (Rogers 407)

As Cicero writes in *De Oratore, animi est enim omnis actio et imago animi vultus* (All action is of the mind and the mirror of the mind is the face). A Spanish proverb echoes the orator: "la cara es el espejo del alma" (the face is the mirror of the soul). Borges absorbs this cliché and takes it further, for if a man cannot see himself, how can he know himself? He may be, or at least feel, transparent to others, but remains mysterious to himself. Laraway places "El espejo" directly in opposition to "Elogio de la sombra": "As "Elogio de la sombra" makes the mirror a key to Borges's identity, "El espejo" hints that the key itself is locked within the mirror, forever inaccessible to the poet in his blindness" (Laraway 312). Borges fears that the mask conceals his true face, bruised and guilt-marked, visible to God and man but not to himself. Borges fears a visual encounter with his essential but all too physical self, doubled, fixed, actualized in the mirror. Nevertheless, this face remains on the plane of the virtual; it instills terror not because of what it is but what it could be.

The inaccessibility of the reflected body finds expression in the memoirs of other individuals who have experienced late-onset blindness. In his memoir *Touching the Rock: An Experience of Blindness*, John Hull describes the gradual disappearance of the face. "To what extent," he asks, "is the loss of the image of the face connected with the loss of the image of the self? Is this one of the reasons why I often feel I am a mere spirit, a ghost, a memory? Other people have become disembodied voices, speaking out of nowhere, going into nowhere. Am I not like this too, now that I have lost my body?" (19). Another memoirist, Robert Hine, asks a similar question: "Think of how much we esteem or deride ourselves because of the way we perceive our own features. When no reflection reveals that face, our very existence is threatened" (50).

Like all of Borges's motifs, the face is a site of paradox, at once horrific, redemptive, and out of reach, both a source of anxiety and consolation. Borges's 1960 volume, *El hacedor*, a volume that contains pieces dating as far back as the early 1930s, as well as texts composed after 1955, registers the face as a stabilizing force. Its epilogue, frequently cited as a justification for any and all variety of biographical readings of the author's work, reads: "A man sets himself the task of representing the world . . . [s]hortly before he dies he discovers that this patient labyrinth of lines is a drawing of his own face" (Coleman 143). In a 1971 interview at New York University, Borges's translator Norman Thomas di Giovanni asked the author if he had found his own face in his writings. Borges responded, as was his wont, playfully: "That's possibly the quotation, but I wonder whether my own face is a tomb? At least I hope it isn't" (Burgin 129).

One recalls the aforecited couplet from "Arte poética": "el arte debe ser como ese espejo / Que nos revela nuestra propia cara." ("Art should be like that mirror / Which reveals to us our own face"; 19–20; Merwin 137.) The poet speaks of art in general, not his own work, and further, that he recognizes himself less in *Borges's* own books than in those of others or "en el laborioso rasgueo de una guitarra" ("Borges y yo" OC II 221). ("in the rich strumming of a guitar"; Coleman 93.) In his response to di Giovanni, Borges resists the charge of solipsism, or of being a hermetic poet writing of himself for himself. Nonetheless, the poet suggests that we can't escape ourselves, our memory: "what the reader finds at the end is our face, our features, though we are quite unaware of it" (Burgin 129). Borges cannot see himself in his works, but that does not mean he does not await self-recognition in the future, or in the works of others.

Many critics have puzzled over the epilogue of *El hacedor*. How can such a passage come from the mind of a writer who continually undermines the notion of authorship, who makes fiction from the very impossibility of mimesis? Funes, whose memory perfectly repeats the universe, dies of a pulmonary congestion; the Aleph is indescribable; the book of sand, the book that is the universe, is finally hidden away in the basement of the Biblioteca Nacional; the map of the world, which corresponds to every point in the world is left to rot in the desert. These are but a few examples of Borges's resistance to representation. In light of this, how can the unseen face signify anything, let alone the universe? The notion of a representation of the world, which is simultaneously coterminous with its progenitor's face, is sustainable precisely because it is never actualized. It remains possible only because it is always merely possible. This imminent revelation, continually deferred, is synonymous with poetic creation. Self-knowledge is not a prerequisite for creativity. In fact, this continually deferred revelation and the disquiet it produces constitute the aesthetic act; the mirror's opacity signals the beginning of art. Borges does not present blindness as unequivocally positive, but he does posit it as a source of artistic creation. He codes the embodied experience of blindness as a series of gifts: a new sense of time, a greater dependence on memory, as well as a new kind of social life. These gifts do not impede the artistic process—they are the artistic process.

This last gift, a new social life, entails a community of authors bound by the experience of blindness, among them Homer, Milton, and Borges's predecessor at the Biblioteca Nacional, Paul Groussac. This literary idealism conflates Borges and Homer in "El hacedor" as well as "El inmortal." For Borges, the prime, mythic blind poet embraces all other poets, or better, all poets are blind Homer. This concept receives elegant treatment in "El poema de los dones" ("The Poem of the Gifts") from *El hacedor*. The poem concerns the simultaneity of two events: the loss of Borges's "vista de lector" and his becoming director of the Biblioteca Nacional. Marveling at the coincidence that Paul Groussac, too, was blind, he wanders the library's galleries, feeling the holy dread that he is in fact Groussac. This prompts the poetic subject to pose these questions which echo "Borges y yo": "¿Cuál de los dos escribe este poema / de un yo plural y de una sola sombra?" ("Which of the two is setting down this poem— / A single sightless self, a plural I?"; 33–34; Reid 97.) Blindness becomes the prerequisite for identification with that other blind writer:

> Groussac o Borges, miro este querido
> mundo que se deforma y que se apaga
> en una pálida ceniza vaga
> que se parece al sueño y al olvido. (37–40)
> Groussac or Borges, now I look upon
> this dear world losing shape, fading away
> into a pale uncertain ashy-gray
> that feels like sleep, or else oblivion. (Reid 97)

Here, the first-person singular "miro" suggests mutual perception, or the eternal return. As a consequence, it transforms the isolated figure of the blind man into the member of a community. Certainly, Borges takes great relish in discovering yet another blind former director, José Mármol.

More so even than Homer, Milton functions in Borges's late work as an archetypal blind writer. By way of an ambiguous referent, "On His Blindness" blurs the line between Milton and Borges. "Una rosa y Milton" ("A Rose and Milton") imagines the last rose Milton held before his face, but could not see. As in a later poem, "El don," the invisible, silent rose, somehow spiritual, immaterial, secures immortality in the poem. On the subject of *Samson Agonistes*, one senses that Borges takes Milton's identification with Samson as a model: "Milton thought on the similarity of destinies, since he, like Samson, had been a strong man who was ultimately defeated" (Weinberger 480). A bond forms within and without the text.

Nonetheless, Borges also reifies the overcoming disability narrative when he describes Milton's life: "Here we have an example—much more important than my own—of a man who overcomes blindness and does his work . . . all of this was executed while he was blind; all of it had to be dictated to casual visitors" (Weinberger 480). Similarly, "Groussac overcame his blindness and left some of the best pages in prose that have been written in our country" (Weinberger 481). Joyce composes *Finnegan's Wake* in spite of his bouts with vision loss. Borges proffers these literary forebears as exemplary men who have written great works not because of, but in spite of, their blindness. His characteristically self-effacing aside "much more important than my own," merely reinforces their exceptionality as blind poets and diminishes his agency. Nevertheless, like each of these forebears, he in fact composes great works not in spite of his blindness, but because of it.

After receiving the Formentor Prize in 1961, Borges began traveling the world in earnest, attending conferences, giving interviews, delivering lectures, and receiving countless awards and honorary degrees. These late, sentimental journeys were often translated into poetry. Whereas Borges's first three books—all published in his twenties—focus exclusively on the city of Buenos Aires, taking their nourishment from it, the poet's later volumes are geographically expansive: their poems concern subjects as varying as Norse eschatology, Shintoism, and the state of Texas. His penultimate volume *Atlas* (1984) constitutes a kind of travelogue, with short prose pieces or poems accompanied by photographs taken by his literary secretary, traveling companion, and eventual second wife, María Kodama. From the early 1970s until his death, to travel meant to experience the world with Kodama, the late love of his life. "Hemos recorrido y saboreado muchas regiones, que sugirieron muchas fotografías y muchos textos" (We have traversed and savored many regions, which have suggested many photographs and texts; OC III 485; [my translation]), the poet writes, describing travel as both deeply sensual and social. The blind man registered no contradiction in the fact that perception included Kodama's verbal descriptions of the immediate visual scene.

One poem, "The Cloisters," about a trip to the famed branch of the Metropolitan Museum in October of 1980, articulates perception as plural, distributed. Approaching the unicorn tapestries, one notes the plural poetic subject: "Vemos en los tapices / La resurrección y la muerte / Del sentenciado y blanco unicornio" ("We see in the tapestries / the resurrection and the death / of the doomed white unicorn"; 22–24; Merwin 435). The other observer, implicitly understood to be Kodama, sees the unicorn tapestries with and for him. Vision, in this case, is likely synonymous with verbal description on the part of the other. For the poet, who after 1955 always described dictation as writing, and being read to as reading, the act of vision becomes vitally blurred with verbal description—*a priori* resembles *a posteriori* knowledge.

Borges's plural poetic subject highlights a pedagogical facet of blind writing: by conflating verbal description with vision, he reveals the mediation that characterizes all experience. He would have found an ally in Georgina Kleege, who writes: "The sighted can be so touchingly naive about vision. They apparently believe that the brain sees out of it" (*Sight Unseen* 96). Discussing a piece by painter Katherine Sherwood, Kleege complicates our notions of aesthetic experience, saying she knows the work through touch and through conversations with the artist about her process and the ideas that went into its making. Ultimately, she enters into the debate about the role of vision in epistemology, asking whether she can really claim to know this painting, to have firsthand knowledge rather than hearsay. By way of response, she poses another question: "I could ask the same question about any viewer—to what extent is understanding of this or any work dependent on knowing the different ideas and elements behind it? Why else do art museums publish catalogues and post biographical and critical wall texts?" ("Brain Work").

Paradox characterizes all of Borges's work, including the treatment of his own "modesta ceguera personal." He embraces psyche over soma, yet continually returns to the blind body. He fantasizes about inner vision, yet depends on ocularcentrism. He conflates his identity with that of Milton and Homer, yet deems it absurd to place his name beside theirs. He celebrates blindness and laments it. Though he reaches for the archetypes, Borges remains bound to particulars. In their seminal work, *Narrative Prosthesis: Disability and the Dependencies of Discourse*, Mitchell and Snyder describe the disabled body as "a reminder of the 'real' physical limits that 'weigh down' transcendent ideals of the mind and knowledge-producing disciplines" (49). Disability's power rests in the difference it makes with normativity. The disabled body, overdetermined, heavy with signification, nevertheless represents "the *hard kernel* or recalcitrant corporeal matter that cannot be deconstructed away by the textual operations of even the most canny narratives or philosophical idealisms" (49). The paradoxical treatment of blindness in Borges's work recalls the last lines of "Nueva refutación del tiempo" (New Refutation of Time). The writer recognizes that time and identity are illusory, yet cannot escape them. Likewise, inner vision posits the unimportance of the body, yet man cannot escape it: "The world, unfortunately, is real; I, unfortunately, am Borges" (Weinberger 332).

## Notes

1. Throughout the essay, OC refers to the multivolume *Obras completas*, published in 1996, EC refers to *Obras completas: Edición Crítica*, published in 2009, and TR refers to *Textos recobrados*, published in 2002.

2. La Revolución Libertadora refers to the September 1955 military coup d'état, which overthrew the regime of Juan Perón. Borges responded to the coup with elation.

3. Beginning in the 1980s, academic, author, and disability rights activist Mike Oliver was a chief developer of the social model of disability. A seminal work in the field is the volume, *Social Work with Disabled People*, which Oliver co-authored with Bob Sapey and Pam Thomas.

4. Ted Lyon writes: "Borges turned the interview into a literary genre, a game, a personal art form that he often controlled more directly than the interviewer" (Lyon 76).

## Works Cited

Bioy Casares, Adolfo, and Daniel Martino, eds. *Borges*. Buenos Aires: Destino, 2006.

Borges, Jorge Luis. *Obras Completas*. 4 vols. Buenos Aires: Emecé Editores, 1996.

———. *Jorge Luis Borges: Selected Non-Fictions*. Edited and translated by Eliot Weinberger. New York: Penguin Books, 1999.

———. *Jorge Luis Borges: Selected Poems*. Edited by Alexander Coleman. New York: Penguin Books, 1999. "Elogio de la sombra." Translated by W.S. Merwin, 298–301. "Arte poética." Translated by W.S. Merwin, 136–137. "Everness." Translated by Alastair Reid, 226–227. "El ciego." Translated by Alastair Reid, 310–311. "Un sábado." Translated by Eric McHenry, 408–409. "Un ciego." Translated by Alastair Reid, 356–357. "El espejo." Translated by Hoyt Rogers, 406–407. "El poema de los dones." Translated by Alastair Reid, 94–97. "The Cloisters." Translated by W.S. Merwin, 434–435.

———. *Textos recobrados*. 3 vols. Buenos Aires: Emecé Editores, 2002.

———. *Obras completas: edición crítica*. Edited by Rolando Costa Picazo and Irma Zangara. Buenos Aires: Emecé, 2009.

———. *Poems of the Night*. Edited by Efrain Kristal. New York: Penguin, 2010. "El don." Translated by Christopher Mauer. 176–177.

Burgin, Richard, ed. *Jorge Luis Borges: Conversations*. Jackson: U of Mississippi P, 1998.

Celan, Paul. *Collected Prose*. Translated by Rosemarie Waldrop. Riverdale-on-Hudson, NY: Sheep Meadow Press, 1986.

Couser, G. Thomas. "Introduction: Disability and Life Writing." *Journal of Literary & Cultural Disability Studies* 5.3 (2011): 229–242.

Derrida, Jacques. *Memoirs of the Blind: The Self-Portrait and Other Ruins*. Translated by Pascale-Anne Brault and Michael Naas. Chicago: U of Chicago P, 1993.

Hine, Robert. *Second Sight*. Berkeley: U of California P, 1993.

Hull, John. *Touching the Rock: An Experience of Blindness*. New York: Pantheon Books, 1990.

Kleege, Georgina. *Sight Unseen*. New Haven, CT: Yale UP, 1999.

———. "The Subject at Hand: Blind Imaging, Images of Blindness." *Social Research: An International Quarterly* 78.4 (2011): 1243–1262.

———. "Brain Work: A Meditation on the Painting of Katherine Sherwood." Golgi's Door National Academy of Sciences Exhibition Catalogue 2008.

n.p. January 15, 2013. www.katherinesherwood.com/sherwood/articles/gogli-door_kleege.html

Kuusisto, Stephen. *The Planet of the Blind.* New York: Delta, 1998.

———. "Digressions on Poetry, Prose and a Lingonberry Bush." In *Beauty Is a Verb: The New Poetry of Disability.* Edited by Jennifer Bartlett, Sheila Black, and Michael Northen. El Paso, TX: Cinco Puntos Press, 2011, 198–199.

Laraway, David. "The Blind Spot in the Mirror: Self-Recognition and Personal Identity in Borges's Late Poetry." *Revista Canadiense de Estudios Hispánicos* 29.2 (2005): 307–325.

Lyon, Ted. "Jorge Luis Borges and the Interview as Literary Genre." *Latin American Literary Review* 22.44 (1994): 74–89.

Magee, Bryan, and Martin Milligan. *On Blindness: Letters between Bryan Magee and Martin Milligan.* New York: Oxford UP, 1995.

Mejia, Jorge, and Justo R Molachino, eds. *Borges ante el espejo.* Mexico City: Editorial Lectorum, 2005.

Michalko, Rod. *The Two-in-one: Walking with Smokie, Walking with Blindness.* Philadelphia: Temple UP, 1999.

———. *The Difference that Disability Makes.* Philadelphia: Temple UP, 2002.

Mitchell, David, and Sharon Snyder. *Narrative Prosthesis: Disability and the Dependencies of Discourse.* Ann Arbor: U of Michigan P, 2000.

Oliver, Michael, Bob Sapey, and Pam Thomas. *Social Work with Disabled People.* New York: Palgrave Macmillan, 2006.

Torrell, Margaret Rose. "Plural Singularities: The Disability Community in Life-Writing Texts." *Journal of Literary & Cultural Disability Studies* 5.3 (2011): 321–338.

Williamson, Edwin. *Borges, a Life.* New York: Viking, 2004.

Yudin, Florence. *Nightglow: Borges's Poetics of Blindness.* Salamanca: Universidad Pontificia de Salamanca, 1997.

Chapter 3

# Negotiating the Geographies of Exclusion and Access

## Life Writing by Gabriela Brimmer and Ekiwah Adler-Beléndez

Beth E. Jörgensen

On May 29, 2011 the Mexican National Congress approved the "Ley General para la Inclusión de las Personas con Discapacidad" (general law for the inclusion of persons with disabilities), a groundbreaking piece of legislation that endorses a human rights approach to policies pertaining to persons with disabilities. It was drafted, however, without the input of any of the prominent disability rights experts in Mexico (Ríos Espinosa). In April 2011, while the "Ley General" was being debated, the rather luxurious new Senate building in Mexico City was completed after a lengthy delay and substantial cost overruns. The new Senate building was not designed to be accessible for people with physical disabilities. The juxtaposition of these events and the exclusion of the disability rights community from matters that directly concern their interests exemplify the enormous gap between the theory and the practice of disability rights in Mexico that scholars and activists continually observe and critique. In the realm of culture, deeply embedded contradictions also exist between the representations of people with disabilities produced by the able-bodied, neurotypical artist or intellectual, and the self-inscription of people with disabilities.[1] This essay treats writing by two people with cerebral palsy, placing the texts within their social context: *Gaby Brimmer*, the collaborative autobiography of the poet and activist Gabriela Brimmer, and poetry by the bilingual writer Ekiwah

Adler-Beléndez. These works, which span a period of thirty years bridging the twentieth to the twenty-first centuries, expose and challenge the limits faced by people with disabilities in their negotiation of the geographies of exclusion and access in Mexico, and they convey knowledge that complements the work being done in contemporary disability studies theory. *Gaby Brimmer* and the selected poems by Ekiwah Adler-Beléndez demonstrate how writing by disabled people constitutes a necessary alternative to traditional depictions of disability in literature.[2]

Those who work for disability rights in Mexico, commonly use one word to describe the experience of people with disabilities in their society: *exclusion*. Exclusion from the spaces of education, employment, politics, culture, and daily activities outside of the home, and the consequent invisibility of and ignorance about persons with disabilities are the principal factors that persist in limiting the exercise of their legal rights, their participation in the life of their community, and their individual development and agency.[3] For those with physical conditions that limit their mobility and those with sensory disabilities, the many barriers that exist in the built environment, the means of public transportation and the means of communication create obvious obstacles to inclusion. These barriers can be addressed with existing technologies, albeit at an initial cost to retrofit buildings, streets, transport, and communications media for universal access.[4] The more difficult obstacles to mitigate are those imposed by social and cultural values that determine the complex, largely negative meanings of disability in Mexico, and in particular the severe stigmatization regarding intellectual and psychosocial disabilities. Karla Calcáneo of Conapred (Consejo Nacional para la Prevención y Eliminación de la Discriminación), the federal agency responsible for combatting all forms of discrimination, traces the sources of discriminatory attitudes in Mexico to a lack of knowledge about the rights of disabled people, the view of disability as illness or deficiency, the perception that a person with a disability is a burden on the family and on society, the idea that providing equal access implies giving special privileges, and the notion that any assistance given is a form of charity.

A paradigm shift is currently underway in Mexico, and both older and newer ways of conceptualizing disability coexist in a complex and contradictory panorama. The prevailing view throughout the twentieth century and still today has been formed by the medical/deficit model, which pathologizes disability and contributes to the labeling of persons with disabilities as defective, abnormal, and in need of a cure. The medical model locates disability in the body of an individual subject and holds him or her responsible for adapting to society's norms and expectations through rehabilitation. While this model has strongly influenced institutional and official discourses and popular culture, the religious, charity, and pity models have also shaped people's thinking. The internalization and reproduction of existing paradigms result in seeing disability as a condition of deficit, and as a divine gift or punishment or a cause for generosity and sympathy, as well as producing a generalized tendency to rejection and fear.[5] The past thirty years, however, have witnessed a paradigm-changing challenge to the long history of medicalization and stigmatization. This challenge, posed in Mexico primarily by the disability rights movement, and by families and scholars, is beginning to effect a transformation in social attitudes and official policies, as seen in legislation that promotes a human rights model and in the funding of gradual, still very limited changes in infrastructure.

Federico Fleischmann, co-founder and president of Libre Acceso, A.C., dates the start of the disability rights movement in Mexico to February 14, 1992, when a group of persons with disabilities staged a protest in the chambers of Congress (48). Ernesto Zedillo is commonly identified as the first president to pay increased attention to the needs and demands of this sector, and under Vicente Fox (2000–2006) and Felipe Calderón (2006–2012) significant legislative milestones were reached: the "General Law for Persons with Disabilities" (2005), the signing of the U.N. Convention on the Rights of Persons with Disabilities (2007) and the "General Law of Inclusion of Persons with Disabilities" (2011). This legislation moves Mexico toward a human rights model that recognizes the full citizenship and equal rights of persons with disabilities, and sees disability as a form of human diversity rather than deficiency and otherness. It is universally acknowledged, however, that these legislative actions have had a very limited impact, given long delays in formulating the regulations to put their provisions into effect and a severe lack of resources to enforce compliance (Gamio Ríos 437–438). Furthermore, while the 1990s and early 2000s were a critical period for legislation, civil society began to attend to this marginalized population long before the government assumed a more active role. Early organizations such as APAC (founded in 1970 and serving persons with cerebral palsy) and Confe (1978, focusing on intellectual disabilities) were created by parents to provide services for their children, and they were oriented toward education, rehabilitation, and employment in segregated or "sheltered" facilities.[6] A more active struggle that focused on rights rather than assistance originated with initiatives taken by people with disabilities to form their own associations. Libre Acceso, A.C. (1989) is a prime example of an organization created by and not merely for persons with disabilities, and Fleischmann estimates that by 2006 there were roughly one hundred and sixty-six NGOs concerned with disability rights in Mexico (47). Today the government is seen as continuing to lag behind civil society, rather than providing leadership in this important arena for human rights (Rosas Barrientos).

The complex relationship between literary writing and the promotion of social movements and human rights has been addressed by disability studies scholars in the humanities who have paid close attention to the pervasive representation of illness and disability in art and literature since ancient times with a view toward understanding their social and cultural meanings and impacts. Numerous studies of European and U.S. literature show how characters with disabilities have been employed to fulfill certain roles in narrative structure and to communicate a variety of messages about society. David T. Mitchell and Sharon L. Snyder, as referenced in the "Introduction," coined the term "narrative prosthesis" to capture the "discursive dependency upon disability" of much of world literature, which leans on disability like a crutch to enhance the disruptive power and analytical insight of narrative (47–48). Mitchell and Snyder go on to point out that the "reliance on disability in narrative rarely develops into a means of identifying people with disability as a disenfranchised cultural constituency" (55), or a means of addressing disability as an experience with social and political dimensions (48). Michael Bérubé concurs in remarking that literary representations, while admittedly figural and not literal, contribute to constructing disability as a cultural category with concrete consequences for human subjects. "The stereotypes, metaphors and images of disability have been primary means by which human cultures have constructed disability in systems of compulsory able-bodiedness. The representation of disability (in both the aesthetic and the political sense of representation) has also been the construction of disability—and needs to be reexamined by scholars in the humanities precisely for its effects on, or its productions of, the actual bodies of actual persons" ("Afterword" 342). Therefore, "there lurk . . . in disability studies profound questions of social and cultural justice" (342).

Just as literature can be complicit in the imposition and normalization of ideologies of exclusion, so, too, can art exercise a subversive challenge to hegemonic values and attitudes. In this regard, texts produced by people with disabilities have the potential to push back against canonical representations and offer alternative ways of conceiving of bodily and cognitive difference. Personal narrative, or life writing, occupies a privileged place in disability studies because it invites the active, shaping participation of those who live in a situation of disability in the narration of their own stories. G. Thomas Couser, the foremost North American theorist of disability life writing, affirms that its value resides in the exercise of the agency of the person with a disability through narrative acts that shape the representation of his or her experience and subjectivity. Relegated to a position of marginalization and preinscription in society at large, the autobiographical subject takes the initiative in representing him/herself through the act of writing ("Disability" 605). Couser highlights the function of these texts as a counter-discourse to the paradigm of deficiency and the common representation of disabled literary characters as defenseless victims. At the same time, he warns that not all disability life writing subverts social and cultural norms. In fact, it can, and often does reinscribe conventional, conservative views manifested in sentimental portrayals of the disabled, narratives of overcoming impairment, or messages of spiritual rewards achieved through patient suffering ("Signifying" 110–111). Disability life writing that resists these trends, however, "can be an especially powerful medium in which disabled people can demonstrate that they have lives, in defiance of others' commonsense perceptions of them" (605). Tobin Siebers, in his book *Disability Theory*, attributes this subversive potential to the analytical power of works written by persons with disabilities. Siebers posits that while it is difficult to analyze and critique prevailing ideologies from a subject position that is located firmly within hegemonic values and privileges, the subject who occupies a social position of exclusion can perceive and question norms in which he or she does not fully participate. Exteriority provides an angle of heightened perception (Siebers, *Disability* 15, 105). Disability life writing, such as *Gaby Brimmer*, may therefore record negotiations of the spaces of exclusion in an innovative and subversive way.

In the introduction to her book *Unruly Bodies: Life Writing by Women with Disabilities*, Susannah Mintz calls our attention to other relevant issues. Mintz says the following about autobiographical texts: "Their overt intention is to challenge the troping of disability in able-bodied culture as deviance, helplessness, insufficiency, and loss, as well as to speak openly about a form of embodiment often excluded from the conversation in both disability and feminist discourse. . . . The autobiographers studied in *Unruly Bodies* . . . train their attention on the family dynamics, medical intrusions, media representations and structural barriers that conspire to make impairments physically and psychologically disabling" (1). These comments apply equally well to *Gaby Brimmer* (1979), which was translated into English in 2009 as *Gaby Brimmer: An Autobiography in Three Voices*.[7] Gabriela Brimmer was born in Mexico City in 1947 to Jewish immigrants who had fled Europe during the Holocaust. Brimmer was profoundly affected at birth by cerebral palsy caused by Rh factor incompatibility. The story of her life and how she was able to communicate by manipulating an alphabet board or a typewriter with the big toe of her left foot is rather well known in Mexico due to the autobiography and the Luis Mandoki film *Gaby: A True Story* (1987), as well as Brimmer's activism in the disability rights movement.[8]

Two substantive analyses of the book have been published to date: Claudia Schaefer's chapter on *Gaby Brimmer* and Elena Poniatowska's *Querido Diego, te abraza Quiela* in her book *Textured Lives: Women, Art and Representation in Modern Mexico* (1992) and Susan Antebi's chapter "Enabling *Testimonio*" in her book *Carnal Inscriptions: Spanish American Narratives of Corporeal Difference and Disability* (2009). Schaefer characterizes *Gaby Brimmer* as conservative in form and thematics when compared with *La noche de Tlatelolco*, Poniatowska's oral history of the 1968 student movement. Antebi's detailed and subtle analysis of the text and its film version links the autobiography to Latin American *testimonio* by comparing and contrasting it to *I, Rigoberta Menchú* and placing it within the debate over *testimonio* and postmodernism. She acknowledges the conservative dimensions of the narrative, while also carrying out "a body-centered reading of agency as an ongoing practice of intercorporeality" (175) that is grounded in disability theory. My study reads the book through the theories developed by Couser, Mintz, and Siebers, that see disability life writing as a "powerful medium" that can defy ableist assumptions and propose theoretical knowledge through narrative.

The writing of *Gaby Brimmer* was an original and even a daring act for the decade of the 1970s in Mexico, long before a disability rights movement existed there. It is important to acknowledge that Brimmer's life story was narrated, edited, and published in a virtual literary and cultural vacuum and in a context of extreme social exclusion of the disabled. In the prologue written by Elena Poniatowska, she describes the process of composing the text on the basis of interviews and letters, and she also reveals her reservations about collaborating in the project with Gabriela Brimmer, her mother Sara (or Sari), and her caregiver Florencia Morales (Nana). In 1977 when the famed journalist first interviewed Brimmer for an article in *Novedades*, all of the messages transmitted by society and high and popular culture conveyed that persons who were ill or disabled were a terrible burden, and their stories could have nothing to do with literature. Poniatowska admits that she had to negotiate among conflicting external pressures and internal obstacles in order to undertake the project, given that her family and friends and her own formation as a writer all cast such an assignment in a negative light. As a consequence, the language employed, which Trudy Balch has scrupulously respected in her English translation, often reflects a way of thinking that many readers today will not accept. Poniatowska writes, for example, of Sara Brimmer's lifelong "torture" that began with her daughter's birth, she compares Gaby Brimmer to her "perfectly healthy" brother David, and she and the text's protagonists use terms such as "invalids" and "cripples" to refer to those with motor disabilities, thus betraying deeply internalized attitudes of condescension and pity.[9] Nonetheless, in spite of this, *Gaby Brimmer* stands as an innovative, positive achievement in Mexican letters that offers an opening into alternative discourses on disability. The passages attributed to Brimmer's own self-expression, in particular, prefigure issues that disability studies scholars continue to discuss today. As Tobin Siebers theorizes, the marginalized experience and excluded subject position of the person with disabilities can prompt a profound critique of the ideology of ableism and its privileging of individual autonomy and self-sufficiency.

Elena Poniatowska composed *Gaby Brimmer* as a montage of narrative fragments attributed to Gaby, Sari, and Florencia, which she arranged in roughly chronological order around the themes of childhood, family relations, school, support for the 1968 student movement, friendship and love, and finally Brimmer's adoption of a daughter, Alma Florencia.[10] The structure offers multiple perspectives on a life lived within a complex web of relationships, by juxtaposing the three voices without any apparent mediating narration.[11] This device highlights the inextricable interconnections among Gaby, Sari, and Florencia, and it is a verbal reenactment of the constitution of the individual subject and the exercise of agency in relationship to others and not in a splendid, illusory isolation. The textual web woven by the testimonies duplicates the system of support and love that sustains the three women and at the same time sets a trap for them. Gaby is the one who is most aware of the double meaning of the web as support and trap, caught as she is quite literally, that is bodily, at its center. The structure and the thematics of the life story, therefore, foreground the constant negotiations of human agency carried out from a subject position defined by uncommon physical limitations.

Disability studies theory reminds us that the human experience of the world depends on the body and its sensory functions, and subjectivity is constituted by the materiality of the body with its inherent imperfection and fragility, as well as by the shaping force of language and cultural discourse.[12] Bodily impairment and severe physical limitations such as Brimmer experienced create restricted options for self-determination and development in a cultural and built environment that demands physical mobility and normative speech as minimum requirements for full participation. In Mexico in the 1960s and 1970s, living with cerebral palsy meant a universal assumption of nonentry into the spaces of learning, work, leisure, and pleasure. The barriers to schools, places of employment and entertainment, and spaces of privacy were virtually insurmountable. As a result, Gaby's exercise of her agency in choosing to study, work, or pursue friendships is inseparable from her bodily condition and her relationship with her caregiver in ways that many readers will not assume they themselves experience.

The collaborative autobiography narrates a limit-case of how an individual is both enabled and constrained by others in a relationship of interdependence, and is not largely in control of her life course. One example illustrates the interplay of bodies, prosthetic devices and cultural discourse in determining agency. In order to attend school, Gaby must be accompanied by Florencia, who drives the car, pushes the wheelchair, carries the wheelchair and Gaby up and down stairs, and pronounces aloud the words that Gaby composes by pointing to her alphabet board. Gaby, Florencia, the wheelchair, and the alphabet board comprise one functional subject position that we might call "student," and Gaby negotiates the multiple obstacles to her intellectual development through these combined, hybrid methods. This composite student, enrolled under the single name of Gabriela Brimmer, then encounters skepticism and dismissal by those who would disable her according to cultural norms: that is, the expectation that people with cerebral palsy who cannot speak clearly are cognitively impaired and therefore the knowledge that the student produces does not originate from the mind residing in her disabled body. Gaby strenuously defends herself against the accusation that Florencia does her intellectual work for her, and she affirms her cognitive and creative independence at the same time that the narrative undermines the humanist ideal of the fully autonomous subject. Hers is a limit-case, but the representation in three voices of a life lived within exceptional physical limitations not only demonstrates Brimmer's unique situation, but also the interdependence and the need for prostheses at the core of our shared human condition.

Another critical factor in the constitution of human subjectivity is the experience of seeing others and internalizing how others see us. The other's gaze, when it is attentive and affirming, is an act of nonverbal communication and recognition that supports the positive development of identity and psychosocial well-being. People with disabilities are often the object of curious, evasive, prying, and even fearful gazes or acts of staring that diminish their value and refuse their humanity. Rosemarie Garland-Thomson in *Staring: How We Look* complicates our common understanding of the phenomenon of the human stare in relation to "unusual bodies" (9) by focusing equally on the agency of the starer and the staree. She quotes the late Harriet McBryde Johnson, a disability activist in New York City, who articulated the dilemma of facing the other's gaze while inhabiting an anomalous body in these few words: "It's not that I'm ugly. It's more that most people don't know how to look at me" (qtd. by Garland-Thomson 188). Johnson practiced visual activism in her daily life by taking control of her visual encounters with others, explaining why her body had an anomalous form, and showing the rare beauty and the capacity for pleasure of a body that others would not desire for themselves.

*Gaby Brimmer* does not record this kind of active engagement with the other's gaze, and in fact it narrates a tendency to avoidance, but it does reflect on the dilemma of meeting the other's gaze from a situation of disability and the corresponding challenge of learning how to look at the anomalous other. Sari and Florencia openly criticize the way that people avoid looking at Gaby, or look at her with morbid curiosity, fear, or disgust, but very rarely with the desire to see her and recognize her as a human being who is uncommonly different and yet equal to themselves. At the same time, the text reveals how difficult it is to embrace bodily difference with an inclusive gaze. Susan Antebi is right to critique Elena Poniatowska's appeal to Gaby's most "normal," "healthy" physical feature—her eyes—as a way to identify with her humanity and see beyond the spasms and the "useless" arms (191–192). Sari's mode of seeing her daughter is, like Poniatowska's, strongly influenced by the medical model, and she despairs over Gaby's condition: "I never resigned myself to seeing her that way . . . I looked for medicines, doctors, some kind of cure . . . I thought something had to be done, that my daughter couldn't stay that way" (31). The reader, cognizant of Gaby's struggle for recognition, may be moved to question his or her own tendency to see only the wheelchair or the spasms when encountering a person with a visible disability. In contrast, the first words attributed to Florencia are as follows: "She was a beautiful little girl, her hair pure gold, such a perfect little face, green eyes, with a nose that turned up at the end. But her hair, how I remember her hair!" (30). There is a great deal at play in this admiring description. One likely factor informing Florencia's perception of physical beauty in the child Gaby is the cultural preference for fair skin and hair and light-colored eyes that is a sign of Mexican prejudice against its dark-skinned (read indigenous) population. Also at play in a positive sense is the acceptance with which Florencia sees and treats Gaby as she is, in contrast to the mother's preoccupation with curing the body that arched and doubled over with frequent spasms. Contradictions aside, Florencia's voice gives witness to a rare beauty that demands an attentive, appreciative gaze in defiance of cultural norms.

Gaby's interventions in the telling of her life story introduce other insights that were ahead of their time, such as her decision to abandon the rigorous physical therapy regimen prescribed for her in order to marshal her energies toward her intellectual life, and her reflections on sexuality and the obstacles to a sexual life that exist for people with disabilities. In so doing, she reveals that in order to negotiate an entry into the closed spaces of school and pleasure, the person with disabilities must defy entrenched norms such as the medical model of rehabilitation, and the taboo surrounding the sexual citizenship of people with disabilities.[13] In closing this section of the chapter and before turning to the poetry of Ekiwah Adler-Beléndez, I return to the idea that disability studies, with its roots in the disability rights movement, has an important social justice dimension. We should not leave *Gaby Brimmer* without asking ourselves about the status of Florencia. Poniatowska's interviews with Florencia Morales resulted in her incorporating Nana's version of Gaby and their common life into the text. Nevertheless, it is easy to read the autobiography and overlook the challenge that Florencia herself poses to the goal of inclusion and equal rights for persons with disabilities. To put it briefly, in a nation with severe income inequality and a history of discrimination against the poor and against people with dark skin, the implications of Florencia's decision to devote her life to Gaby's care are highly problematic. On the one hand, in the Brimmer household Florencia has a level of economic security and personal comfort that she could not have had in her home village with its lack of educational and job opportunities, or in service to a less "humane" family in Mexico City. On the other hand, a middle-class Mexican woman or a woman anywhere who has access to education and a living wage, would not be likely to choose a life of constant service, isolation from her community, lack of freely chosen friends and partners, and lack of schooling, among other constraints and losses that Florencia accepts. In the struggle for access and inclusion for people with disabilities including, I might add, the elderly with their late-acquired needs, society must contend with the reality that their care, as now provided, is often dependent on the limited options available to a differently but also severely marginalized class of people.[14]

In *Gaby Brimmer*, the experience of living with cerebral palsy shapes the narrative structure and determines the predominant themes almost exclusively. In contrast, the writing of the young bilingual, bicultural poet Ekiwah Adler-Beléndez does not immediately call attention to itself as the work of a person with a significant motor impairment, also caused by cerebral palsy. Born in 1987 to a Mexican mother and a North American father, Adler-Beléndez has been writing and publishing poetry in Spanish and in English from a very young age, and at the present he conducts poetry workshops for youth with cerebral palsy, as well as engaging in public speaking and other kinds of activism with the ConNos/Otr@s organization in Cuernavaca. His first book *Soy* appeared in 1999, and he has three more collections of poetry to his credit: *Palabras inagotables* (2001), *Weaver* (2003), and *The Coyote's Trace* (2006), with a new book titled "Love on Wheels" in progress. His work takes up the canonical themes of Western poetry: heterosexual love, the beauty of the natural world, friendship, the desire for spiritual and artistic transcendence, the fear of death, and the art of poetry itself; and it could be said that his poetry thus eludes the gaze of those readers who would look first for the theme of disability in art created by a writer who uses a wheelchair. He also directly addresses the experience of living with a disability from a perspective that defies expectations, and he creates a poetic voice that gives testimony to the frustrations and the pleasures of negotiating the obstacles created by those expectations.

Adler-Beléndez's language can be playful and light, seemingly spontaneous in its generation of images and word play that evoke the beauty of common objects and the ironic dimensions of everyday life. In this, he shows the influence of Pablo Neruda's *Odas elementales*. The poem "Too Bad" from *Weaver* transforms a home remedy for the common cold into a living thing through several linguistic sleights of hand:

> This carrot juice
> (supposed to help my cold)
> Comes effortlessly up the straw
> A rough sunset mingling with my saliva.
> The carrot juice is gone
> A rabbit, leaving but a trace of itself.
> Too bad my cold isn't a dog,
> that leaving its nasal cave
> runs after it. (1–9)

The charm of this brief poem comes from the ingenious, economical use of rhetorical figures and the light tone of the disappointment expressed over carrot juice's medicinal inefficacy. The juice, after rising "effortlessly up the straw," resolves into a "rough sunset" on its way down the raw throat, a metaphor based on the sharing of a common color and enriched by sinestesia. Metonymy transforms the juice into a rabbit—think of Bugs Bunny famously chomping on his carrot—which soon disappears as if in a magician's hat trick. Unfortunately for the sufferer, the common cold is not a dog, invited metonymically by the fleeing rabbit, its natural prey, to leave "its nasal cave," but instead remains inside the nose, a lingering malady. This and other poems place Adler-Beléndez as a poet dedicated to the craft of writing and employing verbal artistry to express a wide range of emotions and experiences, both lived and imagined. Among those experiences, but not occupying a dominant position, is the reality of his cerebral palsy.

Many of us, when thinking of a wheelchair, visualize a clumsy rectangular apparatus with four wheels, heavy and black as mourning. The phrase "confined to a wheelchair" also comes to mind, in spite of recent efforts to say, rather, that a person *uses* a wheelchair. Adler-Beléndez rewrites the relationship between a person with a motor disability and the wheelchair by celebrating mobility, not confinement, and by acknowledging the physical intimacy that exists between the human body and technology. The poem "Joy" from *The Coyote's Trace* inscribes an alternative view—an alternative knowledge—achieved through embodied experience and artistic reflection:

> This turquoise tricycle
> with no pity
> or sense of duty
> carries my weight,
> obeys the natural,
> magnifies the intention
> of movement,
> . . .
> the third wheel
> diminishes the danger of two—
> takes me
> past the smell of compost
> past the facets of time
> past duality! (1–7; 11–16)

The bright color and the three wheels of the wheelchair described here establish its difference from the standard chair whose image we have internalized and normalized. Further, it offers an impersonal assistance, serving its user "with no pity / or sense of duty" in implicit contrast to the experience of too much dependence on other human beings and too much exposure to their sense of obligation. The person and the chair function as one animated unit, with the prosthetic device "obeying" and "magnifying" the body's natural inclination to movement. The final six verses play a highly effective, revelatory game with the numbers two and three. Two, when it designates two wheels, signifies a precarious balance that is hard to hold and prone to the risk of falling. The third wheel of the tricycle gives stability, diminishing the danger implicit in the number two. What is more, the third wheel can be seen as a third term offering an alternative to the divisive duality and apparent stasis of binary oppositions such as ability and disability and, in this interpretation, upsetting a false stability. The duality of mobility and paralysis is superceded by a third option, the body made able through technology. This body, carried by the wheelchair, celebrates an alternative mobility and also reminds us that no one goes very far on "their own two feet." Technology carries us all, and we all depend on its generous impersonality to extend the limited reach of our prized autonomy.

Like Gabriela Brimmer, Ekiwah Adler-Beléndez defies the repression of "disabled" sexuality by openly expressing his sexual desires, both frustrated and realized. Many of his poems represent love and the desire for physical intimacy with a female partner, and his short-lived blog from 2010 "Love on Wheels" treats the relationship difficulties that confront a young person who uses a wheelchair. With honesty and often with humor, the writer contests the common misperception that he is physically and emotionally fragile and must be treated with special care. A poem posted on July 8, 2010, titled "The Woods" captures a moment suspended in space and in time between reality and dream, passion and tranquility, loving encounter with another and reconciliation with oneself. It starts on a decidedly realistic, unsentimental note: "She pushed / my wheelchair / into the woods" (1–3). But, before the poetic "I" can rechannel physical desire into philosophical conversation ("the heavy blanket / of a metaphysical subject" 6–7), the "midsummer night" and a gentle rain overtake the two lovers and they slip, "braided," "into bodies of moss and leaf." The poem concludes with images, both conventional and unexpected, that make tangible the ineffable pleasure of the desiring/desired subject.

> I, with her in my arms . . .
> became at once
> a line of smoke
> where sky meets sea
> over the world's
> curved blue lip
> and one coherent piece
> of cosmic clay
> feeling wanted for the first time
> not in spite of my body
> but because of it
> every one of my cells opening
> into gardens of motion and silence. (17–29)

The shift from a matter-of-fact register in the opening verses to highly idealized imagery later on, might surprise those readers who would seek a more realistic treatment of "disabled" sexuality by a poet with a disability. Nevertheless, I would argue that disabled people have the right—the human right—not only to sexual citizenship as Tobin Siebers describes it, but to the pleasurable idealization of experience in memory, or the outright invention of memories of union and plenitude, free from the limiting reality of everyday exclusions.

Gabriela Brimmer and Ekiwah Adler-Beléndez, whose lives overlapped during a period of cultural and legal continuity and change in Mexico, have made a multifacted contribution to disability rights and to disability knowledge through their writing and their other forms of activism. As Mexico slowly institutes a juridical model of disability based on human rights and inclusion in the twenty-first-century, life writing with its aesthetic and ethical dimension can play a role in the *sensibilización* (consciousness raising) that activists cite as a priority for their society. Reading their work from a disability studies perspective expands our understanding of the complexities and the possibilities of negotiating geographies of exclusion and access in Latin America.

## Notes

1. The term *temporarily able-bodied* or TAB recognizes the contingent nature of "ability" and the potential for entering the category of "disability" at any time. Deborah Marks notes its usage by disability rights activists dating back to the 1980s (18), but the term is surrounded by controversy. For an example of pros and cons, see Liz William's weblog " 'Temporarily able-bodied': and why I don't like it," March 21, 2013.

2. On the distinction between disability life writing and fictional accounts, see Quayson, *Aesthetic Nervousness*, p. 51.

3. In June 2011 and July 2012, I interviewed a number of disability rights activists and researchers and government officials in Mexico City. I am grateful to Federico Fleischmann (Libre Acceso), who met with me and facilitated other valuable contacts.

4. According to American architect Ronald L. Mace, "[t]he universal design approach [means] simply designing all products, buildings and exterior spaces to be usable by all people to the greatest extent possible" (156). Mace advocated for its adoption in order to "assist in empowering people with all types of physical or cognitive disabilities to integrate as fully as possible into the mainstream of daily life" (156).

5. David Pfeiffer's "Philosophical Foundations of Disability Studies" offers an excellent overview of models of disability and their philosophical bases throughout history. Another useful but less easily located summary can be found in Patricia Brogna's essay "Las representaciones de la discapacidad," pages 175–187.

6. APAC is the Asociación Pro Personas con Parálisis Cerebral, and Confe is the Confederación Mexicana de Organizaciones a Favor de la Persona con Discapacidad Intelectual.

7. Textual quotes come from the English translation by Trudy Balch, which captures the individual speaking styles and the vocabulary of disability of the time.

8. Gabriela Brimmer also wrote poetry and she published the collection *Gaby, un año después* in 1980. The autobiography includes some of her poems, but I have chosen to focus on the narrative aspect of the text and the collaborative creation of the life story.

9. In her introduction to the English-language translation, Lauri Umansky addresses these points about the language of the text in greater detail (xviii–xx).

10. In order to maintain a distinction that is critical to the reading of autobiography, I refer to the historical figure as Gabriela Brimmer or Brimmer, and the protagonist of the autobiography as Gaby throughout my study.

11. See Antebi's book chapter for an analysis of Poniatowska's role as co-author and the collaborative nature of the text as regards the theory of *testimonio* (190–198).

12. Critiques of the social model of disability stem in part from the importance of considering the body as central to the human experience of the world. G. Thomas Couser makes the point that illness and disability life writing foreground the somatic basis of human experience (*Recovering* 12).

13. See Siebers's "A Sexual Culture for Disabled People," *Disability Theory* (135–156).

14. National Public Radio (NPR) did segments on October 16 and 17, 2012, on how home health care is provided in the United States. Jennifer Ludden and Marisa Peñaloza focused on two major points: the low wages paid in the home care industry and the high percentage of immigrants, many of them Mexican, who fill these jobs.

## Works Cited

Adler-Beléndez, Ekiwah. *Palabras inagotables*. Jiutepec, Morelos, Mexico: Con Nosotros, A.C., 2001.

———. "Too Bad." *Weaver: A Collection of Poems*. Amatlán, Morelos, Mexico: Ed. del Arkan, 2003, 29.

———. "Joy." *The Coyote's Trace*. Amatlán, Morelos, Mexico: Ed. del Arkan, 2006, 43.

———. "The Woods." *Love on Wheels: Sex, Love, Disability*. July 8, 2010, n.p. Web. December 1, 2012.

Antebi, Susan. *Carnal Inscriptions: Spanish American Narratives of Corporeal Difference and Disability*. New York: Palgrave Macmillan, 2009.

Bérubé, Michael. "Afterword: If I Should Live So Long." Snyder et al., 337–343.

Brogna, Patricia. "Las representaciones de la discapacidad: la vigencia del pasado en las estructuras sociales presentes." In *Visiones y revisiones de la discapacidad*. Edited by Patricia Brogna. Mexico City: Fondo de Cultura Económica, 2009, 157–187.

Calcáneo, Karla. Unpublished interview with the author, June 22, 2011.
Couser, G. Thomas. "Disability, Life Narrative and Representation." *PMLA* 120.2 (2005): 602–605.
———."Quality of Life Writing: Illness, Disability and Representation." In *Teaching Life Writing Texts.* Edited by Miriam Fuchs and Craig Howes. New York: Modern Language Association, 2007, 350–358.
———. "Signifying Bodies: Life Writing and Disability Studies." Snyder et al., 109–117.
Davis, Lennard J. "Constructing Normalcy." *The Disability Studies Reader.* 3rd ed. Ed. Lennard J. Davis. New York: Routledge, 2010, 3–19.
Fleischmann, Federico. "El papel de las organizaciones de la sociedad civil en el monitoreo de los derechos humanos de las personas con discapacidad." *Mecanismos nacionales de monitoreo de la Convención sobre los Derechos de las Personas con Discapacidad.* Mexico City: Comisión Nacional de los Derechos Humanos, 2008, 47–58.
Gamio Ríos, Amalia. "Discapacidad en México: El derecho a no ser invisible." Brogna, 431–445.
Garland-Thomson, Rosemarie. *Staring: How We Look.* New York: Oxford UP, 2009.
Ludden, Jennifer. "Home Health Aides: In Demand, Yet Paid Little." National Public Radio. October 16, 2012, n.p. Web. April 11, 2013.
Mace, Ronald L. et al. "Accessible Environments: Toward Universal Design." In *Design Intervention: Toward a More Humane Architecture.* Edited by W. E. Preiser et al. New York: Van Nostrand Reinhold, 1991, 155–176.
Marks, Deborah. *Disability: Controversial Debates and Psychosocial Perspectives.* London: Routledge, 1999.
Mintz, Susannah B. *Unruly Bodies: Life Writing by Women with Disabilities.* Chapel Hill: U of North Carolina P, 2007.
Mitchell, David T. and Sharon L. Snyder. *Narrative Prosthesis: Disability and the Dependencies of Discourse.* Ann Arbor: U of Michigan P, 2001.
Peñaloza, Marisa. "Immigrants Key To Looming Health Aide Shortage." National Public Radio. October 17, 2012, n.p. Web. April 11, 2013.
Pfeiffer, David. "The Philosophical Foundations of Disability Studies." *Disability Studies Quarterly* 22.2 (2002): 3–23. Web. September 15, 2011.
Poniatowska, Elena and Gabriela Brimmer. *Gaby Brimmer.* Mexico City: Grijalbo, 1979.
———. *Gaby Brimmer: An Autobiography in Three Voices.* Translated by Trudy Balch. Intro. Lauri Umansky. Waltham, MA: Brandeis UP, 2009.
Quayson, Ato. *Aesthetic Nervousness: Disability and the Crisis of Representation.* New York: Columbia UP, 2007.
Ríos Espinosa, Carlos. Unpublished interview with the author, June 24, 2011.
Rosas Barrientos, Ernesto. Unpublished interview with the author, June 22, 2011.
Schaefer, Claudia. *Textured Lives: Women, Art and Representation in Modern Mexico.* Tuscon: U of Arizona P, 1992.
Siebers, Tobin. *Disability Theory.* Ann Arbor: U of Michigan P, 2008.

Snyder, Sharon L., Brenda Jo Brueggeman and Rosemarie Garland-Thomson, eds. *Disability Studies: Enabling the Humanities*. New York: Modern Language Association, 2002.

Williams, Liz. " 'Temporarily able-bodied,' and why I don't like it." *Bread and Roses: A Song of Pilgrimage*. March 2010, n.p. Web. April 12, 2013.

# Part II

# Global Bodies and the Coloniality of Disability

Chapter 4

# Otras competencias

## Ethnobotany, the *Badianus codex*, and Metaphors of Mexican Memory Loss and Disability in *Las buenas hierbas* (2010)

Ryan Prout

In Mexican director María Novaro's most recent film, *Las buenas hierbas* (*The Good Herbs*), dislodgement of Mexico's indigenous cultures—through the forgetting, flight, and appropriation of ethnobotanical knowledge—grows into a structural frame that envelops and continuously informs the narrative.[1] Rather than running toward the site of an authentic culture, in *Las buenas hierbas* the record of an indigenous culture is the marrow of the film. As I illustrate in this chapter, *Las buenas hierbas* tethers traces of pre-Columbian indigenous knowledge to a portrait of a woman experiencing Alzheimer's disease in such a way that a globalized condition is localized while also using individual loss of memory as a route to remembering cultural forgetting.

Subtle special effects of multimedia collage permit pages from the *Codex de la Cruz-Badiano*—the herbal almanac translated into Latin by Juan Badiano, from a Nahuatl text written in the Colegio de Santa Cruz de Tlatelolco in 1552 by Martín de la Cruz, an indigenous botanist—to blend into the film as the visual terrain and background for Novaro's very contemporary narrative about Alzheimer's, and the physical and mental disabilities entailed by the disease. Set in Mexico City, the film's focus is the relationship between Lala, a middle-aged ethnobotanist, and her daughter Dalia, a single mother with a passion for vocabulary and philosophizing.

Initially Lala is presented as an extremely competent person, impatient with her daughter's speculative approach to life. However, the third protagonist in the film is dementia and very soon Lala's high level of cognitive functioning deteriorates: the film's second act opens with her confiding her diagnosis of Alzheimer's to Dalia, and, in the third act, she begins to lose physical as well as mental functionality. Lala's interest in ethnobotany gives Novaro a premise for imbricating in the narrative many references, textual and visual, to the *Codex de la Cruz-Badiano*, and the film's interweaving of a twenty-first-century drama and a sixteenth-century herbal allows the director to make artifacts of Mexico's indigenous cultures speak effectively to the present.

Novaro does not theorize the differences between medical and social models of disability in her film. However, the dialogue between indigenous herbal practice and contemporary biomedicine established by the film's structure potentially disrupts both the notion that the medicalization of disability is an artifact of industrialized and developed societies as well as the sense that progress toward a social model of disability is exclusively a feature of recent history and of Western identity politics. In the reading developed here I propose that the film's negotiation of indigenous and biomedical conceptualizations of the ailing and non-normative mind and body reveals elements of both models of disability in pre-Columbian apprehensions of the diversity of experiences today rendered by notions of the able and disabled body or mind. I suggest that a process of cultural subsidence in *Las buenas hierbas* enables Novaro to show viewers that there is a specifically Mexican understanding of disability informed by pre-Hispanic cultures. Furthermore, the ethnobotanical cultural milieu created by the film allows it to extend its portrait of a family affected by a disability to a critique that politicizes on a national scale the questions it raises about cultural memory and social justice.

The characters in *Las buenas hierbas* talk often about the codex, and animation is used to bring alive the original color illustrations to show the development and flowering of the plants described by de la Cruz. This is one of several unconventional flourishes in the film; it also reifies words, putting them on screen as if three dimensional letters of the alphabet were material parts of the environment inhabited by the characters. Mise-en-scène is used to imply an environment that is quite literally colonized by a language, which, furthermore, takes on some of the aspects of the plants also described by the film, as it grows and establishes itself over a defined habitat.

Among the film's key themes, then, are memory and amnesia, aging and dementia, gender and science, and cultural hybridization and imperialism. And plants. What I want to do in this chapter is first to consider the film under some of these headings—by looking at how understanding the iteration of ethnobotany specific to Mexico can help in seeing how the film fits into a specifically Mexican discourse of disability, indigeneity, and femininity—and then to ask how the third age, and its infirmities, sits within a Latin American cinematic legacy where a political critique informed by the Third Cinema manifesto is privileged. Since Third Cinema queries hybridization and mimesis, the brief incursion into its legacy also allows me to tilt Novaro's film so that it speaks within the still unsettled debate over how to define the cultural identity of the *Codex de la Cruz-Badiano.*

## Foundations of a Mexican Disability Discourse

Mexico City, the megalopolis that gives its name to the world's most populous Spanish-speaking country, is sinking. Built over the network of canals that existed before the arrival of Cortés, the subsidence problem can be seen in tilting buildings and in the flights of steps that have had to be built to permit downward access to the entrances of buildings whose portals used to be at ground level.[2] If this material subsidence creates issues of accessibility for those with mobility impairments in Mexico City, so, too, does the fact that the country's approach to issues of social justice and national identity is also steeped in the layers of history over which contemporary political and institutional structures are built. I do not mean that reference to pre-Columbian cultures automatically creates obstacles or impediments to equality for disabled people in Mexico; the point is a more neutral and descriptive one to the effect that approximations to disability politics in Mexico have recourse to a legitimizing or differentiating discourse of pre-Columbian antecedence, which lends questions arising from physical and mental impairment in Mexico a distinctive framework.

For example, in the preamble to its 2004 statistical assessment of disability in Mexico, *Las personas con discapacidad en México: una visión censal,* the Mexican National Institute of Statistics, Geography, and Technology (INEGI) posits increased recognition of people with disabilities as an interest group, and movement toward the betterment of services and provisions for them, as an index of national development. At the same time, and before summarizing the history of the shift from the asylums of the Porfiriato to the welfare models developed in the 1980s, the *Visión censal* casts its gaze back to a pre-Hispanic North America and discovers indigenous cultural practices that in some ways resembled pre-Christian medieval Europe's animist stigmatization of people with physical or mental deficiencies and, in others, reflected an enlightenment surpassing that of the European colonists:

> Dualism in Nahuatl culture in the explanation and treatment of diseases and deficiencies was apparent in animist interpretations strongly associated with superstitions or auguries, and was also to be seen in the development of an extensive therapeutic practice based around herbalism, something which was a source of admiration among the conquistadors. (INEGI 2)

The colonists' admiration for the pre-Columbian herbal pharmacopeia is also remarked on by Francisco Guerra who says that "The botanical gardens of Nezahualcoyotl and Moctezuma, and the fact that a special market existed in the ancient Tenochtitlan just for medicinal herbs were deeply admired by the conquistadores" (332–333).

INEGI's survey brings this pre-Columbian and—partially—medical model of conditions seen as aberrant or defective very much into the present:

> The influence which Greek and Roman civilizations had in medieval Europe is also reflected in the mixture of Spanish and pre-Hispanic cultures, and can be seen also in the concepts and attitudes which our society currently has towards people with disabilities. (2)

The very fact, then, that disability in Mexican discourse—administrative as well as anthropological—is read as subject to the same syncretizing influences as many other aspects of contemporary Mexican culture and society binds notions of impairment equitably into a specifically Mexican Weltanschauung.[3]

Bridging pre-Columbian practice and post-Hispanic epistemology are the codices, hybrid documents like the *Badianus codex*, which applied the structures of European herbals to indigenous botanical knowledge. As the introduction to INEGI's census puts it:

> Therapeutic practice was based principally in herbalism [and] the degree to which it had developed can be seen in the Badianus and Florentine Codices where there are to be found complex treatments for illnesses, deficiencies, and disabilities such as epilepsy, blindness and deafness, conditions which were addressed in their multiform presentations. (3)

This is significant in terms of this chapter's focus on María Novaro's *Las buenas hierbas*, because it sheds light on the director's conjoining of, on the one hand, a narrative set in 2007 about a woman who becomes disabled due to Alzheimer's and, on the other, an exploration of the relevance to contemporary Mexico of the indigenous knowledge preserved in the *Badianus codex*. The film is punctuated with richly animated illustrations from the codex together with chapter headings taken from the accompanying descriptions of a plant's medicinal or therapeutic properties (see Figure 4.1); if at first this lends it a structural similarity to Laura Esquivel's novel *Como agua para chocolate* (and to the blockbuster film based on it), closer examination reveals a film with a more lacerating underlying political critique than Esquivel's romanticized and magically real cookbook, as I detail further on alongside a brief incursion into Third Cinema politics. *Las buenas hierbas* gives us *recetas* of a different kind, and prescriptions not only for individuals but for social ailments, foreseen, for example, in de la Cruz's inclusion in his manuscript of a plant-based remedy for ineffectual politicians and administrators beset by fatigue and mediocrity.

How do we arrive at a film that, without losing the plot, can shift from animated pages of the *Badianus codex* to scenes set in a community radio station where the presenters decry government corruption and the failure to act on findings like those made by the Mexican journalist Lydia Cacho about sex trafficking? Has there been any sanction for a state crime

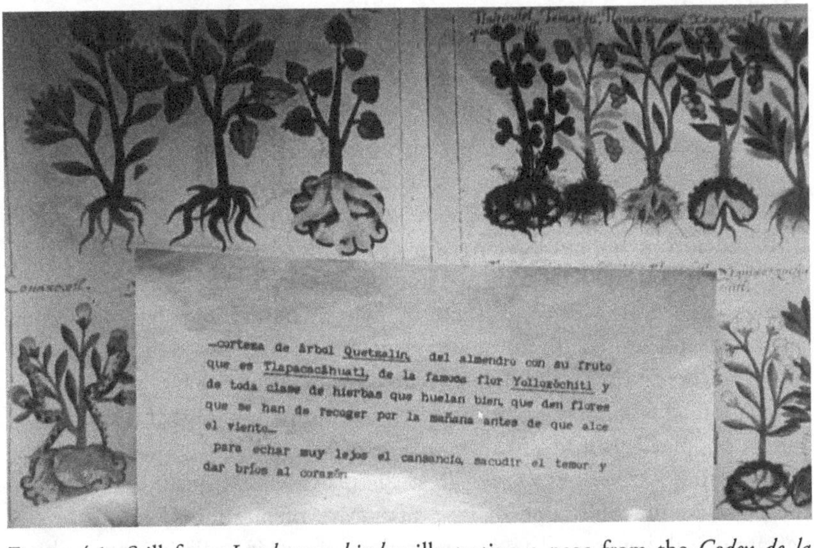


Figure 4.1. Still from *Las buenas hierbas* illustrating a page from the *Codex de la Cruz-Badiano* and Lala's research notes. In the sequence which follows the plants are brought to life in a short animation. Las buenas hierbas © Axolote Cine. 

in Mexico in recent years?," the hosts ask rhetorically, before answering their own question: "There's not a single person in prison: they're governing the country" (Novaro 2010). To understand how Novaro's film about plants and about pre-Columbian botany can also be a film about social (in)justice, disability, women's rights, and unpunished violence, it will be helpful to review Victor Manuel Toledo's work on new ethnobotanical paradigms in Mexico.

Toledo argues that "ethnobotany in Mexico lives by a process [of] 'scientific revolution'; that is, the replacement of an academic tradition with a new way to conceive and carry out research" (85). Mexican ethnobotany, he says, "has entered a new dimension in which it is no longer isolated and a discipline enclosed within itself, but has become part of a new interdisciplinary trend loosely tied to the problems of production and politics" (85). Toledo claims that a confluence of factors has contributed to making the crossroads of demos and indigenous knowledge presupposed by ethnobotany a magnet and rallying point for troublemakers and critics; the growing sense in Mexico that native epistemologies are cultural artifacts requiring preservation and conservation coincided with a realization that while the legacy of indigenous plant knowledge plays a large part in the development of pharmaceuticals, 80 percent of Mexico's medical drugs are supplied by multinationals whose profits remain entirely exogenous.[4] Toledo's key point is that few of the profits from these (re)discoveries (inaccurately claimed as wholly modern and Western) go back to the source and that the convergence of Western pharmacy and indigenous practice around social knowledge of plants is therefore contentious, political, and an arena in which are condensed many of the tensions between globalization and ecological concerns about people and the places they inhabit.

Edward Anderson argues that as an area of inquiry that is by its very nature interdisciplinary, ethnobotany "is a subject than cannot be dealt with from the narrow specialist's viewpoint so common in academic circles" (184) and that it demands "breadth of knowledge in both the social and natural sciences" (193). In Mexico, this already hybrid epistemology has in addition "attracted and united the most dissident, heterodox, and radical investigators [and] become a discipline preoccupied with social change, technological innovation, the country's economic self-determination, and the struggle of Indian peoples" (Toledo 75).

Setting *Las buenas hierbas* in a discursive environment informed by the ethnobotanical research of its protagonist, then, affords Novaro several narratological benefits. The incorporation of an interdisciplinary subject favors the hybridity that critics have underscored as a distinctive feature in the director's work.[5] In light of Joanne Hershfield's and Miriam Haddu's perspectives on Novaro, in particular, I would argue that the approximation in *Las buenas hierbas* to the increasingly global phenomenon of dementia diagnosed as Alzheimer's, and to mental disability through a character whose life work has been an engagement with the pre-Columbian pharmacopeia, allows Novaro to negotiate between the local and the global in a way that retains comprehensibility for an audience outside Mexico while also eschewing an equation between filmic Mexicanness and an aesthetic of violence. Furthermore, the film's invocation and literal representation of the *Badianus codex* establishes a frame of reference for the film that points to the potential for a specifically Mexican conceptualization of disability and of its socialization throughout a history extending much further back than the identity politics of contemporary rights movements.

Comparing Novaro's original screenplay (dated 2004) with the finished film (released nearly six years later) is instructive in that the text makes slightly more obvious the hybridization of the local and the transnational, and of Western biomedicine and pre-Columbian herbalism. For example, in the script a cross-cut between the sixteenth-century codex and a contemporary clinical breakdown of landmarks in the physical and mental deterioration of people with Alzheimer's bridges scenes sixty and sixty-one:

> We see [. . .] reproductions of plants taken from the copy of the *Libellus de medicina libus Indorum Herbis* that Lala had in her office [. . .] We read [. . .] "*Cure for one who has been shaken by whirlwinds or gales*" (Novaro 2004, 65)

And this is followed immediately by:

> A reminder stuck to the wall [that] explains the "STAGES IN THE ALZHEIMER PATIENT'S PHYSICAL AND MENTAL DETERIORATION" (Novaro 2004, 65)

In the screenplay, the turning points in the pathogenesis of Alzheimer's are used as chapter headings for the divisions that break the film up into a series of numbered stages. In the completed film, these chapter headings are not used and their place is taken instead by the animations of pages from the codex, each illustrating a different condition and a different plant-based therapy. The conversation between indigenous and biomedical knowledge is retained, however. For example, the film retains the scene where Dalia researches the arguments for a biochemistry of gendered behavior, and the mise-en-scène of Lala's office and home juxtaposes indigenous knowledge, in the form of the *Badianus codex*, with the accoutrements of an empirically based scientific practice. It is telling, perhaps, that María Sabina, a *curandera* synonymous with non-Western therapeutic practices and knowledge, appears to Lala in her home, rather than in her workplace. The domestication of local knowledge and culture is further reinforced when Dalia rejects the hospital as a source of succor for her mother and decides that the best place for her care and her treatment is, instead, her home.

## A Feminist Ethnobotany

María Novaro has said of her approach to gender and narrative: "I try to narrate things *from* a woman's perspective, and not to narrate things *about* women" (Delon and Quezada 2011 [part I]). Novaro adds to this remark a recollection of a conversation with Carlos Monsiváis in which he emphasized that there had been few stories in Mexican cinema told *by* women. She positions her filmmaking within an attempt to rectify this imbalance. Focusing in *Las buenas hierbas* on the *Badianus codex*, a text written by a man and translated by a man, might seem like a strange choice given the director's preference for telling stories *by* as well as *about* women. However, the work of women scholars in the rediscovery and republication of the codex was vital, as Peter Furst outlines in his ethnobotanically informed history of the text in the twentieth century. The manuscript had languished in European libraries for 450 years, Furst notes, before Charles Upson Clark chanced upon it in the Vatican library in 1929. "These and other facts about the history and content of the Aztec herbal," Furst writes, "we owe to Emily Walcott Emmart" (111). The watercolor reproductions of the manuscript's botanical illustrations were painted by Marie Therese Missionier-Vuilleman and it was Elizabeth Clark and another female member of the Garden Club of America who secured funding—through an award established in honor of the Club's first president, also a woman—for the expenses entailed in the costly color printing of the book.

The film's inclusion of strophes from Maria Sabina's mushroom *velada* positions femininity at the center of the narrative and at the heart of Novaro's concern with her characters. Each line of Sabina's incantation begins with the words "I am the woman" (Novaro 2004, 48) and one of the sections replayed by Lala in the film (apparently—in the diegesis—from a tape recording made during field work) ends with the line "I am the woman who has wisdom of language because I am the woman who has wisdom of medicine." The *curandera*'s equation of lexicographic and medical sapience seems to augur the taking up of ethnobotany as a socially and politically disruptive epistemological framework by Mexican activists and by Novaro herself in a script informed by this context.

Lala will tell her daughter in a later sequence of the film "We women are the ones who pass on words and wisdom" (Novaro 2004, 55) and the resonance with Sabina's incantation implies a feminized transmission of indigenous knowledge between the peoples of Mexico and between generations within a family. Indeed, Lala has named her daughter Dalia, as if she were the child both of her corporeal maternity and of her research into the meanings and uses plants held for Mexico's native peoples. At the beginning of the film Dalia is impatient with her mother's clearly often repeated advocacy of natural plant remedies for her grandson's ailments. In a long suffering tone she echoes Lala's recommendation of a homemade plant-based ointment, which is "better than any cream." Toward the end of the film when, frustrated by the cruel impersonality of the hospital, Dalia is treating her mother at home, she uses the same preparation Lala had made for her and says again, this time with tenderness and regret, "it's better than any cream." While going through her mother's personal belongings, she also speaks aloud her sadness that she did not take the opportunity when it arose to ask Lala about her meeting with María Sabina and what it was like to take part in a *velada*. Her mother's ailing and disabled mind becomes the damaged repository of an indigenous knowledge already once removed from its source. Tellingly, the incarnation of indigenous plant and mycological knowledge in the film is someone who can only be represented posthumously and by the use of a special effect, which conjures an ethereal hologram of María Sabina into Lala's presence.

It is also noteworthy that the greatest tension in the film occurs in a scene where Dalia is trying to help dress her mother before they set out on a visit to the hospital. Lala's incapacity to tell the difference between a skirt and a cardigan, her loss of the ability to dress herself, is interwoven with her tremendous agitation about the need to find some vital textual material in the *Badianus codex*, which lies open on her bed amidst a rapidly growing pile of discarded clothes (see Figure 4.2).

Here, perhaps, is where *Las buenas hierbas* implies most clearly an affinity between the loss of subjective identity and the loss of non-Western cultural knowledge and traditions. Globalization is the Alzheimer's chewing up the store of cultural diversity and memory, and Lala's personal breakdown figures the fragmentation and erosion of a collective subjectivity. The same scene also illustrates some of the paradoxes and contradictions within the film: on the one hand, the evocation of pre-Columbian traditions through the extant codices that record them resists what Ethan Watters describes in *Crazy Like Us: the Globalization of the Western Mind* as "the flattening of the landscape of the human psyche" and a process of diagnostic and iatrogenic contagion that "homogeniz[es] the way the world goes mad" (2–3); on the

Figure 4.2. A still from a pivotal scene in *Las buenas hierbas*. Dalia's struggle with her mother's dementia centres on an open facsimile copy of the *Codex de la Cruz-Badiano* and the disorderly Alzheimer's wardrobe. Las buenas hierbas © Axolote Cine. 

other hand, this same gesture of rhetorical similitude draws the film into the paradigm that Sharon Snyder and David Mitchell have identified whereby disability becomes a metaphor for social and political aberrance and thus becomes harder to see in its own right.

## Localizing a Global Diagnostic Paradigm

Novaro's screenplay and mise-en-scène, as we can see from the previous discussion, bring together the erosion of personal identity due to dementia with concerns about the loss of cultural subjectivity. Finding this narrative device at work in a Mexican film from the 2000s comes as no surprise to anyone familiar with the spate of films made in the last five years or so with a focus on Alzheimer's. It is also consistent with the 2012 estimate that there are now more than 800,000 people with Alzheimer's in Mexico (Secretaría de Salud).

In Spain alone between 2008 and 2011 there were at least three films released with a focus on Alzheimer's: *Nadar* [*Swimming*], *Bucarest: La memoria perdida* [*Bucharest: Lost Memory*], and *Arrugas* [*Wrinkles*]. Korean director Chang-dong Lee's surprise success with *Poetry*, a film released in 2010 about the travails of an older woman as her Alzheimer's symptoms worsen, shows that the pattern is also a global one. While Alzheimer's is experienced on a very subjective level by the patient and by his or her caregivers it lends itself as a paradigm to an international art house circuit because the diagnostically established signs of the progression of the disease are universal. In *Las buenas hierbas* Lala first forgets that she put her keys in the biscuit tin, then forgets how to dress. She begins to have difficulty with hand-to-mouth coordination, and then starts to lose motor control generally: these signposts are common to all the films I have mentioned as they portray the diagnosis and pathogenesis of Alzheimer's. Subjectivities, as they fall apart, begin to look very samey: toward the end of the process there is no individuation.

In spite of, or perhaps because of, the homogenized mileposts in Alzheimer pathogenesis, all the films referred to earlier try not simply to wrest some individuality from the ravages of Alzheimer's but also, paradoxically, to make it function as a metaphor for a cultural specificity under threat of loss or of being forgotten. While *Las buenas hierbas* is not as overtly political as *Nadar* and *Bucarest: La memoria perdida*, which cast historical amnesia as a correlate of Alzheimer's, neither is Novaro's film as lyrical as Chang-dong Lee's *Poetry*. It sits somewhere between the two, inviting the viewer to reflect on the loss to science of the pharmaceutical knowledge that was not preserved in the codices and, at the same time, to draw a comparison between the loss of an individual's memory and cognition and the lacunae in the Mexican people's knowledge of their pre-Hispanic heritage.

Blanquita, a minor character in the film, expresses the metaphorical function of Alzheimer's when she says that despite the asyndetic thinking produced by the disease, it nevertheless reveals a profound truth. From the film's ethnobotanical and anthropological context, we can take this to be a truth about the loss of cultural memory. This is a function that Alzheimer's could not be made to serve in an American approach to the condition, for example, where one of the therapies considered most progressive is to forget memory and to cease to attach any importance to it (Basting 2009).

As I have argued elsewhere (Prout 2012), a problem with using Alzheimer's as a metaphorical vehicle in a personal narrative is that it tasks the patient, who is effectively losing the capacity for executive action, with the further responsibility for safeguarding, and thus for losing, the already tenuous cultural or historical memory, which his or her ailing mind comes to represent. We can see, therefore, that the strand of scholarship that stresses the extent to which disability is the disavowed kernel at the root of critical rhetoric and discourse is highly germane to interpretations of this new wave of Alzheimer's filmic texts.

## Hybrids, Copies, and a Third (Age) Cinema

In *Las buenas hierbas* we see that modern medical science is part of the problem, rather than the cure, inasmuch as it exports through the imperial corridors of technology and knowledge a globalizing and homogenizing set of diagnostic practices and cures. Novaro's film sets against the high-tech panopticon of the MRI scanner the folk wisdom of Mexico's indigenous peoples. Whereas Carla Subirana's *Nadar* segues between high-tech images of her grandmother's brain and the similarly rippled image of her grandfather's fingerprints, as recorded in his criminal record, *Las buenas hierbas* makes a very similar segue, but in the Mexican film the images merge the brain scans and leaves and petals falling from trees until the plant material and the tau tangles characteristic of Alzheimer's seem to become one.

Like Claudia Llosa's *La teta asustada* (*The Milk of Sorrow* 2009), *Las buenas hierbas* brings into dialogue Western and non-Western models of medical practice in an encounter that spotlights the holisticism of pre-Columbian concepts of the relationship between body and soul and the mechanistic approach taken by Western biomedicine. Perhaps slightly more than *La teta asustada*, *Las buenas hierbas* tends toward a syncretic accommodation of both traditional and high-tech medicine. Alongside its inclusion of content from Nicolás Echevarría's *Mujer espíritu*, the documentary made in 1978 about María Sabina, Novaro's screenplay also name checks or includes visual references to people like Julieta Fierro, an astronomer and celebrity scientist, and Constantino Macias, a well-known ecologist. And Lala herself is portrayed as a respected botanist, one in a line of female Mexican scholars going back to Helia Bravo Hollis who was a significant figure in the field in Mexico in the 1940s (Herrera 116–121).

Scene nineteen in Novaro's script is illustrative of its evocation of an idealized knowledge environment where traditional and scientific wisdom are to be found alongside each other. In this scene there is no dialogue: the camera simply tracks across the contents of Lala's offices at UNAM's Botanical Gardens: it first picks out the computer screen on which we see a page about Alzheimer's being loaded and then shifts to other objects: a poster depicting María Sabina, "the mycological sage," a diploma awarded to Eduarda Calderon, "Mexican ethnobotanist," a book, *Plantas curativas en México*, and a large reproduction of illustrations from the *de la Cruz-Badiano Codex*.

The hybridization created here in the mise-en-scène is further reflected in the relationship between the film's content and its structure, more so in the original screenplay than in the finished film, as I suggested previously. In the written text, the same page that we had seen on Lala's computer screen, and a poster that is referred to later on and is headed "Stages in the Alzheimer patient's physical and mental deterioration," provide the subheadings that break the dialogue into chapters with intertitles that read, for example, "Fourth phase: changes to behavior with periods of lucidity," or Sixth phase: loss of the ability to assume sitting position and to hold head up straight." *Las buenas hierbas* thus uses a paradigm from Western biomedicine as a framework for narrative content, which is to a large extent drawn from indigenous traditions of botany and medicine. Here we can see that Novaro's appeal to the *Badianus codex* is not only facilitated by intertextual reference but is also brought into being by creating a textual edifice in which neither European nor traditional science is ever clearly privileged at the expense of the other. In this, the film's organic structure reflects the *Badianus codex* itself: is it an Aztec pharmacopeia ordered after the fashion of a European herbal, or is it a European almanac that westernizes its indigenous content within the strictures of an old-world paradigm? The question has vexed scholars since the reemergence of the text in the 1930s.

In the 1980s Debra Hassig wrote that the only new-world elements present in the codex were the plants themselves; the idea of signature diseases, where the plant is somehow matched with the part of the body affected by an ailment, and of cures that addressed imbalances in humors or in temperature, were clear evidence of contamination of the original knowledge by European concepts, she sustained. Hassig also proposed that the recording of indigenous pharmaceutical practice was not intended for posterity but simply as a means to permit the more efficient annihilation of "suspect religious ritual" (31). In 2008, Millie Gimmel posited, on the other hand, that "in spite of its European appearance the Codex is an indigenously produced work that reflects primarily indigenous sensibilities" (186). She says that "the European contamination seen by so many scholars in the Codex might actually be more a reflection of indigenous ethnocentricity and misinterpretation of European texts rather than the wholesale acceptance of European medicine" (186). Gimmel foregrounds studies of the Aztecs' belief in three animistic entities to propose that where other scholars have seen the imposition of a European humoral notion of medicine, there is also a remnant of indigenous ontology. From this she concludes that the "Codex de la Cruz [is] a work which looks like a European herbal but whose content and composition is almost completely indigenous." The ideal readerships for the text did not exist at the time of its composition, she says and proposes that "As twenty first century readers and scholars we must recognize the hybridity of this text and treat it as the blended text it is" (187). My own contention here is that María Novaro does precisely this and her syncretic alignment of indigenous content within a paradigm drawn from Western medicine's pathogenesis of Alzheimer's makes the codex available to just such a hybrid reading. Here again there is a parallel with the work of INEGI and its emphasis on cultural hybridization within a medical history of disability.

The question of colonial facsimile versus cultural hybridity takes us to a more recent codification of cinematically mediated remedies for social malady: Getino and Solanas's manifesto for a Third Cinema. The authors quote the narration from their film *La hora de los hornos* to the effect that "As early as the seventeenth century the Jesuit missionaries proclaimed the aptitude of the South American native for copying European works of art. If you want to be a man, says the oppressor, you have to be like me, speak my language, deny your own being" (116). By building her film around the *Badianus codex*, a text that plugs so directly into the debate over whether early hybrid texts from the new world are merely slavish copies of European traditions or valuable records of indigenous cultures, Novaro can be seen as having created a work that falls within the legacy of the Third Cinema manifesto: it speaks clearly to the debate opened up and expanded by Getino and Solanas's text over mimesis as oppression and, as my reading of the film through Gimmel's reinterpretation of the codex suggests, uncovers a potential for hybridization, which the manifesto's dichotomizing debate seemed to have foreclosed.

The attention to the third age in *Las buenas hierbas* could be read, furthermore, as an evolution of the Third Cinema manifesto inasmuch as Novaro's film focuses on the elderly and those with presenile dementia, a demographic that cinema prefers on the whole to forget. From this angle, the narrative can be understood as meeting Getino and Solanas's challenge to expose "the whole climate of pseudonormality behind which the warfare of everyday life is hidden" (127). Particularly toward the end when Novaro's perspective turns a spotlight on the impersonal treatment extended to Lala by hospital staff, the film uncovers the disregard for elders and for people who are no longer able to be self-advocates.

*Las buenas hierbas* engages with a disease that is in itself a threat to the imperialistic cult of the individual. In this much the film fits within the prescription for a Latin American Third Cinema: it affords a central role to a section of the population often overlooked by mass media and society, namely the elderly and people affected by the symptoms of dementia. It also calls into question neo-imperialist paradigms of biopower and pharmacracy by situating medical practice within a hybridized narrative that conjoins indigenous and Western traditions and thus confronts the notion that only when the imperialist project, reconfigured as a globalized diagnostic practice, has gained control of the entire planet will order prevail; as Szasz puts it, in a pharmacratic imperialism all "human problems are diseases that medicine will soon conquer" (xv).

In other ways I think it is fair to say that Novaro's film expands out of the Third Cinema box. It is a narrative scripted by a woman and in which women and motherhood are the predominant focus, an aspect of creativity not especially central in the manifesto informed as it is by a machista outlook on filmmaking where guns, testosterone, and guerrillas are predominant. More subtly, I would argue that the film's exploration of memory and of the fragility of individual subjectivity also expands on, or breaks away from, the original manifesto. To find value in the individual life of a woman who is losing her mind, Novaro's film eschews the flight from the past. Memory, on the other hand, is a trickier theme to situate within the Third Cinema legacy. The manifesto privileges novelty, youthfulness, and mobility. Ernesto Guevara is praised as the exemplary new man, while "the cinema fit for a new kind of human being" is contrasted with an execrable cinema characterized as one made "for the old kind of human being." There is not much scope here for making something good out of what is held to be old and infirm and therefore worthy only of the dustbin of history. My point is that a concern with the loss of memory sits uneasily with a manifesto, which is based on a thrusting advance toward a new dawn. Nevertheless, by summoning collective cultural memory alongside the exploration of individual memory *Las buenas hierbas* also responds to the need foreseen by the advocates of Third Cinema not to be drawn into a debate about the conceptualization of post-Hispanic Latin American culture as merely a reiterative or simulative derivation of a European original. This, in turn, as I have sought to set out in the preceding pages, sets a heavy burden on the individual mind as a storehouse for an entire cultural legacy.

## Impressions of Loss

The two strands of memory loss treated by the film—subjective and cultural—could have rendered Lala's experience little more than a metaphor, but *Las buenas hierbas* avoids reducing the individual to a cypher for a larger amnesia and is starkly honest both about the disintegration of Lala's subjectivity and the physical deterioration wrought by the illness. Those who care for people with Alzheimer's are often portrayed as the real victims of the disease; without painting Dalia as a victim, *Las buenas hierbas* nevertheless illustrates the anguish she endures as her mother disappears before her eyes. Ofelia Medina (Lala) and Úrsula Pruneda (Dalia) make the filial relationship tested by Alzheimer's a credible one in scenes that never become mawkish.

Novaro situates herself in a tradition of female botanical artists and researchers, asking questions about how the representation of the natural world has been a labor divided by gender (see, for example, Lightman, and Speirs) and about the relationship between this segregation and the misogynistic violence, which is also referenced in the film. *Las buenas hierbas* brings Mexican cinema into a current of films about Alzheimer's and shows that while the pathogenesis of the disease is the same everywhere, responses to it are imbricated in cultures that remain discrete. Loss leaves a distinct impression, an idea developed in *Las buenas hierbas* both at an historical, national level, and at a personal one.

In her latest film, as in her previous work, María Novaro sidesteps an aesthetic of violence to approach pressing issues within Mexican society. I have tried to read the film in a way that elucidates the political and social connotations of the director's choice of a sixteenth-century Aztec herbal as the cultural medium for her representation of Alzheimer's and mental disabilities. In addition, my argument has pointed to the dialogue between feminist and disability issues in the film and I want to end with Novaro's own assessment of how women's filmmaking is received in Mexico. This quote from the director illustrates, I think, that the shared interests of feminism and of disability rights as cognate political movements have still fully to be worked out:

> I think—and I experience this every time one of my films comes out—that very often our themes [as women filmmakers] are considered to be minor, our films are considered as smaller, our cinematography is considered a minor genre, as if we were . . . as if it were the cinema of the handicapped or of people with different abilities and as if we were being told of our filmmaking, "Well, considering it's made by women, it's not that bad," as if we were in another league, in another competition. (Delon and Quezada, 2011 [part II])[6]

## Notes

1. In contrast, in Novaro's earlier film *Sin dejar huella* (*Without a Trace*), indigenous culture—its potential loss and reappropriation—constitute a plot device.

In this film, a detective chases a counterfeiter of Mayan artifacts across Mexico from the northern border with the United States to the Yucatan peninsula.

2. Tenochtitlan and Tlatelolco (Aztec forerunners of what became Mexico City) were built on islands within Lake Texcoco. In the seventeenth century, the lake was drained and filled in by the Spaniards: this, together with other geological factors and the drainage of aquifers to supply drinking water, is at the root of the city's subsidence. Illades and Lesser estimate that parts of Mexico City are sinking at a rate of between 5 and 10 centimetres each year (13).

3. In *Nadie es ombligo en la tierra / Ayacxictli in Tlalticpc: incapacidad en el México antiguo* (2000) Arturo Rocha portrays pre-Columbian conceptions of disability in light of a Nahuatl injunction against the casting out from ordinary society of those with non-normative presentations of physical and mental capacities. Reviewing the book, Ernesto de la Torre Villar says that Rocha finds: "[An] extensive series of elements which allow us to apprehend how there existed [among the Mexica] people with very diverse disabilities who lived as part of the everyday society (. . .) and how there grew up around the disabled a way of thinking and a form of conduct in which we see not rejection but human comprehension."

4. Research by Fabricant and Farnsworth indicates that 80 percent of "122 compounds of defined structure obtained from only 94 species of plants, that are used globally as drugs [. . .] have had an ethnomedical use identical or related to the current use of the active elements of the plant," and that "most useful drugs derived from plants have been discovered by follow-up of ethnomedical uses" (69, 74).

5. Joanne Hershfield suggests that "If it wants to appeal to a global audience, a [Mexican] national film must supplement its localness with a global aesthetic that appeals to an audience educated through globalizing models of cinema practices" (171). As Hershfield goes on to illustrate, Novaro has found a way in her films to achieve this fusion and yet remain outside the drive toward "a global aesthetic of violence" (172). In a similar vein, Miriam Haddu proposes that "Novaro attempts to rediscover her nation" and "projects in her work a vision of what she deems to be an acute interpretation of a specific sense of 'Mexicanness' on the screen" (104).

6. The final word in this quote from Novaro—"competencia"—means "competition" or "ranking" in the context of the director's conversation about the reception of Mexican women filmmakers' work. In Spanish, the word also denotes competence and competency. The title of my chapter uses "otras competencias" having in mind the parallel meanings of "competencia" in Spanish. Here as elsewhere throughout the text, translations from Spanish into English are the work of the author.

## Works Cited

*Alzheimer Project, The*. Produced by J. Hoffman. 2009. HBO Home Video.

Anderson, Edward F. "Ethnobotany and the Liberal Arts." In *Ethnobotany: The Evolution of a Discipline*. Edited by Richard Evans Schultes and Siri Von Reis. Portland: Discorides Press, 1995, 183–186.

*Arrugas*. Directed by Ignacio Ferreras. 2012. Cromosoma producciones.

Barrier, Michael. *Hollywood Cartoons: American Animation in its Golden Age*. New York: Oxford UP, 1999.

Basting, Anne Davis. *Forget Memory: Creating Better Lives for People with Dementia*. Baltimore: Johns Hopkins UP, 2009.

*Bucarest: La memoria perdida*. Directed by Alberto Solé. 2008. Cameo Media.

*Las buenas hierbas*. Directed by María Novaro, 2011. Action.

*Como agua para chocolate*. Directed by Alfonso Arau. 1992. Arau Films International / Fondo de fomento a la calidad cinematográfica, etc.

De la Cruz, Martín, and William Gates (translator). *An Aztec Herbal: The Classic Codex of 1552*. Mineola: Dover, 2000.

Delon, Erika, and Mónica Quezada. *María Novaro: una visión femenina del cine mexicano I*. *Youtube*. 2011. Web.

——. *María Novaro: una visión femenina del cine mexicano II*. *Youtube*. 2011. Web.

Desnoes, Edmundo. *Inconsolable Memories*. London: André Deutsch, 1968.

Esquivel, Laura. *Como agua para chocolate: novela de entregas mensuales, con recetas, amores y remedios caseros*. Madrid: Mondadori, 1990.

Fabricant, Daniel S., and Norman R. Farnsworth. "The Value of Plants Used in Traditional Medicine for Drug Discovery." *Environmental Health Perspectives* 109 (supplement 1) (2001): 69–75.

*Fresa y chocolate*. Directed by Tomás Gutiérrez Alea and Juan Carlos Tabío, 1993. ICAIC.

Furst, Peter. 1995. " 'This Little Book of Herbs': Psychoactive Plants as Therapeutic Agents in the Badianus Manuscript of 1552." In *Ethnobotany: The Evolution of a Discipline*. Edited by Richard Evans Schultes and Siri Von Reis. Portland: Discorides Press, 1995, 108–130.

Getino, Octavio, and Fernando Solanas. "Toward a Third Cinema." *Tricontinental* 14 (October 1969): 107–132.

Gimmel, Millie. "Reading Medicine in the Codex de la Cruz Badiano." *Journal of the History of Ideas* 69.2 (2008): 169–192.

Guerra, Francisco. "Aztec Medicine." *Medical History* 10.4 (1966): 315–338.

Haddu, Miriam. " 'Welcome to Tijuana . . .': Space, Place, and Identity in María Novaro's *El jardín del Edén*." *Journal of Romance Studies* 6.3 (2006): 103–116.

Hassig, Debra. "Transplanted Medicine: Colonial Mexican Herbals of the Sixteenth Century." *Res* 17–18 (1989): 31–53.

Herrera, Teófilo. *Breve historia de la botánica en México*. Mexico City: Fondo de Cultura Económica, 1998.

Hershfield, Joanne. "Women's Cinema and Contemporary Allegories of Violence in Mexico." *Discourse* 32.2 (2010): 170–185.

Illades, Juan Manuel, and Miguel Ángel Cortés Pérez. "El hundimiento del terreno en la Ciudad de México y sus implicaciones en el sistema de drenaje." *Ingeniería hidráulica en México* 13.3 (1998): 13–18.

Instituto Nacional de Estadística, Geografía e Informática (INEGI). *Las personas con discapacidad en México: Una visión censal*. Aguascalientes: INEGI, 2004.

Johnson, Tim. "Mexico City Copes with that Sinking Feeling." *Seattle Times*. September 24, 2011 [online edition].

Lightman, Bernard. "Depicting Nature, Defining Roles: The Gender Politics of Victorian Illustration." In *Figuring it Out: Science, Gender, and Visual Culture*. Edited by Ann B. Shteir and Bernard Lightman. Hanover: Dartmouth College P, 2006, 214–239.

*María Sabina: mujer espíritu*. Directed by Nicolás Echevarría. 1978. Centro de producción de cortometraje.

McRuer, Robert. *Crip Theory: Cultural Signs of Queerness and Disability*. New York: New York UP, 2006.

*Memorias del subdesarrollo*. Directed by Tomás Gutiérrez Alea. 1968. ICAIC.

Mitchell, David, and Sharon Snyder."Narrative Prosthesis and the Materiality of Metaphor." In *The Disability Studies Reader*. Edited by Lennard J. Davis. Abingdon: Routledge, 2006, 205–216.

*Nadar*. Directed by Carla Subirana. 2008. Benecé / TV3 / Barton Films.

Norden, Martin. *The Cinema of Isolation: A History of Physical Disability in the Movies*. New Brunswick: Rutgers UP, 1994.

Novaro, María. *Las buenas hierbas: guión original de María Novaro*. Unpublished manuscript. 2004.

*Poetry*. Directed by Chang-dong Lee. 2011. Zeus / Khan Entertainment.

Prout, Ryan. "Critical Condition: Alzheimer's and Identity in Carla Subirana's *Nedar* (2008)." *Journal of Iberian and Latin American Studies* 18, 2–3 (2012): 245–263.

Roca, Paco. *Arrugas*. Bilbao: Astiberri, 2007.

Rocha, Arturo. *Nadie es ombligo en la tierra: ayacxictli in tlaltícpac: discapacidad en el México antiguo: cultura náhuatl*. Mexico City. Teletón, 2000.

Secretaría de salud (Mexico). "Comunicado de prensa no. 407—Se presenta el plan de acción Alzheimer." November 18, 2012.

*Sin dejar huella*. Directed by María Novaro. 2000. Venevision.

Speirs, Carol. "Two Women Botanical Artists and their most Famous Works." Reading University. 2007. www.reading.ac.uk/web/FILES/special-collections/featurewomenbotanicalartists.pdf

Szasz, Thomas Stephen. *Pharmacracy: Medicine and Politics in America*. Westport, CT: Syracuse UP, 2001.

Toledo, Victor Manuel. "New Paradigms for a New Ethnobotany: Reflections on the Case of Mexico." In *Ethnobotany: The Evolution of a Discipline*. Edited by Richard Evans Schultes and Siri Von Reis. Portland: Discorides Press, 1995, 75–85.

Torre Villar, Ernesto. "Arturo Rocha, *Nadie es ombligo en la tierra. AyacXictli in Tlaltipac. Incapacidad en el México antiguo*." *Estudios de Cultura Náhuatl* (January 2003): unpaginated.

Watters, Ethan. *Crazy Like Us: The Globalization of the Western Mind*. London: Constable & Robinson, 2011.

Chapter 5

# Cripping the Camera

## Disability and Filmic Interval in Carlos Reygadas's *Japón*

Susan Antebi

In a 2006 comparative study of Juan Rulfo's classic novel, *Pedro Páramo* (1955) and Carlos Reygadas's 2002 feature film, *Japón*, William Rowlandson makes a brief, but intriguing observation. As he describes the opening scenes of the film, he notes that the camera and sound seem to directly convey the perspective of the protagonist. That is, as we experience the film, we simultaneously experience the protagonist's vision, movement, and corporeal sensation, through a process of partial identification. As Rowlandson writes: "The camera . . . walks roughly over the stony ground, to the crunch of footsteps and the man's laboured breathing. Moments later it is revealed that the man walks with a pronounced limp. This simple and easily overlooked technique fuses together in one montage the separate roles of actor, filmmaker, and viewer" (1028).

Part of Rowlandson's project is to compare the processes of identification between viewer, protagonist, and filmmaker, or reader, character, and narrator, in Reygadas's film and Rulfo's novel. As is well known to readers of *Pedro Páramo*, one of the most widely read works in the Mexican canon, the protagonist, Juan Preciado, serves as a guide to the reader as he makes his descent into Comala, an allegorical world of the living dead. Similarly, in Reygadas's film, partial identification between protagonist and viewer takes place, but in this case through specific camera strategies, as noted in the aforementioned example. In both works, the reader/viewer as witness descends into a rural world emblematic of a semi-mythologized Mexican past, of extreme poverty, and *caciquismo*, or a local political system characterized by despotism. Rowlandson pays attention to what he calls "this simple and easily overlooked technique," that is, the identification between the limping movements of the camera, and the revelation that the protagonist walks with a limp. However, his article is not in fact about disability, nor does the author discuss the point further. In my reading of the film and its critical context, I focus on this limp, not simply as an instance of disability representation in film, but rather as an approach to situating disability itself at the center of the dilemma of cinematic communication.

In more technical terms, the dilemma may be understood through the notion of the Deleuzian interval. As Cynthia Tomkins writes, borrowing from Deleuze and Bergson, "the interval defines a specific type of image, which receives actions in certain parts and executes reactions in others" (30). As she also notes, "The notion of the interval acquires especial significance in the work of experimental Latin American auteurs such as Reygadas, whose films call for active participation on the part of the audience in deciphering motivation and eliciting an affective reaction" (30). Use of the limp in the film is also perhaps an instance of what Mitchell and Snyder have famously called a narrative prosthesis, whereby disability does the work of giving a text what it couldn't otherwise represent on its own. In this case, however, prosthetic function occurs at the level of a self-reflexive filmmaking technique that interpolates the viewer, so that disability becomes the gesture of a shared embodied experience, just as character/actor, filmmaker and viewer become momentarily fused as one. The shared experience is no more than a momentary gesture because identification is only partial; we are not the filmmaker, and the camera pulls away to remind us that our gaze is not, finally, the same as that of the limping protagonist.

My purpose, then, in approaching this film, is to explore the overlaps or thresholds between disability representation and personal identification via embodiment as lived, sensorial experience. In analyzing such expressions, I also wish to consider what the film might contribute to a broader discussion of disability in its colonialist contexts—made evident through the camera's and the viewer's allegorical descent into a "primitive" world. I refer here to Aníbal Quijano's notion of the coloniality of power, which extends specifically to the question of disability through global capitalism's historical and ongoing demands for productive bodies, and through institutionalized practices of normalization and subjugation (Grech 54).

Other disability studies critics, including David Mitchell and Sharon Snyder, and Nirmala Erevelles, although using distinct terminology, have effectively demonstrated the historic and ongoing inseparability of disability and what Quijano has called the coloniality of power. Quijano's frequently cited work crystallizes the symbiotic relationship between the idea of race, as a structure used to impose hierarchies between human groups, and the control of labor, resources, and capital (533–534). For Erevelles, race and disability are mutually configured on and through the bodies of enslaved Africans, as part of a process that is in turn inseparable from the evolution of modern global capitalism (40–42). Mitchell and Snyder focus on eugenic practices and policies of the eighteenth and early nineteenth centuries, and describe race and disability as mutually constitutive of one another within the eugenic project (844).

These readings underscore a clearly marked historical trajectory, through which practices of exclusion and subjugation have irrevocably linked the categories of disability and race. Yet disability, I would suggest, also demands its own narratives, which may not always fit neatly into the sweep of compelling paradigms such as the coloniality of power. Much as Víctor Manuel Rodríguez-Sarmiento has argued for a "colonialidad del placer" (coloniality of pleasure) in his reading of queer artistic practices and resistance, reading disability here will mean paying attention to divergences from more familiar narratives of oppression: that is cripping coloniality.[1] In the case of *Japón*, as I suggest further, the structure of disability representation and embodiment certainly carries the echo of a neocolonial narrative, as when the camera's "limping" motion highlights the roughness of the landscape while underscoring an unjust allocation of key resources, such as inhabitable land and water. At other points in the film, race, gender, and poverty become features of disability, and clearly determine the relative values of bodies and access to resources. Yet *Japón* also disrupts the viewer's expectations in this regard, by splintering the visual continuity it at first appears to offer, and hence releasing bodies into unpredicted patterns of affective continuity and symbolic circulation.[2]

In *Japón*, the film's protagonist, an unnamed middle-aged artist from Mexico City, travels to a tiny and isolated rural community at the bottom of a steep cliff. We may note from early in the film that he walks with a limp. And we learn that he intends to kill himself. The man takes lodging in the home of an elderly woman named Ascen—a shortened form of Ascensión. In one scene, he attempts to shoot himself, but instead the scene culminates with a bird's-eye view of his living, breathing body, lying next to the corpse of a castrated horse. In another scene, he asks the elderly woman, Ascen, to have sex with him and she agrees. In the final sequence of the film, the woman's nephew comes to claim the foundation stones of the barn supporting her house, and the townspeople arrive to assist him in moving them. This will mean the destruction of the woman's house. The stones are loaded onto wagons and pulled down the hill by a tractor, with Ascen sitting on top. We later learn of an accident, in which the woman and many of the townspeople perish. At the end of the film, the camera travels slowly over the landscape of fields, scattered stones, and railroad tracks, to finally arrive at the body of Ascen. She wears a jacket she had borrowed from the male protagonist, and her face is covered in a lace-like pattern of blood (figure 5.1).

It may be reasonable to suggest that the film is not really about disability, or that disability is not its central focus. Indeed, critical work on the film thus far has not explicitly emphasized disability. Then again, *Japón* in some sense demands that we question the intention and nature of such classifications. After all, the film is certainly not about the country Japan, nor about anything Japanese. In an article on contemporary Mexican film, Geoffrey Kantaris has noted that the seemingly misplaced title may be intended to underscore this film's "translocality," as the urban character seeks out a remote rural space in which to index or displace what he has lost (524–525). Yet it is not in fact clear from the film whether anything has been lost, or to what degree this is simply a matter of individual perception. In the same sense, within the plot of the film the nature of this hypothetical loss remains purposefully ambiguous, perhaps referring to sexual impotence, to a physical condition that creates a limping gait, to an artistic or existential crisis, or more generally to the alienation intrinsic to contemporary urban life. Kantaris's notion of translocality is useful here in the sense that it allows for a reading of disability that does not insist on the fixed identification of

Figure 5.1. Following the accident, the body of Ascención lies among stones on the railway tracks. The lace-like pattern of blood on her face suggests a textural similarity to the lace shroud of the woman who had arrived, in a previous scene, to announce her death. Japón © 2003 Distrimax S.A. All rights reserved.

a specific body, but instead operates through movements of and between bodies, while layering each body with an index of potential and figurative locations.

Thus, we might argue for the film's disability focus by fixing our attention on the way the camera, in more than one scene, seems to follow the protagonist's limping gait, at times limping along with him, at times pulling back. We might also pay attention to a scene in which the elderly woman assists another character in untying his shoes, as the camera focuses on his limply curled hands. The woman, and the viewer, then focus in on the woman's own aged, arthritic but still strong, working hands, as she holds them up toward the sunlight and rotates them so as to gaze on both the backs of the hands and the palms (figure 5.2). Later on, she listens to the male protagonist's insinuated intention to kill himself, or as he puts it, to "throw away what doesn't work" and she responds: "I don't like my old, sick arms, but even so I wouldn't cut them off."

These seem to be the most explicit disability moments in the film, in the sense that the camera focuses on specific bodies represented as disabled—a man with an unconventional walk, or hands that cannot fulfill the expected function of tying shoes, and hands that work despite age and sickness. In addition, the narrative allows for reflection here on the individual's valuing of body parts and function, while tying the reflection directly into the overarching theme of the film, namely the choice to com-

Figure 5.2. Ascensión gazes upon her hands in bright sunlight, fingers pointing upwards. The scene emphasizes the aged and arthritic quality of the hands, and their status as tools that create affective, intercorporeal ties to other characters. Japón © 2003 Distrimax S.A. All rights reserved.

mit suicide. The suicide choice in this case becomes momentarily equated with the hypothetical choice of cutting off a body part that doesn't work as well as it used to. The narrative sequence also places disability on a relative scale here, so that the supposedly more extreme disability of the hands that cannot tie shoes are contrasted with hands that are arthritic but working. This value scale becomes central to the anti-suicide message, since radical disability implicitly increases the value of the other, less-disabled human bodies and lives with which it is compared. The representation of radical disability, therefore, leads to the implied message that, considering the purportedly unfortunate fate of someone with such a disability, others should be happy they are relatively able-bodied, and therefore should not take their own lives.

This narrative sequence and its clearly implied message are undoubtedly troubling from a disability studies perspective that emphasizes the value and rights of individual human beings. Yet from here the camera quickly travels, following Ascen's gaze, to an extension of the same scene, one that allows for a more complex proliferation of meanings surrounding the disability represented thus far. After assisting Fernando, the secondary character, in tying his shoes, Ascensión continues with her washing. Suddenly, she hears the distinct sound of someone biting into an apple. She and the camera turn and look toward the nearby river bank, where Fernando is seated, now shirtless, eating an apple that he has pierced with a pointed stick so that he can grasp the stick with his toes and bring the fruit toward his mouth. Fernando relaxes in a seemingly carefree manner, surrounded by trees, water, and the quiet buzz of nature. The scene is edenic, yet slightly disturbing, for the depiction of leisurely eating seems calculated in opposition to Ascen's hard work of washing clothes by hand: she stands while he reclines, she is clothed while he appears half-naked, she uses her hands to work while he consumes. And he has access to his feet as tools only because she untied his shoes for him.

The crudely traced economics of this scene situate the disabled person in relation to production, consumption, and value, as one who does not work. Yet disability itself does its own work here by disrupting the presupposed landscape of labor and leisure, and by linking bodies through an unexpected intercorporeal exchange. We may note initially that the opposition between bodies reiterates a commonplace of history; the indigenous woman works, her body tires, she ages, and these processes imbue her with a combination of dignity and suffering. The man, in the meantime, eats and rests, apparently at her expense. Disability, in this context, appears naturalized in the landscape, an element of passive enjoyment, but at the same time troubles the scene by reminding the viewer of the relative values of bodies according to their use and productivity. The violence of the filmic sequence stems from the colonialist economy it cites, in recycling a familiar history of bodies defined by a superficial rendering of their abilities and appearances.

In touching Fernando's disabled body, and lending him her hands to untie his shoes, Ascen reiterates and participates in this economy, defining the value of her work and her body in relation to a body that implicitly does not work. But at the same time, when the scene extends itself to the moment of apple eating—as a secret pleasure, because Fernando remains outside the frame until we hear the crunching sound and Ascen turns her head to discover him—the intercorporeal exchange between the two characters in turn extends itself. Because Ascen has served Fernando in a prosthetic capacity, lending him her hands, she now shares this prosthetic function with the stick that Fernando uses to eat the apple. The affective experience of eating an apple thus passes between the two bodies, and links them at the same time that it objectifies the hands of the elderly woman. Instead of a substitution of hands based on their relative use value, the scene now reveals an extended body, both singular and dual, continuous and ruptured, in which manual labor transforms itself into pleasure, and human flesh becomes a wooden stick, from one moment to the next. Evidently, disability makes possible this unexpected extension of labor, and of the functions, values and pleasures of the bodies in question.

This scene offers an explicit instance of disability representation, while at once illustrating the notion of the interval, as discussed by Cynthia Tomkins in her Deleuzian reading of Reygadas and other Latin American auteurs. The interval, in this sequence, or, "gap between action and reaction" (30) requires the viewer of the film, following Ascen's gaze, to create a subjective perception (31) or more generally, to infer a particular visual and logical continuity in the scene. Because of the interval, or gap, highlighted here through the technique of an abrupt sequencing of shots, which Tomkins calls a "paratactical structuring device" (164), there is a delayed reaction, both for Ascen and the viewer. The delay, for Tomkins, is what allows the interval to create something new. In the scene in question, newness emerges from an unexpected perception and experience of intercorporeal disability, linking and transforming bodies while restructuring their relationships to an implied, and historically pre-inscribed economy of labor and consumption. This particular interval would seem to coincide most closely with the interval's facet referred to as "affection-image." As Tomkins writes, "The affection-image arises in the subject as center of indetermination, between a perception that is somewhat troubling and a hesitant action. The affection-image may be a coincidence of subject and object or a self-reflexive perception. In sum, it associates movement with 'quality' as lived state" (31).[3] Disability here is this hesitation, this uncertain experience, an association and disassociation between body, action, and selfhood. In addition, the filmic creation of a new and unexpected body, made possible by the delayed reaction of the interval, ultimately breaks with the script of the presupposed neocolonial economy and the relative values it ascribes to particular bodies.

The Deleuzian reading of this scene, in relation to the neocolonial economy the film implicitly engages, finds echo in recent Deleuzian-informed disability studies scholarship. In a 2006 article, for example, Margrit Shildrick and Janet Price interweave contemporary globalization, disability, queer corporeality, and readings of the work of Deleuze and Guattari, in order to go beyond materialist approaches to global inequalities, and to "mobilise a productive positivity that overcomes normative binaries, breaks with stable identity, and celebrates the erotics of connection" (par. 3). Thus, rather than focusing on the social and economic inequalities intrinsic to globalization, the authors insist on a "global coming together of bodies" (par. 4), which in turn demands an ethical relationship, a "corporeal generosity" (par. 15).[4] As they write: "Where on the one hand non-disabled and disabled people are always co-implicated in a dis-organised flow between both themselves and other others, the non-normativity active in that intercorporeality can elicit also a break, unforeseen lines of flight, a moment of difference, within the interrelation between bodies" (par. 16).

Here Shildrick and Price refer to modes of contemporary global capitalism as experienced primarily through market relations that bring privileged Western consumers into contact with an unpredictable array of economically underprivileged Others, many from the Global South. While they do not focus specifically on the technology of film, nor on neocolonial structures as those inscribed on the bodies depicted in *Japón*, their emphasis on a Deleuzian flow, on intercorporeality, and on the "interval" of differences, that may produce "unforeseen lines of flight," does suggest an affinity with Reygadas's cinematographic enactment of disability in the scene discussed above.

Reygadas's cinematic articulations of disability, as analyzed here, undoubtedly may be said to operate through a mode similar to the intercorporeal disability envisioned by Shildrick and Price, and alluded to—though in rather different terms—in Tomkins's Deleuzian study of Latin American cinema. The sequence of the camera's "limping" movement, discussed earlier, that is revealed to coincide with the male protagonist's limp, also underscores this point. The camera creates a momentary identification between viewer and disabled man, but at once insists—through use of a delayed reaction, and a pulling back from the protagonist's perspective—on our separation from both the protagonist and the landscape he traverses.

The functions of disability and intercorporeality in the film, however, are also inflected by this work's participation in a specifically Mexican cultural landscape, and a narrative tradition in which local and global economies of life and death play significant roles. Rowlandson's article, cited at the beginning of this chapter, explicitly locates the film with respect to Juan Rulfo's *Pedro Páramo*, highlighting, among other points, the troubled line between life and death. As Rowlandson notes, in the conclusion of the novel Pedro Páramo's body is compared to a heap of stones. At the moment of death, "He struck a feeble blow against the ground and then crumbled to pieces as if he were a heap of stones" (Rulfo 123). Similarly, Ascen's body in the concluding sequence of *Japón* becomes, again according to Rowlandson "scarcely distinguishable from the 'montón de piedras'" (heap of stones) (1034). The comparison becomes especially apt when we consider that the stones from the foundation of the barn supporting Ascen's house were literally essential to her survival there. Thus in their violent removal, they ultimately rematerialize as equivalent to her dead body (figure 5.3).

Analysis of the role of fluid, troubled, ambiguous, or otherwise charged divisions between the categories of life and death in *Japón* at once allows for reconsideration of the roles of disability in the film. This is not simply

Figure 5.3. Stones from the foundation of the barn that once supported Ascensión's house lie strewn along the railway tracks. The house in pieces in a landscape of human remains makes literal Juan Rulfo's metaphor of the body as a heap of stones. Japón © 2003 Distrimax S.A. All rights reserved.

to suggest a logic linking disability to death. Instead, witnessing instances of blurred interchangeability between life and death requires the viewer to reassess the values and expectations conventionally ascribed to particular bodies and objects. In *Japón*, the economy of life and death arguably also works in dialogue and tension with a Christian, and specifically Mexican and Catholic narrative of sacrifice and redemption, which in turn inflects the roles of disability in these texts. Here, too, situating disability in the context of these overarching themes means going beyond a focus on particular instances of disability representation in the film, in order to recognize that disability cannot necessarily be located and reduced to the contours of an individual body, or even to a singular filmic sequence. Instead, disability becomes central to an overarching narrative and cinematic operation, in which the relative values of human—and at times, nonhuman—bodies and lives are negotiated and contested.

Despite the fervent catholicism of Ascen, the female protagonist, and the symbolic function of her name as prefiguration of her sacrificial death, religious allegory does not necessarily offer a definitive structure to the role of death in *Japón*, and in fact has been read in one case as subordinate to a competing paradigm. In a recent article on this film, Craig Epplin suggests that the work participates in a contemporary global and Mexican economy of life and death, characterized primarily by the indifferent generation of death as waste. In reference to Reygadas's films released between 2002 and 2010, Epplin writes, "*Japón* foreshadows a trope that runs throughout Reygadas's oeuvre: the representation of death as something that cannot be recuperated for collective purposes, death as a nonsacrificial event" (294).[5] This reading of death in Reygadas's work, but also in the broader sphere of Mexican culture in relation to contemporary global capitalism, borrows from the work of Octavio Paz and more specifically Claudio Lomnitz, who reads this modern structure of death in relation to the lack of a future vision or project for the Mexican nation.[6] For Epplin, the role of death in modern Mexico is exemplified in the murder of hundreds of women and girls in Ciudad Juárez.[7] At the same time, Reygadas's cinematic aesthetics in *Japón* suggest an expanded recognition of life forms and even inanimate objects, such as rocks in the landscape. As Epplin describes, if New Latin American Cinema incorporated greater recognition of marginalized human subjects—such as the urban poor—into film, Reygadas takes "recognition" a step further by lingering over animals and stones with the same, or greater focused precision than what he projects on human subjects (297).

Such a reading of the film, in which death is part of an indifferent and necessary production of waste, and humans and nonhumans become equivalent elements, subjects, or objects scattered over an affective terrain, suggests strong similarities with Mel Chen's notion of "animacies," as discussed in Chen's recent book with the same title. Chen questions the divisions and hierarchies that have conventionally defined "life" and "death," and construes affect as integral to material objects, whether living or dead. As the author discusses, the flow of affective animacies is not ultimately indifferent; instead, human and nonhuman matter is racialized, sexualized, queered, and contoured according to able-bodiedness and disability (10–11). Troubling expected or mainstream boundaries between the living and the dead, or disturbing predetermined oppositions between subjects and objects, might have everything to do with a disability studies-inflected reading of the contemporary world, as is the case in Chen's work. This is so because animacy may grant previously unrecognized agency to nonhuman animals, objects, and disabled people who had been formerly "stereotyped as passive" (3).[8]

Key differences between, on one hand, Epplin's reading of the indifferent production of waste as intrinsic to global capitalism and to cultural articulations of death in contemporary Mexico, and on the other, Chen's approach to affective continuities between subjects and objects, living and dead matter, point toward a central dilemma in reading disability in this film, as well as in broader global contexts. Specifically, we might ask to what extent the film offers at particular moments a potential, critical salvageability for both the particular bodies and the affective, intercorporeal relationships it portrays. The question is implicitly similar to the one suggested by Shildrick and Price when they imagine the possibility of an ethical approach to disability and otherness in the context of globalization. Does rethinking relationships between center and margins, humans and animals, prosthetics and flesh, life and death, allow for a trangressive and celebratory intercorporeality, or rather does it lead to a flattening of distinctions, an indifferent and violent objectification of all bodies? If the film itself offers no straightforward answers to this vexing question, it may be because the operation in question, whether designated as the violent production of indifferent waste or as the productive generation of animacy, tells only part of the story.

In my reading of the disability interval in the film, exemplified through scenes of the limping protagonist, and of the shared pleasure of the apple, discussed earlier, I insist on the tension between a neocolonial backdrop structuring the roles of gendered, racialized, and disabled bodies, and the production of a different, unpredicted body, a trangressive intercorporeality that disrupts and "crips" visual expectations. Here, too, in paying attention to the repetitive project of death in *Japón*, as a feature relevant to both a uniquely Mexican cultural and narrative tradition, and to a reading of contemporary globalization, as in Epplin's approach, I note a different, though related tension, this time between the obfuscation of the lines that conventionally separate life from death, or human from animal, and a lingering—and emotionally rich—religious economy of sacrifice and transubstantiation. In other words, the blurred continuum of life/death, human and nonhuman objects, acquires a certain emotional appeal due to its links and contrasts with the more acutely felt violence of inequality and injustice. Similarly, the interchangeability of bodies works in counterpoint to the spiritual, and specifically Catholic catharsis of exchange as sacrifice.

In *Japón*, the death of Ascensión clearly replaces that of the man who had intended to take his own life.[9] The juxtaposition of the two main characters is not likely to leave the viewer indifferent. As we have seen, the male protagonist is a privileged, urban mestizo, who descends into a world of rural indigenous poverty in order to seek his own death. His hostess and lover is an elderly indigenous woman, who tacitly accepts that her home be dismantled around her, stone by stone. The lengthy final sequence of the film, in which the camera follows the railroad tracks, strewn with stones and corpses, until it arrives at the body of Ascen, is set to the soundtrack of Arvo Pärt's popular *In Memoriam Benjamin Britten*. It is difficult to watch and listen to this scene without falling sway to its emotivity. The music features Pärt's minimalist, signature technique, known as tintinnabuli. As Benjamin Skipp explains, "Pärt's search for tintinnabuli originated from a desire to imitate the sensations brought about by hearing the tolling of church bells, and he has commented to this purpose that the relationship between the two voices 'can be likened to the eternal dualism of body and spirit, earth and heaven'" (3).[10] The point here is not only that the concluding scene to *Japón*, with use of this music, connotes a Christian spiritual tradition, but in addition that the specific musical technique works through an explicit, structural reference to religious allegory. The film's economy of death goes beyond the indifferent production of death as waste, because the bodies it depicts are inevitably tinged with what's left of this "eternal dualism," and the emotional weight it carries.

The affect rendered by the allegory of exchange as sacrifice does not ultimately represent a strict opposition to the affect of "animacy," whereby life coexists in continuity with death, and the landscape offers up rocks and human bodies interchangeably. Although as viewers we may note the tension between these models, they also appear to work in tandem with one another, so that the indifferent articulation of life and death, humans and nonhumans, paradoxically underpins a more deeply rooted emotional appeal, grounded in the duality of symbolic exchange. Thus, the metaphorical dismemberment of the elderly woman's body, exposed in death as the stones of her house, draws on the affective materiality of the stones themselves. This circuit of emotions, oscillating from human to nonhuman objects is driven by the bland interchangeability of subjects and objects, life and death, but at the same time by the trace and pull of a religious, humanistic affect. In other words, stones replace flesh—and vice versa—as a body of Christ, and as the corpse of an indigenous female Ascensión replaces that of a nameless, urban mestizo man with an unexplained limp; the exchange is both emotionally loaded and strangely flat.

Here again, despite evident contextual differences, *Japón* echoes *Pedro Páramo*. The novel, like the film, may be read as referencing the dilemma of the affective materiality of a "heap of stones," which is at once tied into an overarching allegorical structure that separates spirit from flesh and stone, or disembodied voices from layers of dust. Jorge Aguilar Mora implies this dynamic, while privileging the subsumption of symbolism into pure matter when he writes: "Pedro Páramo hides nothing, and his death is the spectacle of a myth that returns to its matter, to its common origin with earth" (226; my translation). This point of contact with Rulfo's classic text and the critical tradition surrounding it is significant in the sense that it binds the film to a particular cultural landscape; thus the viewer's experience may be mediated by the additional layer of Mexican narrative history, and the familiar dynamic of bodies and voices, living and dead, that it conjures.

The circuit of exchange in the film, inflected by a reference both to allegory and sacrifice and to a blurring of oppositions, an apparent indifference, repeats itself in numerous instances, creating a chain of associations that is at times emotionally compelling, even as it renders a landscape of seemingly interchangeable objects. In one sequence, a reverse angle reveals two horses mating, and a group of young boys who watch them, even as the boys also witness the camera documenting their emotions. The scene, which is also witnessed by the male protagonist, prefigures the human sex scene between the man and Ascen, an octogenarian woman. The awkwardness of this subsequent scene stems in part from its violation of more mainstream cinematic conventions regarding sexual expression and desirable bodies, but also from the suggested partial exchangeability of horses and humans, and the repeating reference to the exposure of the viewer in a compromised position.

An additional sequence of symbolic substitution takes place at the end of the film, when a woman wearing a black lace veil over her face comes to tell the man of the accident, and the death of Ascen. The shot of the woman's head and face, shrouded in black lace, rehearses the film's final image, in which the blood covering Ascen's face appears similarly lace-like. In chronological time, the accident and subsequent death of Ascen necessarily precedes the arrival of the lace-shrouded woman (figure 5.1). The sequence of scenes thus creates a strange temporal reflexivity, in which blood and lace simultaneously project one another backward and forward in time, saturating the film's conclusion with the symbolic weight of death, while at once reducing lace and blood to a material equivalence, a visible texture.

The structures of symbolic exchange, and interchangeability, traced through *Japón* allow us to read the economy of life and death and the material affectivity of humans and objects in the landscape as additional layers determining the possibility of a disability studies-inflected analysis of the film. In a sense, particular sequences invite us to consider relations of sameness and difference between various humans and objects, and implicitly to weigh the loss or death of one, and hence its value, in relation to another, as well as to assess the potential for new juxtapositions of these elements, hence the creation of new intercorporeal continuities. In addition, as I have suggested, both the figurative and the literal landscapes of the film are marked by a trajectory of coloniality, one that ostensibly determines the relative values of bodies, and access to needed resources. Through and against these structures, disability emerges at several key moments as the representation of particular bodies, but most importantly through the technique of the filmic interval. I return briefly here to the early scene of the handheld camera that navigates uneven ground, following the perspective of the limping protagonist, in order to consider how the interval underscores an affectively and historically loaded, yet potentially open-ended moment of exchange, and hence a productively disabled intercorporeality.

The viewer experiences the landscape of grass and rocks through an unevenly moving frame, and then, from a different angle, witnesses the limp of the protagonist as he walks.[11] We are thus reminded that we accompany him on his journey, we make the film with him, forced to see through his eyes while walking in sync with his gait. Yet by pulling back from a fully fused first-person perspective, the camera both shows us the disabled man, and shows us the body that we are, and cannot be. The calculated indifference of this focal shift works because of a deeper and historically specific economy of substitution and identification. As privileged viewers, we can be the urban artist on his journey of self-discovery—the generic cinema-goer par-excellence. Or in slightly different terms, we can be the disabled wanderer who supposedly seeks his own death, just as his personal suffering might seem to fuse with the landscape over which he travels, and its inscribed injustices. But our gaze, our gait, and our intentions cannot quite match his, even if we happen to experience some self-recognition. And similarly, he himself remains an outsider to the community and the landscape, displaced from the metropolis. The limp, as specific embodiment and marker of disability, is the force of cohesion between shots and projected identifications, for without this device we, as viewers, might not easily recognize that the character, cane in hand, is the same one whose perspective we have embodied as we travel, limping over the landscape, watching the film. At the same time, it is only through the moment of de-identification, as the camera shows us the man in a full body shot, and eventually wanders away, that disability becomes literal and apparent.

Despite the fact that disability as such does not appear initially to be a major theme in *Japón*, nor for that matter in Reygadas's other films, by focusing on disability here as the central axis in my reading of the film, my aim has been to propose an approach through which the interactions and identifications between bodies and objects acquire social, political, and historical significance, and project new possibilities. This approach centers on the filmic interval from a disability studies perspective, and argues for the centrality of disability as a facet of analysis in film viewing practices. Reading disability in this case as the structure through which bodies and objects emerge, interact with one another, and establish the possibilities and limits of identification between viewers and characters, suggests its critical applicability beyond the film in question.

The work of disability in *Japón* is ultimately to rehearse the continuities and ruptures of identification and de-identification, to produce and reproduce both alliances and differences over a landscape whose objects and bodies cannot be all the same. Disability, as a constellation of bodies and actions in the film, works at certain points through reference to religious allegory, or to allegories of historically ingrained oppression. Yet these corporeal relations are not finally frozen in time. Instead, they ask us to engage embodiment itself as an opening to new identifications, a fluidly communicative process, with an as-yet-unmapped trajectory.

## Notes

1. The verbal expression of "cripping" comes primarily from Robert McRuer's analysis. See especially his *Crip Theory* 70–72.

2. Here again, I direct the reader to Tomkin's emphasis on the interval, and on Reygadas use of "paratactical articulation" (166).

3. Tomkins refers to Deleuze's designation of "perception-images" as relating to nouns, "action-images" relating to verbs, and "affection-images" relating to adjectives.

4. The authors invoke the work of Roslyn Diprose, specifically her book titled *Corporeal Generosity*, the focus of which is more phenomenological than Deleuzian.

5. Epplin argues that Reygadas's other feature films, *Batalla en el cielo* (2005) and *Stellet Licht* (2007) similarly feature nonsacrificial representations of death, as does his short film, *Este es mi reino* (2010). Epplin does not discuss Reygadas's 2012 feature *Post tenebras lux* as it had not yet been released.

6. Here Epplin mentions Lomnitz's discussion of the 1982 debt crisis, and subsequent failures of the government. As Epplin notes: "In such an atmosphere, the sacrificial sublimation of the dead into the world of the living loses relevance" (292).

7. See Victoria Dickman-Burnett's essay in this volume for analysis of the Juárez femicides in relation to disability and global capitalism.

8. Chen's reading of animacy indicates an affinity with the Deleuzian notion of "becoming-animal" (146) and in this sense alligns with Shildrick and Price's similarly Deleuzian approach.

9. Her name, as she states at the beginning of the film, refers to Christ who rose up to heaven "without any help from anyone," as opposed to Asunción, a reference to the Virgin Mary, whom the angels carried up to heaven.

10. The citation within Skipp's description comes from Paul Hillier's *Arvo Pärt.*

11. As Tomkins writes: "The shaking image of the ground is almost dizzying, yet it is naturalized when we notice that the man, who is nearly lame, walks only with great difficulty, aided by a cane" (161).

## Works Cited


Aguilar Mora, Jorge. "Novela sin joroba." *Revista de Crítica Literaria Latinoamericana.* 33.66 (2007): 225–248. *JSTOR.* Web. December 7, 2012.

Chen, Mel. *Animacies: Biopolitics, Racial Mattering, and Queer Affect.* Durham: Duke UP, 2012.

Epplin, Craig. "Sacrifice and Recognition in *Reygadas's Japón.*" *Mexican Studies/Estudios Mexicanos* 28.2 (2012): 287–305. *JSTOR.* Web. December 13, 2012.

Erevelles, Nirmala. *Disability and Difference in Global Contexts: Enabling a Transformative Body Politic.* New York: Palgrave, 2011.

Grech, Shaun. "Disability and the Majority World: A Neocolonial Approach." In *Disability and Social Theory: New Developments and Directions.* Edited by Dan Goodley, Bill Hughes and Lennard Davis. New York: Palgrave, 2012, 52–69.

Hillier, Paul. *Arvo Pärt.* Oxford: Oxford UP, 1997.

*Japón.* Directed by Carlos Reygadas, Mexico, 2002.

Kantaris, Geoffrey. "Cinema and *Urbanías*: Translocal Identities in Contemporary Mexican Film." *Bulletin of Latin American Research.* 22.4 (2006): 517–527. Web. December 15, 2012.

McRuer, Robert. *Crip Theory: Cultural Signs of Queerness and Disability.* New York: New York UP, 2006.

Mitchell, David, and Sharon Snyder. *Narrative Prosthesis: Disability and the Dependencies of Discourse.* Ann Arbor: U of Michigan P, 2003.

———. "The Eugenic Atlantic: Race, Disability and the Making of an International Eugenic Science, 1860–1945." *Disability & Society* 18.7 (2003): 843–864. *Taylor & Francis Online.* Web. October 20, 2011.

Quijano, Aníbal. "Coloniality of Power, Eurocentrism and Latin America." *Nepantla: Views from the South* 1.3. (2000): 533–580. *Project Muse.* Web. December 15, 2011.

Rodríguez-Sarmiento, Víctor Manuel. "La colonialidad del placer: Experiencias artísticas desde América Latina para un mundo *queer.*" South by Midwest International Conference on Latin American Cultural Studies. St. Louis, Missouri, March 28, 2013. Conference Presentation.

Rowlandson, William. "The Journey Into the Text: Reading Rulfo in Carlos Reygadas' 2002 Feature Film, *Japón.*" *The Modern Language Review* 101.4 (2006): 1025–1034. *JSTOR.* Web. March 15, 2012.

Rulfo, Juan. *Pedro Páramo.* Translated by Lysander Kemp. New York: Grove, 1969.

Shildrick, Margaret, and Janet Price. "Deleuzian Connections and Queer Corporealities: Shrinking Global Disability." *Rhizomes* 11/12 (Fall 2005/ Spring 2006). Web. May 15, 2013.

Skipp, Benjamin. "Out of Place in the Twentieth Century: Thoughts on Arvo Pärt's Tintinnabuli Style." *Tempo* 63.249 (2009): 2–11. *Scholars Portal.* Web. May 15, 2013.

Tomkins, Cynthia. *Experimental Latin American Cinema: History and Aesthetics.* Austin: U of Texas P, 2013.

Chapter 6

# Bodily Integrity, Abjection, and the Politics of Gender and Place in Roberto Bolaño's *2666*

Victoria Dickman-Burnett

The story surrounding Vincent Van Gogh's removal of his own ear has contributed to a certain mythos of the "troubled artist": a romantically passionate fellow who totters on the brink of madness as he feels the pain necessary to motivate him to produce the best possible artwork. Any less pain, and the artist fades into mediocrity. In Roberto Bolaño's novel, *2666*, English artist Edwin Johns takes the violation of his bodily integrity a step further than Van Gogh when he severs his painting hand and displays it with his final painting in an artistic exhibition. In doing this, Johns has made the severing of his hand an act of performance art and established a link between his arm and the embodied experience of painting. Johns's hand, like Van Gogh's ear, raises the question of what is to be made of the willful self-mutilation of bodily integrity and violence toward the body. What does it mean to alter one's own bodily integrity and what are we to make of Johns's act against his own body? Why, in a novel full of hidden meaning is Johns's self-amputation dismissed as either madness or publicity stunt because he needed the money?

Within the discussion surrounding Johns's hand lies the answers to the violation of bodily integrity elsewhere in the novel, particularly that of the women of Santa Teresa, a fictional version of the real life Ciudad Juárez. Johns's act of self-harm illuminates not only how we understand bodily integrity within the novel, but also how such mutilation functions in relation to place and power, reflecting the disproportionate privilege of Europe and the Global North in relation to Santa Teresa as the gateway to the Global South. Using critical disability studies to read both the treatment of Johns's body and the treatment of the murdered female bodies in the novel enlightens the tenuous, troubled relationship between Europe and Latin America that Bolaño often explores in his work. Onto the bodies we can map privilege and disprivilege, wealth and poverty, agency and invisibility; however, issues of disability and embodiment in *2666* cannot be reduced to simple metaphors. Instead, the novel highlights the politics of embodiment as indicator of related structures that shape both Bolaño's literary world and the world in which we live.

This essay begins with an exploration of Johns's mutilation from a disability studies framework, examining the possible explanations offered in the novel for Johns's actions. Using transability, a controversial issue in the field of disability studies, to examine the conversation between Johns and Piero Morini, a scholar and wheelchair user, better illuminates why Morini, and consequently the other characters ultimately dismiss Johns's actions as incomprehensible or financially motivated. From here I shift focus to the women of Santa Teresa, using Jasbir K. Puar's idea of debility to argue that the culture that made their violent deaths inevitable denies them bodily integrity and renders them disposable, noting that the contrast between body-as-art and body-as-waste demonstrates a fault line between Global North and South in *2666*.

Performance and art, abjection and uncanniness converge upon each other in the self-amputation, but the characters that are familiar with Johns's story are unable to make meaning of his actions, and so he is relegated to the realm of madness, the act treated first as incomprehensible and then as purely capitalistic. We must move beyond both the conventional understanding of Johns's act (as madness) and the co-opted understanding of the act (as purely motivated by money), to an understanding that takes into account the embodiment of abjection, the transformation into the uncanny, and the control one exerts over one's body in a context that is informed by the existing systems of power in a transnational world. Because, as Lisa Jean Moore and Monica J. Casper write, "Bodies are socially constructed within social orders, including patterns of dominance and submission along lines of race, ethnicity, gender, age, and physiological normativity" (1–2), we can see the intersections of gender, race, and global capitalism crystalized in the treatment of bodies in *2666*.

Johns's act is a voluntary amputation of bodily integrity and it raises larger questions of what we make of acts of violence against one's own body. The novel offers several responses to Johns's actions. The implied response is to treat the act as an indicator of mental disability. Given that we later find Johns in a psychiatric hospital and it is stated that he went mad after severing his hand, it's fair to say that there is a good chance that madness was also a factor in his amputation, but that did not end Piero Morini's exploration of Johns's motive, so it will not end ours. In *Visions of Excess*, Georges Bataille explores the severed ear of Van Gogh and sacrificial mutilation. He briefly examines the idea of madness in relation to sacrificial mutilation, stating "But how is it possible that gestures incontestably linked to mental disorder (even if they can never be seen as the symptoms of a specific mental illness) may be spontaneously designated as the adequate expression of a veritable social function, of an institution as clearly defined, as generally human as sacrifice?" (67). While Johns's act may have been an act of madness, like Bataille's discussion of Van Gogh it can be understood as a sacrifice, in this case, a sacrifice for Johns's art, and therefore given meaning beyond madness.

Couched in paradox, Johns's actions cause both revulsion and curiosity. The commercial success of his exhibit signifies the public's fascination, perhaps a Nietzschean fascination with horror—the Dionysian aesthetic that draws people to that which should repel them. Johns's artwork is associated with excess and decadence from his first introduction—he is associated with the new decadence movement and English animalism, and the act of cutting off the arm is perceived as an act of extreme decadence, which led other artists to decadence as well (52–53).[1] We see that what repulses the audience also draws them in. Johns's artwork spawns an entire movement, his exhibition is a commercial success, and the previously low-income neighborhood in which he established his studio quickly becomes gentrified as a result of his fame. The fascination with Johns outweighs the repulsion and fear, and so his actions become co-opted by the art community. His hand becomes a commodity, a piece of art that has monetary value.

As in the case of Van Gogh, Johns's self-amputation is treated as artistic eccentricity, though he ultimately uses it to turn a profit. Putting to the test the old maxim that an artist's work is more valuable when he is dead, Johns's amputation of his painting hand is symbolic suicide, as he has effectively removed himself from the artistic world. Without dying, he has managed to create the same level of fame—by more or less guaranteeing that he will never paint again he has raised the value of his existing paintings, yet he gets to enjoy this success in a way that no artist has before.[2] At the same time, by featuring his mummified hand prominently in an exhibit with his last painting, he elevates the act of cutting off his hand into the realm of performance art. By cutting off the hand for the purpose of the exhibit, he has linked the hand that paints, his artwork, and his act of self-amputation.

In his exploration of the performance art of Bob Flanagan, Robert McRuer examines how Flanagan's sadomasochistic performance art that incorporates signs of his cystic fibrosis such as hospital masks is counter-hegemonic and transgressive in a way that suggests awareness of the possibility of cooptation of his work by mainstream culture (193). For Johns, the transgressive performance of self-amputation has been co-opted by a mainstream culture that has found enjoyment in the shock of the artist's exhibit while the commercial success of his artwork suggests that the shock of the audience was also performed. The sterilized response to his act shows how it has been co-opted, though Johns's willingness to make self-amputation into performance art suggests that he is also aware of this potential and that he is not completely averse to this outcome. Because it is clear that Johns severs his hand with the intention of displaying it in an exhibit (he contacts a taxidermist to mummify it in advance and makes up a story for the hospital after the severing), his art takes on a performative dimension—he intends for the world to see what he has done to his body. Like Flanagan's performance art, Johns's work also pushes the boundaries of art, attempting to make his audience uncomfortable with the limits of pain and the human body. Johns and Flanagan both perform disability as part of their artwork in their own way—Johns even goes to the extreme of acquiring a physical disability in the process of creating his masterpiece.

Rosemarie Garland-Thomson writes, "Disability, then, is the attribution of corporeal deviance—not so much the property of bodies as a product of cultural rules about what bodies should be or do" (6). Johns's artwork is the performance of such corporeal deviance. Before he severs his arm, his body (presumably) conforms in appearance to the cultural rules that mark out the nondisabled person, whom Garland-Thomson calls the normate. The implied presence of mental disability complicates Johns's ostensibly self-transformative act, yet in the act of cutting off his hand for his masterpiece, Johns has transformed his physical body from conforming to deviant.

Johns's hand has special significance precisely because it is the hand of a painter, a hand used to create masterpieces. The hand is able to become a work of art because it represents the ability to create artwork—Johns's talent and artistic genius[3] is embodied in his hand. To put it simply, the hand is elevated to the level of artwork because of its connection to artwork. Were anyone who is not an artist to put his or her severed hand on display, it would not be received the same way—the fact that it is an artist's hand, severed with the purpose of creating art makes it meaningful. Were we to replace the hand of the artist with a hand severed in an industrial accident at a *maquiladora*, for instance, the significance of the severed hand as artwork would be lost, speaking to both Johns's privilege as an artist in the global North, and also to the painterly hand as the embodiment of its ability.

Piero Morini is perhaps the only character in the novel with an openly discussed physical disability, as a wheelchair user who also experiences temporary blindness at various times in the first section of the novel. He is also the only character who interacts with Edwin Johns, and he soon chalks the self-amputation up to purely financial motives (Bolaño 97). Ultimately, the Morini/Johns encounter strikes a parallel with the conversation surrounding the idea of transability. On the subject of transability, Bethany Stevens writes, "Transabled people are individuals who *need* to acquire a physical impairment despite having been born or living in physically unimpaired bodies" ("Interrogating Transability"). She links transability to art through body modification, contending that disability can be body art and that "Including transability within the spectrum of body modification provides a useful point of departure to begin to consider disability as body art" ("Interrogating Transability"). However, many people with disabilities are resistant to the idea of transability, Stevens notes, adding that she herself is hesitant and conflicted about the subject. The idea of disability as art is especially useful when discussing Johns. Perhaps, the fascination and failure to understand Johns that Morini experiences arises from similar skepticism to the idea of voluntarily acquiring a new disability. When the two meet, the first thing each notices about the other are the indicators of disability: Morini's wheelchair, the absence of Johns's right hand (Bolaño 89). In the exchange the two talk past each other, Johns asking twice, "Do you think you're like me?" and Morini responding that he is not, suggesting that neither is sure what to make of the other or how they should relate to each other, mirroring disjunction between the disability rights community and people who identify as transabled (Bolaño 91).

Johns's act engages both abjection and the uncanny. For Julia Kristeva, the point of intersection between these two is the corpse, which is of the body, resembling the self, yet not the self. Kristeva says of corpses, "There I am at the border of my condition as a living being. My body extricates itself, as being alive, from that border. It is no longer I who expel, it is 'I' that is expelled" (3). The body without life is uncanny: it resembles the living body but the element that makes it human—recognizable, familiar—is gone. On this subject of death and the uncanny, Sigmund Freud writes, "To many people the acme of the uncanny is represented by anything to do with death, dead bodies, revenants, spirits and ghosts" (148). In severing his hand, Johns has created a hand-corpse, dividing his body (familiar) from the newly amputated limb. The process of creating the hand-corpse is a symbolic death. In *Animacies*, Mel Y. Chen notes the role hands play as indicators of humanness, emphasizing a strong connection between the hand and creativity. Johns's "creative death" is thus twofold: in creating a hand-corpse he has ended his creative capacity in the eyes of the world and he has severed a symbol of his humanity (119).

Just as Kristeva treats the corpse as waste, the discovery that the non-living body is nothing more than matter, that there is little separating a living being from abject waste is intrinsically linked to Johns's artwork. Death transforms people into bodies—corpses—abject, lifeless matter. This encapsulates the horror surrounding Johns's hand: by cutting off his hand he has not only harmed his body, he has also made his hand, a part of himself, into an object, which he treats as a work of art rather than garbage. However, other bodies throughout the novel are treated as garbage when they are quite literally thrown away by their murderers.

Gloria Anzaldúa characterizes the border between Mexico and the United States as an open wound (25), embodying the social problems that arise at the intersection between Global North and South as a sore, a site of pain. In *2666* the Santa Teresa murders, a loosely veiled fictionalization of the real life murders in Ciudad Juárez, again shows the body as an object, cast aside and removed from all life, with little evidence of previous humanity. As Laura Barberán Reinares notes in her article no heroine ever emerges in the novel, because we never meet the women who die, we only find their bodies after the fact (62). The women of Santa Teresa are not just disposable; they have already been thrown away. Reinares's analysis of *2666* converges on Kristeva's study of the corpse as the "most sickening of waste," paying special attention to the fact that only corpses remain. Johns's corpse hand is the first signifier—in symbolically murdering himself, Johns has been left with a partial corpse, which he proudly displays for the world as a work of art. In contrast women's bodies are discovered only after they have been discarded as waste.

If we compare the violent alteration of Johns's bodily integrity to the violation of the bodies of the women found in Santa Teresa, agency is the key difference between the two. Motive aside, Johns's self-amputation was an autonomous act. Johns has chosen to cut off his own hand, and regardless of the harm done to his body, he has had control of his course of action. While he may have made himself abject in the process, he is the one responsible for his actions. The women of Santa Teresa, on the other hand, are disposable to their society. There will always be more than enough people to work in the *maquiladoras* and the tasks that they perform there are not so difficult that any one of them is indispensible. The intersection of globalization and general capitalistic excess has created a world where an entire class of people, mostly female, does not matter, and faces the marginalizing forces of global capitalism as it colonizes Santa Teresa. Johns wields control over his body that the women of Santa Teresa will never experience.

The female bodies that continue to be found in Santa Teresa highlight the disposability of the female body within the novel. In addition to the sheer number of women who vanish, only to be found as corpses, the narration of the novel further supports the claim that the female body is disposable in Santa Teresa. "The Part about the Crimes" is devoted to the account of the femicides. There is little central plot beyond chronicling the bodies and the half-hearted attempts of the police to solve the murders of women. The narration of the crimes is interrupted by an episode in which the police officers tell sexist jokes about women that often advocate rape or domestic violence (Bolaño 552–553). The episode does not advance the plot in any way, but it highlights the prevailing attitudes toward women by the police.

Zygmunt Bauman's discussion of the increase of superfluous human beings as the by-product of modernity offers explanation for the growth in numbers of refugees and other displaced persons. While many of the young women from Santa Teresa had individual families who were looking for them, most of the murders go unsolved, because the police are unwilling to devote department resources to finding their killers. Cynthia L. Bejarano discusses the role of *maquiladoras* and globalization in the murders in Ciudad Juárez, suggesting that global capitalism plays a role in the murder of the women in Juárez.[4] She contends,

> I see these communities as an extension of myself and wanted to expose the underbelly of "the new era of globalization and progress" veiled in the *maquiladora* industry, which is acted out—unintentionally or not—through the exploitation and killing of young brown women, while highlighting the "organic" leadership powers emanating from subaltern/colonial shantytown communities through the mothers of these disappeared young women. The racialized, sexualized, and gendered practices along the borderlands within and around the global economy and the production of the *maquiladoras* prompted me to investigate these social and cultural diseases. (405)

Bejarano identifies globalization as responsible for the localization of violence, noting that the *maquiladoras* give rise to shantytowns, impermanent living conditions and displaced persons, a dynamic not overlooked in *2666* (404–405). Just as Bauman contends that refugees are lives gone to waste, that is to say their displacement results in their inability to be productive members of an increasingly globalized world, residents of a shantytown are refugees of globalization itself. Global capitalism and the overabundance of unskilled laborers for the *maquiladoras* have destabilized life in Juárez/Santa Teresa, and made it possible for people to be refugees in their own land.

The skewed focus of the police leading to the murders of the women of Santa Teresa going unsolved has further manifestations that can be seen in "The Part about the Crimes." For example, when the detectives of the Santa Teresa police force pursue an unknown man given the pseudonym "the Penitent" for defiling churches with excrement, the utter lack of power of the women of Santa Teresa becomes evident. The targets of the Penitent's crimes are church relics, not people. Yet these crimes are taken more seriously than the crimes against the women. This is because the church holds more power in society than the women who work in the factories of Santa Teresa. Additionally, the Penitent's actions defile the holy relics of the church, creating more fear in Santa Teresa because of the role those relics play as part of the Catholic religion, which provides order and security in Santa Teresa. Excrement plays a role in abjection because it is expelled from the body; it is quite literally what the body rejects because it has no use for it. The Penitent incidents exemplify the idea that when the abjection of excrement intersects with the idea of the sacred or holy, the result is defilement.

Kristeva positions defilement as the "Two-Sided Sacred," noting that an object or ritual cannot be sacred without the possibility of being defiled, with the possibility of defilement arising from a number of sources, specifically excrement and menstruation (57–58). She writes, "excrement and its equivalents . . . stand for the danger to identity that comes from without: the ego threatened by the non-ego, society threatened by its outside, life by death" (71). Likewise, the Penitent is positioned outside of society, believed to be harmless, yet hostile to religion (here representing order), and given to impulses (Bolaño 382). In contrast to the defilement arising from excrement is the defilement arising from menstruation, which she asserts, "stands for the danger issuing from within the identity (social or sexual); it threatens the relationship between the sexes within a social aggregate and, through internalization, the identity of each sex in the face of sexual difference" (71). Both the Penitent and the women of Santa Teresa represent a type of defilement through abjection, and while conventional wisdom would suggest that the murders of multiple women pose more of a threat than someone who defiles holy relics, the police treat the Penitent as if his crimes have much more gravity because he promotes abjection, while the murders dispose of bodies, which have been deemed abject because of their femaleness.

The abjection of the women in *2666* makes them a source of fear in Santa Teresa. Elvira Campos, the psychologist consulting the police in the Penitent case offers the following opinion, "Or gynophobia, which is fear of women, and naturally, afflicts only men. Very widespread in Mexico, although it manifests itself in different ways. Isn't that a slight exaggeration [Juan de Dios Martinez interjects]? Not a bit: almost all Mexican men are afraid of women" (382). Kristeva contends that women's abjection leads to fear of women because of her "generative power" as a mother. The fear of women in Santa Teresa has led to widespread violence against them. The fear of women that Campos discusses is responsible not only for the murders, but for the fact that no one seems to care that women are being murdered. "The Part about the Crimes" chronicles several hundred deaths, and while the police do investigate the crimes, there is no acknowledgment of the underlying problems that are responsible for the deaths of women. Elvira Campos compares Juan de Dios Martinez's denial of her claim of widespread gynophobia in Mexico to symbolic optophobia (the fear of opening one's eyes). Dios Martinez is so afraid of what his admission of male fear of women would say about him that he and the rest of the police force are unable to admit to the problem. This is not because the information is unavailable to them, but because they refuse to open their eyes.

Jasbir K. Puar introduces the idea of debility from Lauren Berlant's idea of slow death, which she defines as "the debilitating ongoingness of structural inequality and suffering" ("The Cost of Getting Better" 177). While debility or slow death has not been applied to violent environments in the past, it stands to reason that there are certain types of inevitable deaths that would also result in debility. The women of Santa Teresa illustrate such inevitable death—because they are superfluous, there is a sense of inevitability to their death and subsequent disposal, as illustrated in the second and third section of the novel when Amalfitano expresses his fears for his daughter in this dangerous environment. Whether the women die or survive does not change this debility, because all live with the constant threat of a violent death, and as superfluous persons, they are interchangeable, and any of the women who survive could have easily been one who did not survive. They thus encounter "structural inequality and suffering," at the hands of global capitalism and modernity.

Debility is also apt when discussing the women of Santa Teresa because it destabilizes the binary between disability and ability. As Puar notes elsewhere,

> The political mandate behind such rethinking about disability—or, as I argue, a move from disability to debility—would not be

> to disavow the crucial political gains enabled by disability activists globally, but to invite a deconstruction of what ability and capacity mean, affective and otherwise, and to push for a broader politics of debility that destabilizes the seamless production of abled-bodies in relation to disability. ("Prognosis Time" 166)

Because, as Garland-Thomson notes, able-bodiedness has traditionally been defined by male standards, a collapse of the binary between able-bodiedness and disability is useful in examining the women of Santa Teresa. Debility completely refigures how we look at embodiment and ability, and the women of Santa Teresa, as women, as persons in the Global South, as persons made redundant through globalization and late capitalism, have diminished capacity that partially excludes them from the realm of the able-bodied.

The narration of the fourth section of the novel, which is devoted to the crimes themselves, can be difficult to follow because the murders are detailed with clinical precision, stripped of the pathos associated with murder, offering a factual depiction of the events of the murders that seems more fitting for a police report than a work of fiction. However, the style of narration employed in "The Part about the Crimes" emphasizes the abjection and disposable nature of the women. While this section attempts to chronicle all of the murders that occur in Santa Teresa since the first body was found, it begins with a caveat that suggests the larger problem:

> This happened in 1993. January 1993. From then on, the killings of women began to be counted. But it's likely there had been other deaths before. The name of the first victim was Esperanza Gómez Saldaña and she was thirteen. Maybe for the sake of convenience, maybe because she was the first to be killed in 1993, she heads the list. Although surely there were other girls and women who died in 1992. Other girls and women who didn't make it onto the list or were never found, who were buried in unmarked graves in the desert or whose ashes were scattered in the middle of the night, when not even the person scattering them knew where he was, what place he had come to. (353–354)

In hindsight, Esperanza Gómez Saldaña was the first of the bodies to be counted not because she was the first murder, but because she was the first murder that suggested that the murders of women were a trend. Her status of being "the first victim" is contingent on the existence of other victims, and it is the awareness of a pattern, not the first murder, that her death commemorates. The narrator raises the question of the nature of the list, revealing just how easy it is to throw away the women of Santa Teresa, who wound up in unmarked graves, superfluous lives that were denied acknowledgment.

While the narration about the bodies does not eulogize the lives of the women, it reflects awareness about the women's being treated as disposable, and therefore serves to rectify the way their deaths seemed to "throw them away." While the narrator's tone does not reanimate long-dead corpses, it does offer details about the lives that would have been passed over in the anonymity of unmarked graves. Not all of the women are identified, but the narrator makes an attempt to reunite the bodies with the memory of their former lives and with an awareness of their identities. It is difficult to remember a single name given the sheer number of women who have been murdered, but the accounts of the crimes make clear that these bodies were at one time more than the "waste" they appear to be in their final state. Because the women of Santa Teresa can be thrown away, we need not see them alive, we need not get attached. As superfluous persons they have no hope of survival; the individual lives before their deaths are measured by the brief description of the bodies found mutilated in shallow graves.

Chen's discussion of animacy hierarchies is particularly apt in a discussion of the women of Santa Teresa. Because the women in the fourth section are from the Global South and are superfluous persons in the perpetuation of global capitalism, they are already lower on an animacy hierarchy than Johns, a man from the Global North who is able to make a living as an artist. The fact that the women are introduced as dead bodies gives them an even lower standing on the animacy hierarchy than if they were alive when introduced. The clear difference between the embodiment of Johns's art and the embodiment of the women of Santa Teresa is that they are inanimate from the very beginning, which is a clear statement of the agency and value of the women of Santa Teresa.

Johns is animate, he gets to speak, to act. The reader is introduced to him and sees his death. In contrast the women of Santa Teresa are not given a voice or even a live presence. Not only do they never speak, the reader never as much as sees them silently going through their lives before their murders. Never once do we see the "before" to compare it to the gristly "after." However, Bolaño subtly subverts the dichotomy of animacy he has created, and while he reports the deaths with extreme detachment and almost scientific precision, he manages to continually remind the reader of the women's humanity, giving them names and attaching humanity to the bodies that have been discarded. The narrator often includes the reactions of friends and family, allowing the reader to see that these women were loved and valued by someone, often someone who can do nothing about their deaths.

*2666* presents the reader with a conundrum: the body is art, but the body is also waste, and little separates the two. Is it the fact that Johns is an artist and his painterly hand embodies the talent with which he painted that makes his severed hand art while the bodies of the women of Santa Teresa are discarded as waste? Is the hand art because Johns called it art and people believed him? Does the fact that the hand is art mean that it is not waste? And perhaps the most pressing question of all: in writing "The Part About The Crime," has Roberto Bolaño elevated the bodies of the women of Santa Teresa to the realm of art in a fashion similar to that of Edwin Johns's elevation of his own severed hand? The parallels between Bolaño and Johns carry the risk of undermining the subtle critiques of the violence toward the women of Santa Teresa as an attempt to make art out of bodies. Johns is not Bolaño's perfect double, as the former uses his own body as material for creating his masterpiece, while Bolaño has used the bodies of women who are disenfranchised by where they are positioned geopolitically, bodies that global capitalism has rejected, bodies discarded in deserts, and, perhaps most importantly bodies that correspond to real bodies of the women murdered in Ciudad Juárez. We can speak of Johns as elevating the body to the realm of art, because it is his body, but when the bodies that make up the art are those of the disenfranchised, who have no way of consenting to be art and have become part of the work of art because of the violent nature of their life, and the invisibility of their death, has Bolaño elevated their bodies at the expense of devaluing their lives? Is Bolaño guilty of the same dehumanization responsible for the environment that led to the violent deaths of hundreds of women? There is no easy answer, but the accounts of the misogyny of the policemen and the conversations between Campos and Dios Martinez suggest a greater awareness of the problems in Santa Teresa that led to the deaths. In his work, Bolaño often grapples with the relationship between Europe and Latin America, Global North and South, privilege and invisibility, and *2666* is no exception. Positioned at the intersection of all of these elements, the women of Santa Teresa illuminate the complexity of how each relates to the others. Unfortunately the women are never given the opportunity to speak, and so we do not see an exchange between Bolaño (or his alter-ego Belano) and the women to mirror the exchange between Morini and Johns. But it is not difficult to imagine the writer asking the women "Are you like me?" only to be met with silence.

## Notes

1. Such artistic movements do not exist outside the world of *2666*. Although there are artists whose work mirrors that of Johns, because we get no real description of his artwork other than his mummified hand, to comment on his other artwork or link him to real world artistic movements would involve a great deal of conjecture.

2. While Johns could learn to paint again in another way, he has at least created the illusion of being unable to paint again.

3. If it exists. The reader is not informed of the quality of Johns's other paintings.

4. Because there is a clear link between Santa Teresa and Juárez in the critical conversation surrounding *2666*, scholarship regarding the women of Juárez is applicable to my analysis of the role of women in *2666*.

## Works Cited

Anzaldúa, Gloria. *Borderlands/La Frontera*. San Francisco: Aunt Lute Books, 2007.

Bataille, Georges. *Visions of Excess*. Translated by Allen Stoekl. Minneapolis: U of Minnesota P, 1985.

Bauman, Zygmunt. *Wasted Lives*. Cambridge: Polity Press, 2004.

Bejarano, Cynthia. "Las Super Madres de Latino America: Transforming Motherhood and Houseskirts by Challenging Violence in Juárez, México, Argentina, and El Salvador." In *Violence and the Body: Race, Gender, and the State*. Edited by Arturo Aldama. Bloomington: Indiana UP, 2003, 404–428.

Bolaño, Roberto. *2666*. Translated by Natasha Wimmer. New York: Picador, 2008.

Casper, Monica J., and Lisa Jean Moore. *Missing Bodies: The Politics of Visibility*. New York: New York UP, 2009.

Chen, Mel. Y. *Animacies: Biopolitcs, Racial Mattering, and Queer Affect*. Durham: Duke UP, 2012.

Freud, Sigmund. *The Uncanny*. Translated by David McLintock. 1919. New York: Penguin, 2003.

Garland-Thomson, Rosemarie. *Extraordinary Bodies: Figuring Physical Disability in American and Literature*. New York: Columbia UP, 1997.

Kristeva, Julia. *Powers of Horror: An Essay on Abjection*. Translated by Leon S. Roudiez. New York: Columbia UP, 1982.

McRuer, Robert. *Crip Theory: Cultural Signs of Queerness and Disability*. New York: New York UP, 2006.

Puar, Jasbir K. "Prognosis Time: Toward Geopolitics of Affect, Debility, and Capacity." *Women and Performance: A Journal of Feminist Theory* 19.2 (2009): 161–172. *JSTOR*. Web. March 15, 2013.

———. "The Cost of Getting Better." *The Disability Studies Reader*. 4th ed. New York: Routledge, 2013, 177–185.

Reinares, Laura Barberán. "Globalized Philomels: State Patriarchy, Transnational Capital, and the Femicides on the US-Mexican border in Roberto Bolaño's *2666*." *South Atlantic Review* 75.4 (2010): 51–52. *JSTOR*. Web. September 19, 2012.

Stevens, Bethany. "Interrogating Transability: A Catalyst to View Disability as Body Art." *Disability Studies Quarterly* 31.4 (2011): n.p. Web. April 15, 2013.

Chapter 7

# Violence, Injury, and Disability in Recent Latin American Film

Victoria L. Garrett

## Introduction

In the last decades Latin American film has met unprecedented international success. Despite important changes in production and distribution methods, as well as marked aesthetic differences, a significant number of films continue to advance the agenda of the New Latin American Cinema of the 1960s and 1970s defined by Ana M. López as: "a pan-Latin American cinematic movement dedicated to the people of the continent and their struggles for cultural, political, and economic autonomy" (136). Although, as Luisela Alvaray details in her incisive essay on contemporary Latin American film, globalization has complicated the question of autonomy, the commitment to probing Latin American social realities remains central to an important body of films. Within this body, a number of such socially committed films privilege the image of disability to carry out critiques of physical and structural violence in the last half century. This chapter analyzes the relationship between the representation of injured bodies and political and social critiques in *El violín* (*The Violin*, directed by Francisco Vargas, 2005) and *La teta asustada* (*The Milk of Sorrow*, directed by Claudia Llosa, 2009). The disabilities of the protagonists of both films intersect with their racial, social, aged, gendered, and/or political alterity to indict the social injustice existing in their respective societies.

Through an analysis of these two films, this essay seeks to intervene in critical debates on disability in postcolonial contexts to consider how recent Latin American cinema treats the injury that results specifically from structural violence and violent States. The exemplary films *El violín* and *La teta asustada* engage with key facets of two intricately connected periods: the dirty wars of the 1960s through the 1990s and globalized societies after neoliberal structural adjustments from the 1980s to the present. In these two contexts, disability makes visible the processes by which authoritarian and capitalist regimes actively produce precarious bodies. Moreover, by reading cinematic fictions of human rights and neoliberalism through the lens of disability studies, this essay examines the metaphor of healing to call for future societies that produce more socially just conditions instead of injury. Finally, I address the cultural solutions proposed in *El violín* and *La teta asustada* as key to this metaphoric social healing.

## Disability in Global Contexts

The field of disability studies is very much in dispute and has received important critiques. Substantial claims have been made that since its emergence in the 1980s and 1990s, the field has been dominated by the concerns of white scholars, writers, and activists predominantly from the first world (Bell 3). Clare Barker and Stuart Murray note that the field's limited scope is especially glaring in postcolonial contexts, where "the history of colonialism (and its post/neocolonial aftermath) is indeed a history of mass disablement . . . and the acquisition of disability may be tied into wider patterns of dispossession—the loss of family, home, land, community, employment" (230).[1] They posit that adverse material environments and historical contexts problematize key assumptions of the field, such as the blanket rejection of medical discourses since the rise of the social model of disability, which can hold importance for raising awareness of (neo)colonial abuses (230).

Likewise, in her groundbreaking study *Disability and Difference in Global Contexts*, Nirmala Erevelles significantly expands the race-based critique of disability studies to consider also class and material inequality. Though she focuses on case studies in the context of the United States, she develops an important theoretical framework relevant for the Latin American context. Drawing on political economy, theories of difference, queer theory, and postcolonial theory, she "situate[s] disability as the central analytic, or more importantly, the ideological linchpin utilized to (re)constitute social difference along the axes of race, gender, and sexuality in dialectical relationship to the economic/social relations produced within the historical context of transnational capitalism" (6). Noting that in advanced capitalism one's experience of disability and possibility of survival depend heavily on economic realities conditioned by unequal social relations of class, Erevelles argues that disability must be studied in tandem with the historical conditions of diseases (12–17). She underscores the connection between high rates of disability in the Global South and adverse conditions such as high incidence of war, unhealthy living conditions, natural disasters, and pollution (18). Erevelles brings such historical material conditions to bear on theories of disability in order to complicate postmodern theories of posthumanism, such as those of Gilles Deleuze and Felix Guattari, who embrace the disabled subject as "an unstable and transgressive Body-without-Organs (BwO)" for its capacity to deconstruct the norm (27). By considering physical and structural violence in relation to how disability is actively produced in many cases, as well as how socioeconomic inequality affects access to care and healing, she effectively exposes the limits of postmodern conceptions of disability in contexts of violence (16). Wary of the pitfalls of ableism[2] and of an implicitly genocidal desire for the disappearance of disabled people, she still cautions that disability can only be desired in a historic context "that does not reproduce economic exploitation on a global scale" (29).

Erevelles blames transnational capitalism for exacerbating disability, which makes it a problem to overcome rather than a difference to be celebrated. She coincides with critics from other fields, such as Tauti Heron and Tina Mai Chen, in a strong critique of transnational capitalism as the current global order that reproduces the social and economic exploitation to which Erevelles attributes the production of disability. In her discussion of how human agency has been diminished in the context of neoliberalism, Tauti Heron recalls that violence and making certain bodies matter more than others have been at the root of capitalism since its birth with the colonization of the Americas in the sixteenth century. The neoliberal values system that calculates worth based on the potential for capitalist accumulation produces lives that do not matter in the Global South if they stand in the way of accumulation (90).[3] Tia Mai Chen signals another peril of neoliberalism in the fantasy that equates "inclusion" (i.e., market integration) with liberation:

> As critical feminists have long argued with respect to gender, and which is equally applicable to race and ethnicity, inclusion does not necessarily redress inequality nor does it produce equality. Adding to a never-ending list of members in "the global village" merely draws peoples into the capitalist system, complete with racial, patriarchal, and global unevenness[, . . .] cedes too much

> ground to a universalized neoliberal subject[,] and ignores the subject's particular ideological, economic, and cultural location. (13–14)

Though she does not mention disability alongside gender, race, and ethnicity, her comments on the uneven power relationships in neoliberalism are pertinent here. Her critique of inclusion undermines the premises of identity politics sometimes associated with disability activism and scholarship but actually parallels disability studies' strong critique of reinforcing normalcy, or ableism as constituting an affront to embodied diversity. Moreover, she also signals the intricate relationship between neoliberal capitalism and military force: "the coexistence of conspicuous consumption, free trade, and military force, in the Cold War and now, is yet another internal relation of globalization and popular culture" (12). As Erevelles argues, as long as lives are evaluated based on the productive calculations of neoliberalism, the lives of those with disabled bodies will continue to matter less than those considered able-bodied, who are deemed a valued investment rather than a liability to the State. Additionally, disability will continue to be produced by the violence that sustains capitalist accumulation.

In the colonial period, the Cold War, and under globalization, Latin America has been a select battleground of the West's civilizing project, both through military interventions and as a laboratory for neoliberal structural adjustment experiments. As Erevelles and Heron have argued, both have produced disability, exacerbated inequality, limited people's access to modes of redressing disability, and passed the cost of care onto the most vulnerable sectors. According to the aforementioned critiques of neoliberalism and globalization, neither the posthuman, which dissolves identity to celebrate difference, nor identity politics, whose politics of inclusion lacks a critique of the neoliberal subject, provide adequate models for addressing disability in contexts of social injustice. Rather, one must engage the violence of capitalism and its mechanisms for producing bodies and assigning them value in order to advance an egalitarian, nonviolent ethos. In this way, the above approaches resonate with Judith Butler's critical concern with why some bodies matter more than others. Though some disability studies scholarship has drawn explicitly on Judith Butler's *Gender Trouble*, drawing parallels between performative identities of gender and ability (McRuer 10, Meekosha and Shuttleworth 60), I argue that disability studies—at least in postcolonial contexts—could also be enriched by her more recent writings on the United States' war on terror.

In her philosophical writings on torture after September 11, 2001, Butler has called for an ethics grounded in the shared precarity of the body.

Such an ethics would recognize a universal human responsibility to care equally for the vulnerable bodies and lives of others:

> each of us is constituted politically in part by virtue of the social vulnerability of our bodies—as a site of desire and physical vulnerability, as a site of a publicity at once assertive and exposed. Loss and vulnerability seem to follow from our being socially constituted bodies, attached to others, at risk of losing those attachments, exposed to others, at risk of violence by virtue of that exposure. (*Precarious* 20)

From this fragility, she argues, emerges the potential to "crucially rearticulate the possibility of democratic political culture here and elsewhere" (40). In her subsequent text *Frames of War*, Butler posits the importance of representation, or of framing lives in certain ways, to alter relationships in which some matter more than others and thus are differentially exposed to violence and injury. In the global context of armed conflict, it is precisely this differential exposure—which she terms "precarity"—to violence in bodies that do not "matter" that produces injury and, thus, some forms of disability. By drawing on Butler's interventions on precarity, the perspective of Disabilities Studies would shift from how disability is valued in society to how one's value determines one's relationship to disability. This critical approach would emphasize the shared condition of injurability as well as advance a commitment to refrain from exploiting the vulnerability of others.

Through a privileged image of the disabled body, the recent Latin American films studied here make such an intervention in the way lives are framed and, consequently, valued. They foreground some of the ways in which both the dirty wars of the Cold War period and neoliberalism (as well as colonial legacies in which these are grounded) violently produce disabled bodies in peasant communities.

## War and Disability

Francisco Vargas's 2005 critically acclaimed debut feature film *El violín* addresses the Mexican guerrilla period (1960s to 1970s) to establish a direct relationship between war and disability.[4] The narrative of this neorealist black-and-white low-budget film follows three generations of a family of musicians and peasant corn farmers in their struggle against the Mexican military occupation of their community's land. Don Plutarco, patriarch of the family, refuses to let his old age and injured body—he has no right hand—relegate him to the role of raising his grandson Lucio while his son Genaro participates in the rebellion as a guerrilla leader.[5] Instead, he uses the pretext of tending to his cornfield to slip past the occupying soldiers so that he can smuggle weapons out of the field, and he ends up playing a vital role.

The film establishes an implicit link among socioeconomic inequality, war, and disability through Plutarco. His character is introduced in the context of the Mexican *guerra de baja intensidad* in Guerrero, which took place during the 1960s and 1970s in the broader contexts of widespread Mexican State violence and of the Cold War.[6] Though Plutarco is never subjected to violence on screen, a parallel is established between the disproportionate exposure to physical violence suffered by other peasants from his community of corn farmers and his own injury. His old age and high level of functionality (which suggests that he lost his hand in the distant past) evoke the specter of the Mexican Revolution of 1910, when he would have been a young man. His disability is thus linked to a tradition of subaltern armed resistance in Mexico. In the film as in history, the regions of Mexico with the largest indigenous populations and the highest rates of poverty, malnutrition, and illiteracy coincide with both the strongest tradition of rural guerrilla movements and the most pervasive military occupation and repression (Montemayor 21–23). His charged silence when a military captain asks how he lost his hand, coupled with his interrogative response, "When will you leave us in peace?"[7] suggest that the conflict stems from the nation's historic cultural impasse that continues to inflict violence on subaltern communities. His disability is thus both literal and symbolic, serving as a metaphor for the vulnerable social body of the Mexican peasants.[8] In this way, his injurability and resulting physical alterity are inseparable from his racial, aged, ideological, and socioeconomic marginality.

In addition to situating the armed struggle portrayed in the film within the history of the continued struggle for land and freedom that motivated peasants like Plutarco to fight in the Mexican Revolution, his character also institutes powerful links between present challenges and colonial legacies of structural violence, which perpetuate inequality and lead to continued exposure to physical violence. *El violín* uses the trope of a scriptocentric colonial encounter between Spaniards and the indigenous to illustrate these links. After their village has been occupied, Plutarco and the young Lucio visit the *patrón* (landowner) to ask to buy a donkey that, as the viewer later discovers, Plutarco will use to ride back to his occupied fields in an attempt to recover hidden munitions. The patrón and Plutarco address each other with feigned mutual respect as they negotiate, agreeing verbally that in exchange for the donkey Plutarco will bring this year's corn harvest when it is ready. The patrón, however, insists that Plutarco sign a blank document as a guarantee, stating that he will fill out the contract later. In a performative act that evokes the colonial scene in which indigenous people were divested of their land on the pretext of not holding written titles—a tragic consequence of their lack of access to the written word in the language of the conquerors—this moment underscores that people like Plutarco are still subject to such legal manipulations centuries later.[9] The fact that this scene takes place the day after Plutarco uses Mayan myths to explain to Lucio their community's current struggle as a direct continuation of the power dynamic established in the colonial encounter strengthens this parallel and highlights Plutarco's social and political consciousness.[10] He is fully aware of his limited possibilities of maneuvering beyond the physical and structural violence that mutually reinforce one another and keep indigenous people in a heightened state of precarity.

Plutarco's disability, then, intersects with the conceptual link that the film establishes between the violent legacies of the colonial encounter and the revolutionary present, as well as with its indictment of the intersection of non-Western ethnicity and ideology with socioeconomic and physical precariousness. The mutual reinforcement of these conditions exemplifies the critical concept of intersectionality, which addresses overlapping structures of marginality such as race, gender, and ability (Meekosha and Shuttleworth 61). In this context, his disability serves as a powerful visualization of how the uneven distribution of precarity allows some populations to be differentially exposed to violence.

Any concern with individual healing is conspicuously absent in *El violín*. Plutarco is committed to the collective project of defending communal lands, whether it cost him his hand or his life (as it presumably does at the end of the film). Instead of focusing on individual security through, for example, rehabilitation or prosthesis, *El violín* emphasizes the persistence of the violent conditions that create and sustain Plutarco's physical precarity—along with that of thousands more like him—and that produce disability. Instead of focusing on healing, the only solution presented in the film is to continue resisting, inexorably, with the hope that future generations will triumph where the previous ones failed. Like the forms of physical and structural violence that produce the peasants' intersecting categories of alterity, Plutarco's strategies for resistance crisscross categories of socioeconomic class, ethnicity, age, and ability. In Plutarco's case, he overcomes the limitation that his disability might have posed by making music, which he does for both subsistence and resistance. His violin is a source of informal work and a tool he uses to cross the military checkpoint and attempt to recover weapons from his field. Though he remains in a position of inferior power, within certain limitations Plutarco exploits the soldiers' prejudices and presents himself as a harmless (re: old, weak, impotent), innocent man only interested in continuing his work as musician and farmer. Moreover, one night in the refugee camp he teaches his grandson a *corrido*,[11] at first seemingly as a way to alleviate Lucio's fear, much like he does for all the refugees on their first night in the camp after their village is raided. By the end of the film, we discover that the corrido also transmits orally to Lucio the story of the resistance, linking the guerrilla with "so many villages time has drowned in oblivion" and thus preserving and transmitting an unofficial, collective, historic memory of the conflict through song.[12]

The significance of this song as a cultural weapon inherited by Plutarco's grandson becomes apparent in the final scene of the film: Lucio appears in a town, alone, playing his guitar and singing his grandfather's corrido. The song suggests that his father and grandfather have been killed, but he continues their struggle by transmitting the song's unofficial history to new listeners. The final shot is of Lucio and a young girl, another presumably orphaned refugee, walking off together into the distance, with Lucio armed with both a guitar and a gun (also his grandfather's). The potentially foundational couple and the open ending of this scene evoke the hope for a socially just society-to-come. The couple's success will depend on the continued struggle to combat all the forms of violence to which they are subjected, a struggle reliant on the physical and cultural weapons Lucio inherits from previous generations. Until structural change is achieved, he will continue to be differentially exposed to violence, thus forcing him into the paradoxical position of resorting to violence to resist it. The fact that these two children would be adults during the viewer's present creates a link with the current context, one in which the livelihoods and physical security of Mexican peasants are still threatened.[13] The film thus places a demand on the viewer for ethical actions, which it spurs on through the child as a symbol of hope for a nonviolent future created through historic memory, popular culture, and armed struggle.

## Trauma and Disability

While Vargas's film revises the revolutionary period in Latin America to evoke hope for an end to persistent structural and physical violence, *La teta asustada* addresses the legacies of the same history in the present, focusing directly on trauma, memory, and oblivion.[14] The protagonist of Claudia Llosa's visually rich, highly stylized film embodies the traumatic effects of war on the postconflict generation. Despite the temporal differences, there are many striking similarities between *La teta asustada* and *El violín*. They both employ subaltern perspectives, a minimalist style, a slow tempo, an emphasis on music, and relatively little dialogue in their treatment of historic State violence. Moreover, the two films' treatment of disability invite a productive comparison. Fausta's disability, like Plutarco's, is both literal and symbolic. Fausta appears paralyzed by *la teta asustada*, a phenomenon explained by the indigenous theory of how the psychological effects of violence are transmitted through nursing to the victim's child.[15] According to her family, her soul has hidden under the ground out of fear because she was nursed by her mother, a direct victim of violence. Her symptoms, which persist into young adulthood, include social isolation, frequent nosebleeds, and fainting spells. Fausta must confront three connected personal challenges that both lead to her personal healing and resonate with broader social concerns. First, she must overcome her fear of going out alone so that she can bury her mother Perpetua. The latter dies at the beginning of the film, and Fausta must earn money to transport the body to the hometown they fled to escape the armed conflict in which Perpetua was raped and her husband was killed. To do so, she takes a job as a housekeeper for Señora Aida, a wealthy concert pianist whose class- and race-based abuse Fausta must confront when Aida plagiarizes her songs and cheats her. Finally, Fausta must overcome her visceral fear of men, learn to trust, and open herself to a romantic relationship with the worthy suitor Noé, a Quechua-speaking gardener who also works for Aida. Her healing process is complete when she recovers her payment from Aida—pearls from a broken necklace—opens herself physically and emotionally to Noé, and buries her mother.

Like Plutarco in *El violín*, Fausta and her mother also cross multiple categories of alterity (gender, ethnicity, socioeconomic status, geographic marginality), which increases their exposure to violence during Peru's armed conflict. Her trauma is a direct consequence of the widespread terror suffered disproportionately by highland indigenous peasants during the years of terrorist and state violence (1980–2000): her mother sings that Fausta witnessed Perpetua's rape from within the womb,[16] and her aunt and uncle attribute her trauma to *la teta asustada*. As with Plutarco, Fausta's subaltern status and trauma are linked to a violent state that actively produces disability in marginalized people through war. In the case of Fausta, the fact that she was a fetus when the traumatic event occurred evokes a limit situation in which the victim is among the most absolutely vulnerable, but also innocent, of society. She carries this trauma into her adult life, in which the violation of her mother's body lives on perpetually—as her name "Perpetua" suggests—in Fausta. Even though she suffers no specific threat of rape in the present, her visceral fear of men and of being alone in public spaces causes her to live as if the abuses of the past were repeated in the present, as if history were cyclical.

As in *El violín*, such physical abuses are linked here to cyclical colonial legacies of structural violence, again hinging on Fausta's gendered, aged, and ethnic alterity and symbolized by her lack of access to written authority. The protagonist's disadvantaged position with regard to the dominant culture is first illustrated in her dealings with the Western medical establishment. Fausta is excluded from any dialogue with the male doctor, who explains her nosebleeds and fainting spells to her uncle Lúcido. The doctor—armed with the authority of Western medicine—denies Lúcido's non-Western explanation of her fainting episodes in terms of *la teta asustada*, thus refusing to recognize the family's cultural understanding of her trauma. Instead, he insists that her nosebleeds result simply from superficial capillary vessels, but that she faints because she has a potato in her vagina, which is infected and causes uterine inflammation. While the doctor assumes the potato is intended as a form of contraception and Lúcido says it must have gotten there by accident, Fausta insists that rather than a marker of her ignorance, it is intended to protect her from rape. Independent of these competing theories of her multiple symptoms, when Fausta has another nosebleed and faints, the doctor denies her access to medical services for a seemingly trivial reason that marks her cultural distance from the ineffective state bureaucracy: she did not bring her medical record number.

These conflicts parallel Fausta's relationship with Aida, in whose character colonial power legacies, the army (suggested though military portraits of family members), and capitalist exploitation in an unregulated domestic labor market intersect. Aida's exploitation of Fausta's songs hinges on the lack of a written contract documenting their agreement, an already unequal exchange that in addition to denying Fausta's authorial rights to her creations also carries an extreme emotional cost for Fausta. When coerced into singing what will become Aida's signature song, Fausta must overcome tears and trembling to meet the demands of her patron, who remains impervious while she passes Fausta her first pearl. Moreover, as the indigenous girl trades her treasure for trinkets,[17] the absence of a contract later allows Aida to throw her out of the car after the concert—subjecting Fausta to psychological trauma and potential bodily harm—for breaking her implicitly required silence as an invisible subordinate. The film thus underscores how colonial legacies allow structures of inequality to persist in new guises, such as domestic work, the commercialization of indigenous culture for the profit of the elites, and differential exposure to violence.

At the same time that Aida functions as an agent of neocolonial exploitation, her demand for Fausta's songs sets in motion the latter's healing. As for Plutarco, music plays a crucial role in empowering Fausta by serving as a form of economic gain, transmission of collective, cultural memory, and personal comfort. As Gastón Lillo has argued in his analysis of memory and oblivion in the film, Aida "activates the process of memory that contributes to Fausta's resuming a relationship with the cultural objects of her past, the memories she shares with her community, which will help her to repair her wounded identity" (443). At the beginning of the film, both Fausta and her mother sing in Quechua of their personal trauma, and Fausta sings to her mother (both alive and dead) about the preparations for her funeral (washing her so she will not smell of sadness, going to heaven to pick flowers, and taking her back to the village so her father will no longer be alone with the maggots). In these moments, her songs respond to her mother's demand to keep memory alive, a demand first expressed when she sings, "I'll eat if you sing to me and freshen my drying memory. I don't see my memories, it's as if I no longer lived," and later visually when she lies on a pillow embroidered with the words "no me olvides" (don't forget me).[18] When Fausta sings for her mistress, she refers directly to overcoming fear and to the process of healing.[19] Fausta struggles between her mother's demands for memory that tend to perpetuate Fausta's traumatic experience, her mistress's demand for songs-as-commodities, and the men in her life's insistence that she break free from the weight of the past: Noé's insists that she can choose whether to live in fear, and her uncle accosts her to shock her into breathing and fighting to live. These events unleash a transformative sequence in which Fausta finally overcomes her fear and sneaks into the house to "steal" the pearls that she had earned, embraces Noé when he finds her passed out in the driveway, and wraps her legs around him to be carried off to get the potato removed from inside her, thus literally opening herself to him. When her healing process is complete, she releases her mother's embalmed corpse to the sea and steps out of her cyclical, closed-off life by singing, "Look at the sea, Mum. Look at the sea."[20] She thus releases herself from the demand of her village and opens herself to a new life on Lima's coast.

Lillo argues that Fausta's healing provides a positive model for postconflict societies: her contact with her cultural memory (through music, Quechua, and Noé) allows her to process her memory, to comprehend it, and then to liberate herself from her traumatic paralysis. In this regard, *La teta asustada*'s treatment of disability in contexts of violence differs significantly from that of *El violín*, despite other remarkable parallels. Both protagonists and the cultures with which they identify have faced intersecting forms of physical and structural violence from the colonial encounter to the present under nominally democratic regimes. Their markers of disability are inextricable from other forms of marginality that situate them among society's most vulnerable members. It is no coincidence that both characters evoke the specter of rural peasants caught in the crossfire of the Cold War who, like each of these characters, are direct or indirect victims of the military's dirty war tactics. Thus, they lay bare the parallels between physical and structural violence, making visible the way both colonialism and modern capitalism create disabled subaltern bodies. Likewise, they employ any number of subaltern strategies, including physical and cultural weapons such as song and collective memory, to survive. Despite these powerful parallels, Fausta is, in effect, restored to physical normativity through an operation, and her individual emotional healing is evidenced in her receptiveness to Noé, both before her operation and after. The film ends with an image of fertility as Fausta accepts the gift of a flowering potato plant from Noé. Unlike *El violín*, in which the structures that produce disability remain unchanged, *La teta asustada* suggests that structural change can be enacted in unison with the healing process through cultural agency.[21] In the absence of explicitly political solutions, the cultural space represented by music provides Fausta with the agency to process her memory and thus liberate herself from the scars of the past, as well as to confront her exploiter. In the context of posttraumatic societies lacking historic memory and with unclosed processes of mourning, this emancipatory healing carries a positive value for those afflicted by the legacies of postcolonial violence.

## Conclusions

The films studied here form part of a common project based on the use of protagonists with injured bodies to advance a critique of persistent colonial legacies of structural violence as well as military violence. The central issue is social justice, which is intricately tied up with making visible past and present abuses. As Erevelles has persuasively argued, disability does not exist independently of the material conditions in which it is produced. As we have seen, the critical concern of these films is not aligned with a traditional U.S. disability politics of inclusion or of valuing disabled people, but neither does it imply the disappearance of disability. Rather, the focus is on military and market structures that violently produce disability as one among many other categories of marginality. *El violín* and *La teta asustada* critically underscore the oppressive nature of a global society that relies on systematic violence to produce disproportionately higher incidences of injury and disability in subaltern populations. In this context, disability acquires a central cultural significance and functions as a tool of resistance. The films share a common project of producing a powerful desire in the viewer to imagine, and thus make possible, more just conditions free of violent abuses. Recognition of these disabling conditions as well as disability's political and cultural potential is crucial for both films' framing projects.

## Notes

1. Helen Meekosha and Russell Shuttleworth, as well, signal that "[d]isabled people in the majority world have been marginalised often as a result of colonisation, colonial rule and post-colonialism; these cases constitute 80 percent of the 650 million disabled people in the world. The UN reports that for every child killed in warfare, three are injured and permanently disabled (UN 2006). Invasion, war, nuclear testing, mining, the export of pollution and the militarisation of the globe have all contributed to the increasing number of disabled people in the global south" (64).

2. "Ableism" refers to discrimination against people with disabilities. Central to disability studies is a critique of compulsory normalcy or able-bodiness, which functions similarly to compulsory heterosexuality (McRuer 7–10).

3. Heron maintains a loosely defined opposition between Western (capitalist, individualist) and non-Western (noncapitalist, collective) societies. She recognizes, however, that the relationship between the spaces of capitalist exploitation and accumulation can be reconfigured and reterritorialized in different circumstances. The structure of the relationship matters more than the geographic location of the relationship between these two loose categories.

4. For the production, distribution, and reception history of the film, see Alvaray 74 and Mraz 247–250, and especially Spaner 205–218.

5. Don Plutarco is played by Ángel Tavira, a nonprofessional actor whose outstanding performance earned him the 2006 Cannes Film Festival's Best Actor Award in the *Un Certain Regard* section. His musical talent and work toward preserving traditional music from Tierra Caliente is documented in Francisco Vargas's 2004 documentary *Tierra Caliente*.

6. For in-depth historical studies on Mexican social movements and guerrilla struggles, see Laura Castellanos's *México armado, 1943–1981* and Carlos Montemayor's *La guerrilla recurrente*; for a documentary account of Lucio Cabañas, professor and guerrilla leader in Guerrero alluded to by the name of Plutarco's grandson Lucio, see *La guerrilla y la esperanza: Lucio Cabañas*. Because of the widespread use of torture, summary executions, and forced disappearances, this conflict is also referred to as the Mexican Dirty War, which situates it in relation to the better-known Dirty Wars of South America that took place at the same time in the context of the Cold War.

7. I quote the films' English subtitles throughout this essay.

8. Though scholars such as David Mitchell and Sharon Snyder criticize the use of disability as a metaphorical "crutch" for literary narratives (49), Barker and Murray persuasively argue that in narratives culturally situated in postcolonial

contexts, "[d]isability metaphors may be meaningful . . . as part of foundational cultural and historical disability narratives" (233). Noting that "in communities experiencing mass disablement (due to war, disaster, or industrial accident) people with disabilities often constitute a numerical majority," the Western category of "normal" might be drastically altered, thus problematizing disability studies' criticism of narratives of healing as expressing desires for normalcy (229). They argue for reading practices that "highlight how particular disability experiences can shape cultural histories and are written into artistic and representational practices" (234).

9. This kind of manipulation of peasants to circumvent Mexico's constitutional commitment to land reform is traced in Warman's essay "El neolatifundio mexicano: Expansión y crisis de una forma de dominio."

10. Plutarco recounts: "In the beginning of time the Ancient Gods created the earth, the sky, fire, the wind, and all the animals. Then they created man and woman. They all lived in harmony. But one of those Gods was mischievous and he gave mankind envy and ambition. When the other Gods found out, they punished the mischievous god. Then they removed the ambitious people of the earth. But some of them were accidentally left behind. Then there were more and more, and more, and they wanted to own everything. They deceived the good people, and little by little, they took away what they owned, until they owned everything. They drove them out of their forests. They good people felt this was not fair, so they turned to the Gods for help. But the Gods told them to fight on their own, that their destiny was to fight. The ambitious people had become powerful, so the good people decided to wait. And their land became dark and desolate. . . . Then, the good people returned to fight for their land and their forest, because it belonged to them. Because their parents had given it for their children, and the children of their children. And that's what we'll do, we'll go back."

11. The corrido is a traditional musical genre used to transmit orally the exploits of popular heroes. Vargas has emphasized the importance of the corrido as a motif, stating that the film itself is a corrido (Guillén).

12. Plutarco's use of music to perpetuate his cultural memory and consciousness contrasts with the military captain, whose lack of music is directly connected with forgetting and with his participation in the occupation: "I would have liked to learn how to play but it wasn't possible. . . . When my father was killed, I was only a kid and from that moment it was an everyday fight. We didn't even have enough food, so, music, you can imagine. . . . Then I got involved in this, and you see, you forget."

13. For example, the deepening of Mexico's neoliberal policies motivates the EZLN's continued activity in Southern Mexico. In the time between this chapter's composition and its publication, the Mexican State's complicity with the drug cartels that disappeared forty-three students in Guerrero and put countless others in mass graves has sparked renewed conflict in the region.

14. Although *La teta asustada,* Llosa's second feature film, received mixed reviews in Peru, it was internationally acclaimed. Its more significant awards include the Berlin Golden Bear, the Guadalajara International Film Festival, the Montreal

World Film Festival, and the Havana Film Festival, as well as its nominations to the Goya Awards and the Oscar for Best Foreign Film.

15. It is well documented that Claudia Llosa's film was inspired by Kimberly Theidon's work on *la teta asustada* in Ayacuchan communities affected by terrorist and state violence, and published in her book *Entre Prójimos* (2004) (Largaespada, Chauca et al. 46, Sitnisky 263).

16. Though the film does not specify which armed group victimized Fausta's family, military forces more often practiced the kind of group rape suffered by Fausta's mother (Ugaz). Moreover, Fausta's visceral reaction to an official military portrait in Aida's bedroom suggests that she holds the national army responsible. For important historical studies of the conflict, see Gorriti, Manrique, Theidon, and Degregori. See also the Final Report of the Truth and Reconciliation Commission of Peru, which estimates the number of dead and disappeared people at 69,280.

17. Sitnisky and Lillo have both noted the parallel between the pearls and the glass beads and mirrors of the early Spanish conquistadors.

18. When Noé and Fausta clean up the pieces of Aida's piano, which the latter had shoved out the window in frustration, Noé tells Fausta in Quechua, "It's broken, but it still sings. Can you hear it?" Memory, music, and Quechua culture are thus linked in opposition to Aida's sterile attempts at composition.

19. She sings, "we must sing to hide our fear, cover our wound," and later, "My little lost dove, you ran away out of fear and you lost your soul, little dove. I'm sure your mother brought you into the world during the war, and perhaps your mother gave birth to you with fear. Even if they hurt you there, you shouldn't walk crying, there's no reason to walk suffering. Search for, look for your lost soul, look for it in the darkness, look for it in the earth."

20. Bloch-Robin notes that the extradiegetic music of the film, a repetitive ostinato, evokes Fausta's obsessive enclosure and highlights the film's cyclical temporality. Velez reads this final liberation as a necessary form of matricide that allows Fausta to assume her independence from her mother's injuries (38).

21. Likewise, Theidon emphasizes in a published interview the importance of economic reparation and justice for the healing process: "I would like to add that when I think of healing I think of justice, of the lack of justice, and of impunity. Because for me, a part of healing would include sentencing the rapists, and economic and symbolic reparitions for these women. Justice can be very healing. And none of the women I know have found justice, many still suffer from rage" (Largaespada).

## Works Cited

Alvaray, Luisela. "Are We Global Yet? New Challenges to Defining Latin American Cinema." *Studies in Hispanic Cinemas* 8.1 (2011): 69–86.

Barker, Clare, and Stuart Murray. "Disabling Postcolonialism: Global Disability Cultures and Democratic Criticism." *Journal of Literary and Cultural Disability Studies* 4.3 (2010): 219–236.

Bell, Christopher M. "Introduction: Doing Representational Detective Work." In *Blackness and Disability*. Edited by Christopher M. Bell. East Lansing: Michigan State UP, 2011.

Bloch-Robin, Marianne. "De *Madeinusa* a *La teta asustada* de Claudia Llosa: La música en la visión del mundo de un autor." *El ojo que piensa. Revista de cine iberoamericano* 3.4 (2011): n.p. Web. January 29, 2013.

Butler, Judith. *Gender Trouble*. London, New York: Routledge, 1990.

———. *Precarious Life: The Powers of Mourning and Violence*. London, New York: Verso, 2004.

———. *Frames of War: When is Life Grievable?* London, New York: Verso, 2009.

Castellanos, Laura. *México armado. 1943–1981*. Mexico City: Ediciones Era, 2007.

Chauca, Edward, Rafael Ramírez, and Carolina Sitnisky-Cole. " 'No pretendo retratar la realidad. Pretendo interpretar un tema para sacar discusiones que tenemos reprimidas': Una entrevista con Claudia Llosa." *Mester* 39.1 (2010): 45–55.

Chen, Tina Mai. "Thinking Through Embeddedness: Globalization, Culture and the Popular." *Cultural Critique* 58 (2004): 1–29.

Davis, Lennard J. *Enforcing Normalcy: Disability, Deafness, and the Body*. New York: Verso, 1995.

———. *Bending Over Backwards: Disability, Dismodernism, and Other Difficult Positions*. New York: New York UP, 2002.

Degregori, Carlos Iván. *Qué difícil es ser Dios. El Partido Comunista del Perú-Sendero Luminoso y el conflicto armado*. Lima: Instituto de Estudios Peruanos, 2011.

*El violín*. Directed by Francisco Vargas Quevedo. México: Cámara Carnal Films, 2007. DVD.

Erevelles, Nirmala. *Disability and Difference in Global Contexts*. New York: Palgrave Macmillan, 2011.

Garland-Thompson, Rosmarie. *Extraordinary Bodies*. New York: Columbia UP, 1996.

Gorriti Ellenbogen, Gustavo. *The Shining Path: A History of the Millenarian War in Peru*. Chapel Hill: U of North Carolina P, 1999.

Guillén, Michael. "*El violín*. Interview with Francisco Vargas." *Twitch*. n.p. December 31, 2007. Web. November 28, 2012.

Heron, Taitu. "Globalization, Neoliberalism and the Exercise of Human Agency." *International Journal of Politics, Culture, and Society* 20.1 (2008): 85–101.

*Informe de la Comisión de la Verdad y Reconciliación*. Lima, Peru, August 28, 2003. Web. November 28, 2012.

Largaespada, Mildred. "*La teta asustada*: la historia detrás de la película." *Periodismo humano*. n.p. October 25, 2010. Web. February 18, 2013.

*La guerrilla y la esperanza: Lucio Cabañas*. Directed by Gerardo Tort. Facets Video, 2007. DVD.

*La teta asustada*. Directed by Claudia Llosa. Peru: Cameo Media, 2009. DVD.

Lillo, Gastón. "*La teta asustada* (Perú, 2009) de Claudia Llosa: ¿memoria u olvido?" *Revista de Crítica Literaria Latinoamericana* 37.73 (2011): 421–466.

López, Ana M. "An 'Other' History: The New Latin American Cinema." *Radical History Review* 41 (1988): 93–116.

Manrique, Nelson. *El tiempo del miedo: La violencia política en el Perú, 1980–1996.* Lima: Fondo Editorial del Congreso del Perú, 2002.

McRuer, Robert. *Crip Theory: Cultural Signs of Queerness and Disability.* New York: New York UP, 2006.

Meekosha, Helen, and Russell Shuttleworth. "What's So 'Critical' About Critical Disability Studies?" *Australian Journal of Human Rights* 15.1 (2009): 47–75.

Mitchell, David T., and Sharon L. Snyder. *Narrative Prosthesis: Disability and the Dependencies of Discourse.* Ann Arbor: U of Michigan P, 2001.

Montemayor, Carlos. *La guerrilla recurrente.* Mexico City: Debate, 2007.

Mraz, John. *Looking for Mexico: Modern Visual Culture and National Identity.* Durham: Duke UP, 2009.

Sitnisky-Cole, Carolina. "Review of *La teta asustada,* directed by Claudia Llosa." *Journal of Iberian and Latin American Research* 17.2 (2011): 262–265.

Spaner, David. *Shoot It! Hollywood Inc. and the Rising of Independent Film.* Vancouver: Arsenal Pulp Press, 2012.

Theidon, Kimberly S. *Intimate Enemies: Violence and Reconciliation in Peru.* Philadelphia: U of Pennsylvania P, 2013.

*Tierra caliente . . . Se mueren los que la mueven.* Directed by Francisco Vargas Quevedo. 2004. DVD.

Ugaz, Paola. "Es un sueño para cualquier investigador que tu trabajo motive a los demás. Entrevista exclusiva con Kimberly Theidon, la antropóloga que estudió el mal de 'la teta asustada' " *Terra.com.pe.* Terra Networks Perú, S.A. March 3, 2009. Web. February 18, 2013.

Velez, Irma. "Matricidio y ob-scenidad en la (est)ética de Claudia Llosa." *Lectures du genre* 8 (2011): 28–52. Web. January 29, 2013.

Warman, Arturo. *Ensayos sobre el campesinado en México.* Mexico City: Editorial Nueva Imagen, 1979, 39–63.

Part III

# Embodied Frameworks

## Disability, Race, Marginality

Chapter 8

# Sô Candelário's Inheritance

## Leprosy as a Marker of Racial Identity in João Guimarães Rosa's *Grande Sertão: Veredas* (1956)

Valéria M. Souza

*Grande Sertão: Veredas* (*GSV*, 1956) is the story of Riobaldo, a former *jagunço* (or hired bodyguard) in the Brazilian *sertão* (backlands). Now elderly and disabled by rheumatism, Riobaldo relates his autobiography to a silent male visitor from the city. The novel is intimately shaped by disability and populated by large numbers of disabled characters. Yet disability and disabled characters in the text are often overlooked or, when not ignored, conveniently allegorized away by canonical critics. Within the fictional universe of Riobaldo's sertão, the majority of disabled characters fall into two categories—those with what I refer to as either "biblical" or "modern" afflictions (Souza 129–35). Leprosy, though technically an overlap of "ancient" and "modern," remains one of *Grande Sertão: Veredas*' "biblical" afflictions. These interlocking, at once complementary and contradictory representations of leprosy, are embodied in the novel in the persons of the anonymous backwoods "lazar" and the venerated jagunço chief Sô Candelário, respectively. In this chapter, I first read the powerful but critically neglected episode of the "lazar" by examining how it dialogues with and reworks ancient and medieval representations of leprosy. I then explore links between Gilberto Freyre's doctrine of Lusotropicalism and the central tenets of tropical medicine, arguing that Lusotropicalism and the medical designation of leprosy as a "tropical" (read: nonwhite) disease cannot be logically disentangled from one another. A close reading of relevant passages involving Sô Candelário reveals that, in the modern Brazilian literary, cultural, and medical imagination, leprosy became a coded way to talk about tensions and *ambiguities* of race and racial identity.[1]

I opt throughout for "leprosy" in favor of the more revisionist "Hansen's Disease," because "Hansen's Disease" lacks the etymological, cultural, and historical richness with which "leprosy" is imbued. The disease featured in João Guimarães Rosa's novel is undoubtedly leprosy (or, better yet, an amalgam of several different "leprosies" rooted in more than one historical period) and it is important to note that this condition—with all of its biblical and medieval subtext—differs substantially from the microscopically constructed, late nineteenth-century bacillus discovered by Gerhard Armauer Hansen. At this juncture, readers may wonder why leprosy should even qualify as a "disability" at all, as well as how my analysis of leprosy will prove relevant to Disability Studies. This brings me to the issue of "disability" versus "illness." Much of Disability Studies theory draws a clear distinction between illness and disability, although some critics including Susan Wendell make an excellent case for illness-as-disability (19–33). For reasons on which I elaborate further in my discussion of *GSV*'s "miracle girl," I use "disability" to refer broadly to *any* deviation from bodily norms, including (but not limited to) cognitive impairments, blindness, deafness, amputation, paralysis, disfigurement, deformity, physical wounds, chronic/acute illnesses, and speech disfluencies. Where other terminology like "disease," "condition," "ailment," and so forth appears, it is solely to avoid excessive repetition and should always be understood as falling under the rubric of "disability" as defined here.[2]

In Rosa's novel, the narrator-protagonist's encounter with the "lazar" unfolds toward the end of the narrative, as Riobaldo recounts how, in the wake of a minor spat with his love interest and fellow jagunço, Diadorim, he wanders farther away than usual from the band of jagunços:

> And I met [the lazar]. He looked as though he were lying in wait, hiding in the top of a tree, like an *ararambóia* snake. It gave me a start. He was [a man] covered with disgusting sores, truly leprous—[done for]. I'd rip my eyes out not to see things like that! I reached for my revolver. That thing suddenly shrank back, trembling; it trembled so violently that the branches of the tree coiled up the sound of a strong wind. He didn't scream or say a thing. Did he have any voice whatsoever left? I had to crush that inhuman thing. (400, trans. altered)[3]

The "lazar," according to Riobaldo, is poised atop a tree—concealing himself in order to hunt or kill, which suggests a degree of malice and hostility. However, the man may just as well be hiding out of fear of the approaching narrator-protagonist.[4] Riobaldo likens the lazar to an emerald tree boa [*ararambóia*], a nonvenomous, arboreal species of snake found in the Amazon rain forest. This clue implies that the narrator has wandered into the Meio-Norte region of Brazil, if not the actual rainforest. He is "outside of civilization" in relation to the sertão, in much the way that the sertão represents the "outside of civilization" for characters like Riobaldo's urban interlocutor. The comparison to this particular snake is noteworthy for another reason: its scales are emerald green, save for the many alabaster "lightning bolt" patches covering its back. The shape, size, distribution, and (white) discoloration of these patches strongly resemble those found on patients with borderline leprosy (BB).[5] According to Ridley and Jopling, pioneers in leprology, borderline leprosy is the most unstable form of the disease. Its manifestations make it difficult to determine whether patients are at the tuberculoid or lepromatous side, but they will generally progress with time to one or the other (Ridley and Jopling 255–261; Jopling 7–43).

The narrator continues, painting a picture of this lazar who is, at minimum, a borderline case, but more than likely has full-blown lepromatous leprosy (LL)—as evidenced by the presence of "disgusting sores"; he is "truly leprous—[done for]." As Riobaldo reaches for his gun, the leper recoils and trembles, and the narrator scorns him via the third-level demonstrative *aquele*.[6] "That one" or "that thing," he says, describing how the lazar shrinks back, withdrawing into the tree. The choice of the verb "to coil (up)" (*enroscar* in Portuguese) reinforces the idea of the leper as serpentine. In fact, since the original text's expression *cobra ararambóia* is already redundant—akin to saying "emerald tree *boa snake*" in English—the use of coil (up) marks the third instance of a snake metaphor in less than a paragraph. This phenomenon of "stacking" or repetition in *GSV* performs an augmentative function similar to the Lusophone suffixes *–ão/zão* and *–ona/zona*.[7]

Riobaldo emphasizes the leper's silence, noting that he neither screams nor says anything, and wonders if he has any voice left at all. As leprosy progresses, it is known to cause hoarseness via "obliteration of the vocal cords and changes in the trachea and larynx" (Boeckl 12). More than just a clinical symptom, the lazar's muteness is also tied to his nonhuman status. Like an enormous serpent in the treetops, the character communicates through motion and physical behavior, but seemingly lacks the capacity for speech. Indeed, Riobaldo affirms his desire to "crush that *inhuman thing*" (emphasis mine). The overall description of the character situates him within the medieval tradition of so-called wild lepers (not to be confused with their counterparts, the "tame lepers"). Wild leper was an epithet attached to itinerant diseased people, many of whom traveled about in order to beg for alms. The moniker encapsulated ecclesiastical and urban fears regarding the communicability of leprosy and its potential "movement" from town to town, country to country, or even *leprosaria* to *leprosaria* (Rawcliffe 86–87, 284–285).

The episode continues with another "leper story" Riobaldo recalls overhearing: "[. . .] Medeiro Vaz spotted a leper like this one in a guava tree. The man had [come] to lick the ripe guavas on the tree, one by one, in order to pass his disease on to [other people] who would later eat the fruit. Some do that" (400, trans. altered). This jagunço tale is a reworking of an infamous fourteenth-century French legend, according to which hundreds of lepers maliciously plotted to infect all of France by poisoning the nation's drinking water (Boeckl 49; Edmond 1). Allegedly, "[t]his would be done by poisoning the wells with a mixture of reptile parts and human excrement" (Watts 61). There was no truth to the rumor, but Philip V responded by ordering that all lepers be investigated and, if found guilty, burned at the stake. His decree resulted in a ruthless wave of violence against anyone suspected of having leprosy. In *GSV*, the storyline has been adapted to the sertão, with a guava grove replacing wells and fountains but virtually every other detail unchanged. Riobaldo makes clear that he believes the incident recounted by Medeiro Vaz doesn't just pertain to an individual leper, but is rather characteristic of lepers in general: "Some do that." Vaz, mirroring Philip V's actions, assassinates the leper—a decision Riobaldo deems "just and correct" (Rosa, *Devil* 400).

The tale about the leper in the guava grove remains at the forefront of the narrator-protagonist's mind as he tries to determine what to do about the lazar in the tree:

> [What they'd told me] was echoing in my ears now. The revulsion in me, strong fear: the lazar probably stank, and wherever he might be, no matter where he went, he probably left a slimy trail worse than a gigantic slug, contaminating everything with his cursed disease. Such that all the guavas of every guava grove in existence would turn into poison fruit . . . — and as for pulling my trigger, there was Medeiro Vaz's example. . . . (400, trans. altered)

The remark "the lazar probably stank" (with *feder* as the original verb) calls forth an entire classical and medieval vocabulary associated with leprosy. Luke Demaitre observes that leprosy "[. . .] was called 'feda,' an adjective whose meaning ranged from 'ugly' and 'foul' to 'hideous' and 'abominable' " (98). The term *feda* is related to the Latin *fetor*, or "stench," from which feder in turn derives. Prior to the Renaissance, when authors and physicians began to stress the visually unappealing aspects of the disease, they focused primarily on its olfactory symptoms. Hence, the sick were described as having "fetid breath," body odor (Boeckl 97), and "fetid ulcers" (Demaitre 99). Riobaldo touches on the leper's appearance when he mentions "disgusting sores," but what really bothers him—provoking feelings of intense fear and revulsion—is the thought of how the man must smell. It is the mention of scent that leads Riobaldo to expand on Medeiro Vaz's story and conclude that the lazar is worse than a gigantic slug and that he will infect "everything," poisoning all existing guava groves.

Riobaldo wants to kill the leper but struggles to do so, imagining what Diadorim might say (Rosa, *Devil* 401–402). Before long, Diadorim appears, while the narrator-protagonist continues mulling over which course of action to take:

> As long as a lazar like that existed, even far away, in this world, everything remained sickly and dangerous, for that man hated all that was human. Condemned and damned by every law, that wreckage of a man was. Marked: his body, his blame! For otherwise, why did he not rid himself of the evil, or allow the evil to do away with him? That man, he was dead already. (402, trans. altered)

Riobaldo cannot stand the thought of the lazar existing in the world—but why? Why is the narrator so convinced that a single leper will render everything "sickly and dangerous"? Here, the narrator slightly modifies his position by ceasing to label the "lazar" as "inhuman," instead referring to him as a "man" (albeit one who harbors hatred for his fellow man). Yet he also obviously blames the leper for his disability, branding him "condemned and damned," in addition to "that wreckage"—someone who has been corporeally "marked" as a result of his own "fault." The narrator rationalizes this attribution of blame by questioning why the lazar doesn't simply cure himself or, alternately, "allow" himself to perish from the disease. Surely if he is not to blame for being leprous he must choose one of these two options. For the narrator, the mere fact that the man continues living with a chronic disease constitutes proof of his "guilt" in becoming and remaining disabled. In the narrator's eyes, the man is already dead, his very survival an affront to the universe.[8] Riobaldo pictures Diadorim playing devil's advocate, arguing that the lazar is a living entity no different from any other (Rosa, *Devil* 402). The narrator-protagonist, however, vehemently rejects this proposal, preferring instead to view the man as defective—as a thing that needs to be corrected or eliminated.

Riobaldo's momentous encounter with the backwoods leper can be paired with an earlier episode that tells of a young girl who becomes ill, stops eating, and avoids fluids save a few drops of holy water per day. Miracles begin to happen all around her, and a government-sponsored intervention soon follows:

> But the regional chief of police came, bringing along his soldiers, and ordered the people to disperse. They took the girl to an insane asylum in the capital, and it is said that there they force-fed her through a tube. Did they have the right to do that? Were they justified? In a way, I think it was a good thing. Because, in no time at all, thousands of invalids condemned to die appeared there, seeking to be cured: leprous lazars, horribly deformed cripples, people covered with sores, the staring blind, madmen in chains, idiots, consumptives, the dropsical, all sorts: creatures that stank [. . .] And those people screamed, clamoring to be healed at once, praying aloud, arguing with one another, despairing of their faith—what they wanted was only to be cured, they had no interest in Heaven. (48)

The episode is semantically linked to that of the lazar via the reference to "leprous lazars," but also through terminology including "condemned" (which recurs on page 402) and the verb "to stink" [*feder*]. It acts as an important parable in that it wrestles with differing models of and responses to disability—in this case folk/religious versus medical/institutional. The community's reaction to the girl who exhibits what would probably be classified as anorexia (according to the criteria of the *DSM-IV-TR*) consists of noninvasively observing the miracles with which she is credited. Essentially, the girl is treated like a saint. Her decision not to eat and to limit what she drinks is honored. But once the regional police inspector arrives everything changes. The official avails himself of military power and orders those gathered around the girl to disperse. She is then seized and committed to a mental institution where she is force-fed through a gastric tube. The twofold brutality of the inspector's actions needs to be stressed: not only is the girl dislocated—ripped from her native, presumably rural community and shunted into an urban institutional setting—she is also subjected to an aggressive medical intervention (force-feeding) that some characterize as torture and by which she is viciously denied agency over her own body (Barnes n.p.).

Riobaldo remarks that he "more or less" approves of what was done. He opines that forced treatment is a positive solution, because it motivates other disabled people in the community to voluntarily seek out medical attention. It turns out to be a dubious "blessing," though: following the incident with the girl, swarms of people suddenly come forward demanding to be cured. The description of this group is crucial because it lumps together individuals with a vast array of disabilities, including chronic and acute illnesses, physical deformities, and mental illnesses. Among those listed are "leprous lazars," cripples, people covered in sores, the blind, madmen in chains, "idiots," consumptives, and people with dropsy (now called edema). In one fell swoop, Rosa's novel situates a wide range of ailments within a single category—that of "the condemned sick [. . .] creatures that stank." On *GSV*'s terms, there is no difference between illness (chronic or acute, mental or physical) and disability (congenital or acquired).[9]

Sô Candelário ostensibly suffers from the same condition as the backwoods lazar, but the two characters and the narrator-protagonist's relationship to them could not be more different. To begin with, Sô Candelário is a well-respected jagunço chief. As documented in *GSV*'s canonical criticism, little is known about Candelário's origins (Galvão 44). However, the text provides numerous hints that can be used to (re)construct a portrait of this individual, whose personality is closely tied to his family legacy of leprosy. Candelário is introduced at the beginning of the book in a random comment interspersed with Riobaldo's jumbled and still quasi-incoherent monologue.[10] In a statement that could serve as the epigraph to Candelário's biography, the narrator-protagonist says: "Sô Candelário endeviled himself, thinking he had an evil disease" (11, trans. altered). The character's race is touched on briefly when he is described as "the color of blue wheat, almost black, with a yellowed beard" (200, trans. altered), implying that Candelário is not white, and is most likely of Afro-Brazilian and/or indigenous descent.

Riobaldo delivers the next bit of significant information pertaining to Sô Candelário's origins when he muses: "Where was he from, where had he come from? They told me: Bahian deserts" (203, trans. altered). Like the comparison to the emerald tree boa that locates the backwoods lazar in either the Meio-Norte region of Brazil or, deeper still, in the Amazon rainforest, Bahia serves as a topographic marker that furnishes data about more than just Sô Candelário's homeland. The designation "Bahian deserts" is at the same time culturally specific and geographically ambiguous. It is geographically ambiguous because Bahia is a state, as opposed to a town or city, and furthermore, because an impressive 68 percent of Bahia's territory—including its sertão—is classified as having a semi-arid or "steppe" climate ("Bahia" n.p.). Technically, these regions are regarded as "intermediate zones" between pure desert and humid climates ("Köppen-Geiger" n.p.). However, "hot semi-arid" zones such as Bahia (and, for example, areas of the Australian outback) are virtually indistinguishable to the layperson from desert land. Saying "Bahian deserts" is similar to saying "forests of the rain forest" in the sense that all of the rain forest is comprised of forest and, indeed, the vast majority of Bahia hypothetically qualifies as "desert."

"Deserts" appears three times in *GSV*, two of which are relevant to this chapter: the reference to Sô Candelário's birthplace (cited above), and its mention in an early description of the Sussuarão Desert (Rosa, *GSV* 50; *Devil* 26–27), a place that—like "Bahia" in this strictly geographical and climatological sense—represents a nonplace, a foucauldian *heterotopia* ("Spaces" 184–185). In multiple ways, Sô Candelário hails from a place outside of place: he could be from anywhere in Bahia and as such is not from any particular place in Bahia. The overall impression is that Sô Candelário is from a remote, unknown location whose geographical limits are very loosely delineated and identifiable based more on climatic features than on maps or names. This is because where Candelário is from geographically matters far less than where he "comes from" genealogically. For if the label "Bahia" is geographically indistinct, it is anything but culturally vague. Going by Diadorim's birth certificate (Rosa, *GSV* 620; *Devil* 489–490) and a handful of other contextual clues, the narrative of *GSV* is set in the República Velha, between the late nineteenth and early twentieth centuries (Galvão 63–64). During the period in question, Bahia had already established itself demographically as an Afro-Brazilian province (Romo 4). In short, Riobaldo's phrase "deserts of Bahia" bolsters the hypothesis that Sô Candelário is most likely Afro-Brazilian, making this commentary on the character's origins less about geography than about race and/or ethnicity.

Within the same passage, the narrator fleshes out his sketch of Candelário, confiding in his interlocutor some rumors he has heard about the jagunço chief:

> [. . .] what Sô Candelário hunted was death. He drank, almost constantly, his strong *cachaça*. Why? I'll tell you: he was afraid he might be leprous. His father succumbed to it, and his brothers too, afterwards and afterwards—the ones that were older. Leprosy—say no more: that's when a man licks at the wound of cursed punishment. Punishment, what for? Because of that, certainly, Sô Candelário was possessed by hatred. He lived with his mind afire. Leprosy takes time, retarded in the body, then suddenly sprouting forth at any moment, taking many forms. (203, trans. altered)

According to buzz in the backlands, Sô Candelário seeks out death, spurred on by fears of leprosy. This anxiety is grounded in the idea of the disease as a "family curse," a trope whose import should not be underestimated. The narrator suggests that leprosy is self-explanatory ("say no more") with a set of preunderstood meanings based on biblical leprosy, which is consistently depicted as divine punishment for sin (2 Kings 15). Yet Riobaldo also challenges scriptural readings of the disease when he indicates that Sô Candelário is angry because he cannot understand for what reason(s) he and his family are being "punished." The narrator underscores his empathy for Candelário's predicament when he wonders aloud, "Punishment, what for?" and remarks that it was "because of *that*, certainly"—with "that" referring to unwarranted castigation—that the jagunço is filled with rage. Candelário is furious because he and his family have done nothing to "deserve" leprosy, notwithstanding biblical ideology, which locates blame for this illness in individuals and their families.

In the passage's conclusion, Riobaldo identifies leprosy as characterized by temporality, even as he delivers another subtle nod to Candelário's origins. Leprosy is a disease both slow and sudden, anticipated and surprising. It is delayed in the body, ever-lurking but invisible until the moment it erupts. Riobaldo's description is clinically accurate because *Mycobacterium leprae* is a slow-growing bacillus and, as the narrator notes, can present in a variety of ways (Boeckl 8–23). Leprosy's latent presence in the body may also be seen as referring to nineteenth-century conceptions of Bahia, viewed by the Brazilian elite as "backward" due to its predominantly nonwhite racial makeup (Romo 14). The "backwardness" of leprosy mirrors the alleged backwardness of the Afro-Brazilian region that—we are led to surmise—is Sô Candelário's birthplace. That the disease is simultaneously foreseeable and unpredictable relates back to the matter of family history. Having watched his older male relatives develop the disease, Candelário, too, is expecting to fall ill. If (or when) he does, though, it could still come as a shock: having proliferated inside his body for years, the disease will give the impression of striking swiftly via the eruption of cutaneous lesions or other disturbing symptoms. The disease is linked explicitly to the patriarchal branch of the Candelário line; no female family members are ever declared leprous. Leprosy in *GSV* is a masculine affliction, an unexpected finding given that it was associated, in most other literary and cultural (con)texts, with women (Edmond 56).

Riobaldo expounds on how Sô Candelário's disease affects every facet of his life and identity:

> Sô Candelário had a habit: he was constantly lifting up his shirt, staring at his arms, the tip of his elbows, and scratching at his

> skin until it bled. And he carried a little mirror in his pocket, in which he would steal glances at himself. Totally damned. We knew he took certain remedies—he was the first one up every morning at daybreak, and he'd drink theriac and then head down toward the edge of the creek going naked, naked, like a Jabiru's leg. (203–204, trans. altered)

The character is consumed by fear of his "family curse" and is continuously peeking under his clothing, inspecting his bare flesh, even clawing at his skin to the point of drawing blood—as if desperately trying to excise the leprosy from within. Candelário probably uses his pocket mirror to inspect areas of his body that would otherwise be impossible to view (for example, his shoulders or back, or the backs of his limbs). Riobaldo says that Sô Candelário "steals" [*furtar*] glances at himself, suggesting an element of fear, shame, or some combination thereof at play in this behavior. The jagunço may secretively sneak glimpses of his body because he's frightened of what he'll find, or concerned that others will see him scrutinizing his flesh and label him leprous. Based on Riobaldo's previous comments, Sô Candelário's family legacy is well known in the backlands, but what remains unclear is the extent to which Candelário knows that others possess this knowledge. The "family curse" may be the subject of gossip behind his back, leading him to erroneously believe that his comrades are less aware of his predicament than they actually are.

Despite the jagunço chief's secrecy, it is common knowledge that he takes "certain remedies." The character's daily ritual consists of rising at dawn, imbibing theriac, and bathing nude in local streams. That theriac is a central part of Candelário's regimen is germane to this analysis because of the drug's ancient and medieval provenance, list of ingredients, and history of use. Originally formulated by the Greeks, its name means "pertaining to animals" (Rawcliffe 220). Because one of the four humoral types of leprosy was identified with snake-like characteristics, theriac, with its serpentine components, was thought to be a particularly effective therapy for the prevention and treatment of the disease (221). Rawcliffe emphasizes the drug's role as "a central pillar in medieval pharmacopoeia" (220). Its production was tightly regulated, restricting use of the panacea to the wealthy, although knockoffs—what Rawcliffe refers to as "bastardized" versions—were available to individuals of varying socioeconomic backgrounds (221). Theriac was available for purchase as late as 1884 and, since no effective treatment for leprosy emerged until the mid-twentieth century, continued to enjoy popularity as a homeopathic medication up until the end of the nineteenth century. Sô Candelário's diligent bathing is another important signal, as medieval leprosy patients were often advised to bathe and scrub vigorously at their skin in an effort to "restore lost feeling to desensitized limbs" (Rawcliffe 227).

The combination of approaches that the jagunço employs in order to detect, monitor, and prevent or treat leprosy reveals quite a bit. Given the high price and difficulty in obtaining theriac, it is fair to assume—barring the usage of bastardized formulas—that Candelário is well-connected and at least reasonably affluent. The character's status as a leper, like his birthplace and race—both attributes with which his leprosy is inextricably bound up—is ambiguous (does he already have the disease or is he merely paranoid about developing it because of his family history?), and his choice of theriac and morning baths do nothing to dispel this uncertainty, because these methods were used prophylactically and therapeutically. Candelário's chosen regimen situates him squarely on the divide between ancient/medieval and contemporary: during the period in which the narrative of *GSV* unfolds, leprosy was still articulated, by and large, as an "ancient" or "biblical" disease, with the only available treatments antiquated remedies that happened to persist into the modern era.

It is by returning to the issue of race that we can begin to probe in greater detail the "modern" dimension of the jagunço's disease. In the passage cited earlier, Sô Candelário's race is reintroduced via the comparison to a Jabiru bird. What is most memorable about the beast is the color scheme of its feathers and body: Its head, upper neck, and legs are featherless and black, whereas its plumage is typically white. This chromatic pattern, like that of the emerald tree boa, vividly evokes biblical "white leprosy" (2 Kings 5:27; Numbers 12:10; Demaitre 177–178) and the often dramatic presentation of hypopigmented, hairless patches or spots on the bodies' of darker-skinned victims of tuberculoid leprosy. Candelário's nudity is likened to the Jabiru's leg, in what is perhaps a comment on his race (Afro-Brazilian) and build—long and slender.

During the late nineteenth and early twentieth century, leprosy was becoming increasingly racialized and sexualized (Edmond 9). Nancy Leys Stepan, who pioneered research on international constructions of "the tropical," notes that "the category 'race' was removed from the Brazilian national census after 1890," adding: "Since no census was held in 1900 or 1930, and race was not counted in the censuses of 1910 and 1920, [race] was not counted as a factor in the Brazilian population for 40 years" (131). Paradoxically, even as this category was being removed from the national census, Brazilian physicians were becoming increasingly embroiled in a series of debates on the subject of race and the transmission of leprosy, which played out in a dramatic fashion in the pages of the *Gazeta Médica da Bahia*

(Romo 25). One camp downplayed the role of race in epidemiology, while their detractors swore by racially deterministic models of disease transmission. Unlike European leprologists, Brazilian experts complicated the neat separation of people into totally distinct racial categories like "black" and "white," preferring instead to make vaguely defined "intermediate" racial groups—in particular *mulatos*—the nuclei of their projects, as the principal figures onto whom disease was projected (Rodrigues 20: 105–113).[11] Brazilian sociologist and anthropologist Gilberto Freyre is notorious for having based an entire theory of national identity—Lusotropicalism—on racialized tropes of family. Lusotropicalism emphasized "hybridization" as a tool of nation-building that originated with the Portuguese in Europe and was then carried over into Brazil via Portugal's colonial enterprise (66–69). For Freyre, the history of Brazilian *mestiçagem* is intimately bound up with that of certain diseases such as syphilis and leprosy. What racial hybridization introduces is the possibility of the *uncertain*—the "intermediate"—a category whose propagation became synonymous with the spread of disability.

Members of the international scientific community, including Brazilians like Freyre, shared a common understanding of the "tropical"—that is, the concept of environment and race as interconnected, with special differences in how "tropical" versus "temperate" zones acted on white and nonwhite bodies who inhabited "the tropics" for any length of time. In this sense, the work of Brazilian thinkers and the development of tropical medicine as a discipline cannot be logically disentangled from one another. Just as Freyre's Lusotropicalism depends on the enmeshment of geographical and genealogical factors, tropical medicine departs from the principle that most Europeans, by virtue of their origins in "temperate" climates, are inclined to become sick when traveling or living for extended periods in "tropical" zones, to which they are (culturally and racially) maladapted. Both models posit racial characteristics as climatologically dependent, with different races best suited to the climates that originally produced them and the "hybrid" offspring of various races portrayed as hazardous disease vectors. In addition, both Freyre's doctrine and tropical medicine share a vision of "the tropics"—and by extension their progeny—as fundamentally "unhealthier" than "temperate" zones (Freyre 78), a perception that would later become refigured in Brazilian literature as the "sick rural" (Klanovicz 49–51).

This digression brings us full circle, back to the two characters through whose stories the central tenets of tropical medicine and Lusotropicalism play out in Rosa's novel. Sô Candelário and the lazar are in many ways polar opposites, but it would perhaps be more accurate to say that they exist along a spectrum—one that incorporates a variety of overlapping and frequently contradictory beliefs about the nature, clinical manifestation, and modes of transmission of leprosy. Riobaldo's interaction with the lazar can be regarded as a postcolonial encounter because it inverts the power dynamic of the stereotypical "first encounter" found in classics such the *Carta* of Pêro Vaz de Caminha. If—as I have been asserting throughout this essay—constructs of race and leprosy are interconnected in *GSV*, then all signs point to the lazar being white. Though the lazar's race is never identified, this is perhaps due to what some scholars call the "invisibility" of whiteness (Garner 42–46; Frankenberg 72–96). There is only one substantive indication of the lazar's race: he suffers from lepromatous leprosy (LL), the subtype most common among Caucasians of European descent (Boeckl 9).

If the character is indeed white, then Riobaldo's meeting with him is effectively a rendezvous with Brazil's "European granddaddy"—the colonizer who invaded and brought leprosy with him, both directly in the form of his own infected body and indirectly through the importation of West African slaves he had sickened earlier in his travels, prior to the eighteenth-century boom in the slave trade (Monot et al. 1040–1042; Grimm 936). The lazar, viewed from this perspective, would be the patriarch of leprosy in Brazil. Since Riobaldo is probably not white (Bolle 276–277) and the lazar probably is, the men's chance meeting in the forest rewrites the "first encounter": instead of Europeans disembarking on Brazilian soil and marveling over the sight of scantily clad "natives," the narrator-protagonist, himself of native blood, ventures into the periphery of the sertão and accidentally discovers the horrifying sight of a (European) leper in the advanced stages of the most aggressive form of the disease. And, like European colonizers who regularly compared indigenous and African peoples to beasts and who sought to dominate and control their bodies, Riobaldo envisions the man in the tree as serpentine and wrestles with the desire to exert the ultimate form of control over him by ending his life.

Sô Candelário and the lazar embody, as characters, various facets of leprosy. If the lazar is a classic "wild" leper, Candelário is a "tame" one. Like the two furthest extremes of the Ridley-Jopling scale, Sô Candelário is "tuberculoid" (TT) and his counterpart is "lepromatous" (LL). While the lazar is more clearly associated with medieval and ancient ideas about leprosy—cementing his status as archaic—Sô Candelário incorporates overlapping elements of both medieval and modern notions of the disease. The racialized component of leprosy, in conjunction with other textual clues, reinforces the idea that the lazar is white and Candelário is at least part Afro-Brazilian. As the jagunço chief scours his flesh in search of "spots"—lighter areas of discoloration that are often the first manifestation of tuberculoid leprosy—he evokes (Luso)tropical theories about the "whitening" and "darkening" of Brazil (Skidmore 64–69). At any moment, a tinge of "whiteness" may peek through Candelário's darker skin—or be subsumed by his overall coloring of "blue wheat, almost black" (Rosa 200, trans. altered). The threat of these lighter "spots" for which the jagunço searches exhaustively (even as he dreads finding them) can also be read as traces of the lazar waiting to sprout forth. For while the lazar's disease is contagious, the jagunço chief's is undeniably inborn. With the colonization of Brazil regarded as a "family affair" à la Freyre's doctrine of Lusotropicalism, leprosy "runs in the family" more broadly speaking. Sô Candelário's inheritance may well come from his father and older brothers, but farther back—way back in the woods, at the very edge of the sertão—it descends from the branch of a much older tree. It is Brazil's colonial legacy, passed down from Europe.

## Notes

1. It was within this cultural and historical milieu of beliefs about "the tropical" that a young João Guimarães Rosa came of age. Born in Minas Gerais in 1908—just a decade after the publication of Manson's *Tropical Diseases*—the author began his education at the College of Medicine of Minas Gerais University in 1925. In his career as a medical student, a practicing physician, and eventually a Brazilian diplomat traveling through Europe and Latin America, Rosa would have been widely exposed to the burgeoning new field of tropical medicine, along with prevailing theories about relationships between race, climate, and illness espoused in texts by Freyre and his contemporaries

2. The impairment/disability binary posits "impairment" as an underlying biological or medical condition and "disability" as the position of subjugation created by environments hostile towards non-normative modes of embodiment. The problem with the biologically deterministic formulation of "impairment" is that, like the "sex" of feminism's sex/gender binarism, it presumes a neat separation of "biological" and "social," which arguably cannot be said to exist. Just as "sex, by definition, will be shown to have been gender all along" (Butler 11), "impairment" and "disability" can be conceptualized as synonyms, each referring to an interactional configuration simultaneously biological and social in nature (Schriempf 68).

3. All English translations have been adapted from James L. Taylor and Harriet de Onís' 1963 version of Rosa's work.

4. The *British Medical Journal* reported, as late as the nineteenth century, that "lepers instinctively hide themselves" ("Spread" 1056).

5. Although there are several different systems for classifying leprosy, it is helpful to think of the disease in terms of two basic subtypes: tuberculoid and lepromatous. Individuals with low or no resistance to leprosy are most likely to develop the more aggressive lepromatous form (LL), whereas those with some or high immunity are prone to the potentially benign tuberculoid variety (TT). Historically, lepromatous leprosy was most common among Europeans, indicating that genetics play a role in immunity or lack thereof (Boeckl 9).

6. *GSV*'s most despised characters are consistently referred to using either the third-level demonstratives *aquele(s)/aquela(s)* or the second level demonstratives *esse(s)/essa(s),* both of which mean "that one" or "that thing." João Adolfo Hansen identifies this pattern as a revamping of the Latin deictic *iste,* used to connote contempt (147).

7. These suffixes (with *–ão/zão* being masculine and *–ona/zona* feminine) function by conveying the idea of amplification or intensification—usually to communicate that a given noun is "bigger" than average, but sometimes also adjectivally to indicate that something or someone is extra "impressive," "powerful," and so on. Some concrete examples include: *livro/livrão* (a book/a big book); *mulher/mulherona* (a woman/a striking woman).

8. Foucault famously asserted that medieval lepers were "declared dead" (*Madness* 6–7), but this is not historically accurate (Rawcliffe 13–43). Interestingly, *lazarar-se* appears once in *GSV* as a reflexive verb meaning "to die" (Rosa, *GSV* 37), but this does not reflect its overall meaning in Rosa's work.

9. The novel thus anticipates and, in its own unique way, responds to ongoing contemporary debates in Disability Studies regarding the taxonomy of "illnesses" versus "disabilities."

10. Besides featuring a nonlinear narrative with no chapter or section breaks for more than 600 pages, *GSV* is exceedingly difficult to read (much less translate) as a result of having been written in an artificial language, comparable to Homeric Greek, which uses Brazilian Portuguese as a base but incorporates elements from dozens of other languages and freely mixes archaic and colloquial registers. For this reason, it is somewhat absurd to suggest that Riobaldo's monologue becomes any less "jumbled and quasi-incoherent" as the book progresses, but it in fact does. The first 50 to 100 or so pages of the 600-plus page text are the most incomprehensible, reading like a discombobulated stream-of-consciousness written, as one Brazilian student aptly put it, "in Hungarian" (Hansen 119, trans. mine).

11. See also Rodrigues 20: 205–211, 301–314, 358–368, 404–409 and 21: 121–132, 225–234, 255–265, 445–455.

## Works Cited

"Bahia." November 1, 2014. www.bahia.com.br/en/page/geography

Barnes, Djuna. "How it Feels to Be Forcibly Fed." Web. November 1, 2014.

Boeckl, Christine M. *Images of Leprosy: Disease, Religion, and Politics in European Art*. Kirksville, MO: Truman State UP, 2011.

Bolle, Willi. *grandesertão.br*. São Paulo: Duas Cidades, 2004.

Butler, Judith. *Gender Trouble: Feminism and the Subversion of Identity*. New York and London: Routledge, 1990.

Demaitre, Luke. *Leprosy in Premodern Medicine: A Malady of the Whole Body*. Baltimore: Johns Hopkins UP, 2007.

Edmond, Ron. *Leprosy and Empire: A Medical and Cultural History*. Cambridge: Cambridge UP, 2006.

Foucault, Michel. *Madness & Civilization: A History of Insanity in the Age of Reason.* New York: Vintage, 1965.

———. "Different Spaces." In *Aesthetics, Method, and Epistemology.* Edited by James D. Faubion, translated by Robert Hurley et al. New York: New Press, 1998, 175–185.

Frankenberg, Ruth. "The Mirage of an Unmarked Whiteness." In *The Making and Unmaking of Whiteness.* Edited by Birgit Brander Rasmussen, Eric Klinenberg, Irene J. Nixeca, and Matt Wray. Durham, NC: Duke UP, 2001.

Freyre, Gilberto. *Casa Grande & Senzala: Formação da Família Brasileira sob o Regime da Economia Patriarcal.* 51a ed. revista. Apresentação de Fernando Henrique Cardoso. São Paulo: Global Editora, 2006.

Galvão, Walnice Nogeuria. *As formas do falso: um estudo sôbre a ambigüidade em Grande Sertão: Veredas.* São Paulo: Editôra Perspectiva, 1972.

Garner, Steve. *Whiteness: An Introduction.* New York: Routledge, 2007.

Grimm, David. "Global Spread of Leprosy Tied to Human Migration." *Science* 308.5724 (May 13, 2005): 936–937.

Hansen, João Adolfo. *O o: A ficção da literatura em Grande Sertão: Veredas.* São Paulo: Hedra, 2000.

Jopling, W.H. *Handbook of Leprosy.* 2nd ed. London: Heinemann, 1978.

Klanovicz, Jó. "O Brasil no mundo rural doente: A construção do agricultor na literatura em dois momentos da história brasileira (1914 e 1970)." *Luso-Brazilian Review* 44.1 (2007): 45–60.

Monot, Marc et al. "On the Origin of Leprosy." *Science* 308. 5724 (May 2005): 1040–1042.

Rawcliffe, Carole. *Leprosy in Medieval England.* Woodbridge, UK: Boydell Press, 2006.

Ridley, D. S., and W. H. Jopling. "Classification of Leprosy According to Immunity: A Five-group System." *International Journal of Leprosy* 34.3 (1966): 255–273. PDF file.

Rodrigues, Raimundo Nina. "Contribuição para o estudo de lepra no Estado de Maranhão." *Gazeta Médica da Bahia* 20 (1888–1889): 105–113, 205–211, 301–314, 358–368, 404–409. Web.

———. "Contribuição para o estudo de lepra no Estado de Maranhão." *Gazeta Médica da Bahia* 21 (1889–1890): 121–132, 225–234, 255–265, 445–455. Web.

Romo, Anadelia A. *Brazil's Living Museum: Race, Reform, and Tradition in Bahia.* Chapel Hill: U of North Carolina P, 2010.

Rosa, João Guimarães. *The Devil to Pay in the Backlands.* Translated by James L. Taylor and Harriet de Onís. New York: Knopf, 1963.

———. *Grande Sertão: Veredas.* [1956]. 19th ed. 3rd printing. Rio de Janeiro: Nova Fronteira, 2001.

Schriempf, Alexa. "(Re)fusing the Amputated Body: An Interactionist Bridge for Feminism and Disability." *Hypatia* 16.4 (Fall 2001): 53–79.

Skidmore, Thomas E. *Black into White: Race and Nationality in Brazilian Thought.* Durham and London: Duke UP, 2005.

Souza, Valéria M. "Challenging Bodies: Representations and the Aesthetics of Disability in João Guimarães Rosa's *Grande Sertão: Veredas* (1956)." Diss. U of Massachusetts Dartmouth, 2013.

"The Spread of Leprosy." *British Medical Journal* 2.1402 (November 12, 1887): 1054–1056.

Stepan, Nancy Leys. *Picturing Tropical Nature.* London: Reaktion, 2001.

Thomson, Rosemarie Garland. *Extraordinary Bodies: Figuring Physical Disability in American Culture and Literature.* New York: Columbia UP, 1997.

Watts, Sheldon. "Dark Hidden Meanings: Leprosy and Lepers in the Medieval West and in the Tropical World Under the European Imperium." *Epidemics in History: Disease, Power, and Imperialism.* New Haven and London: Yale UP, 1997, 40–83.

Wendell, Susan. *The Rejected Body: Feminist Philosophical Reflections on Disability.* New York and London: Routledge, 1996.

"World Maps of Köppen-Geiger Climate Classification." Web. November 1, 2014.

Chapter 9

# "A solidão da escuridão"

## On Visual Impairment and the Visibility of Race

Melissa E. Schindler

It has been more than sixty years since the first staging of Nelson Rodrigues's controversial play, *Anjo Negro* (*Black Angel*), in Rio de Janeiro, yet its content remains as inflammatory as ever.[1] *Anjo Negro* depicts the torturous marriage between Ismael and Virgínia, a black man and a white woman, characters whom Abdlas de Nascimento describes as "monsters created by racism" (De Nascimento, "Teatro experimental" n.p.). Full of hatred for his own skin color, Ismael blinds his white brother; rapes the woman who would become his wife and then locks her away so she can see no other white people; and then blinds his daughter, Ana Maria, so she won't know he is black, only to teach her to hate all black people, sleep with her, and lock her away, too. His wife, Virgínia, successively murders three of their mixed-race children, citing their skin color as a motive, and then has sex with Ismael's blind brother, Elias, in an attempt to exact revenge on Ismael. In order to "know" race, the play suggests, one must see it. More significantly, it claims that in order to *hate* someone because of his or her race, one need not see at all.

If *Anjo Negro* exposes and criticizes the truth of racism in mid-twentieth-century Brazil, it only succeeds in this critique because it also portrays visual impairment. Blindness makes the entire piece possible; it functions as an analog for metaphorical short-sightedness and serves as the crux of the play's irony. Visually impaired characters Elias and Ana Maria act as indices against which the audience is meant to measure the depth of metaphorical blindness—in this case, the immorality and ignorance that produces racism. The play denounces racism by casting racist people as "blinder" than those who are physically blind. *Anjo Negro* operates by a particular kind of irony, one that is derived from the juxtaposition of three widely held assumptions: that knowledge of self and other is achieved through physical sight (also known as "ocularcentrism"), that race is always and only visibly marked on the body, and that "blindness" is a pejorative term.

*Anjo Negro* raises the question: What is the relationship between race and disability? More specifically, what is the relationship between race and visual impairment?[2] Robert McRuer has effectively shown that disability, like gender and non-normative sexuality, had to be made visible on the body in order for heterosexual able-bodiedness to become compulsory (10). Although scholars and activists have long argued that race is a social construction, one of the impediments to changing people's perceptions of race is the fact that the effects of racism are often physical, especially "in the historical context of transnational capitalism, where bodies encounter each other often in violent collision such that captivity and mutilation are no longer metaphors" (Erevelles 28). This is exacerbated by the casting of nonwhiteness as a disability. Historically, nonwhite bodies have been described variously as hyper-able (e.g., the hypersexualized African man), incapable (e.g., the myths of the so-called primitive, savage, uncivilized "native" invented to justify colonial and imperial presence), or, finally, physically dis-abled (e.g., science's numerous attempts to map out racial inferiorities through physiognomy). Race and disability, therefore, have always been inextricably linked. This is especially true of the Americas, where, as Nirmala Erevelles argues, the institutionalized enslavement of people of African descent "imbricated . . . race and disability in [the] collective formation of the black disabled body" (39).

Given the wealth of twentieth- and twenty-first-century scholarship dedicated to deconstructing the depictions of enslaved peoples and their descendants in the Americas, the relative dearth of work on the intersection of race and disability comes as a surprise. Little has been published on the subject since Leonard Kriegel's landmark essay "Uncle Tom and Tiny Tim: Some Reflections on the Cripple as Negro" (1969). In addition to Robert McRuer's and Erevelles's earlier-cited monographs, the work of the late Chris Bell perhaps most conspicuously addresses the relationship between blackness and disability. Bell highlights and deconstructs this glaring lacuna in an essay for the second edition of *The Disability Studies Reader* (2010), in which he makes a "modest proposal" that we change the name of the field to "White Disability Studies" to reflect its current audience and object of study (275). While these publications certainly point to a growing interest in the study of the intersection of race and disability in the United States, scholars like Bell and Kriegel struggle with the task of "speak[ing] to both [Disability Studies and African American Studies] on their own terms" (Newman n.p.).Within the Brazilian context, examination of the intersection of disability and blackness in a text such as *Anjo Negro* is made even more challenging by the relative newness of both disability and Afro-Brazilian identity and history as recognized areas of study. And much of what makes these fields "new" has less to do with a recent surge in their academic popularity—as the concepts of disability and blackness are recognized as subjects that scholars in other countries take up—and more to do with concerns about what those concepts will mean in and for Brazil. As the title of this chapter suggests, some Brazilian authors perceive a kind of overlap between the experiences of blackness and of disability. Through the phrase "*a solidão da escuridão*," or the "loneliness of darkness," Afro-Brazilian author Miriam Alves equates the darkness of blindness with that of blackness, pointing to a shared perspective based on a mutual experience of sociocultural isolation. Indeed, I would like to suggest that by bringing a Brazilian perspective to the junction of disability and African diaspora studies, as well as by limiting the concept of disability to visual impairment, we gain an example of how to speak productively and simultaneously to both fields in the Americas. If race is popularly thought to be a physical characteristic, then people with visual impairment stand to make a significant contribution to notions of race. Meanwhile, if sight is popularly construed as the foremost avenue to knowledge, then Afro-Brazilian approaches to the way that black identity is both envisioned and embodied likewise add much to our notions of visual impairment.

To that end, this chapter examines how a range of texts represents the relationship between blackness and blindness. The first section analyzes a narrative by a European medical doctor in the nineteenth century who treated enslaved Africans afflicted with visual impairment caused by the Middle Passage journey. The second section looks at the short story from which this chapter takes its title, Miriam Alves's "A Cega e a Negra—Uma Fabula," in order to think about how contemporary authors are repositioning blackness and blindness with respect to one another. The third section discusses the way that a children's book, *The Black Book of Colors*,[3] conceives of sight and color through the juxtaposition of what Vera Godoy has called the book's "three scripts," that is, its use of Braille, Roman alphabet, and drawings. Though in some cases separated by centuries, together these texts confirm that blackness, to the degree that it is supposedly visible, and blindness, to the degree that it is supposedly characterized by a lack of vision, are undeniably linked in our discourses about race in the Americas.

## "Victims of a Physical Darkness"

The texts chosen for this study span different centuries, countries, and artistic genres, and the scope of this heterogeneous archive attests to the cross-cultural, transhistorical and cross-linguistic nature of the assumed link between blackness and blindness. That being said, conceptualizations of blackness and blindness in Brazilian literature and philosophy make a unique contribution to the discussion about how race and disability are mutually constituted. Due to Brazil's largely mixed-race population, the country has long cultivated a definition of race that differs from that most prevalent in the United States. Whereas the "one-drop rule" rendered blackness hypervisible in the United States, insomuch as the identification of supposedly visible characteristics of race could expose and incriminate those who sought to "pass" as white, Brazil instituted no such legal code or social norm. In theory, one could not be "outed" as an African, black, or Afro-descendent individual attempting to "pass" as white if the expectation was that everyone would strive to whiten themselves, either through miscegenation or through nongenetic markers like education, wealth, marriage, and the accumulation of property. By the beginning of the twentieth century, social and genetic whitening (*embranquecimento*) had quite literally become a national project, and today, many Brazilians continue to allege that a "one-drop" identification would be moot in a country where the "new race"—a Brazilian, *mestiço* race—emerged from the mixing of African, European, and Native American genes, cultures, and social codes.[4]

Theoretically, then, race cannot be sighted on a Brazilian body, and so the myth goes that racism does not exist (or exists differently) in Brazil. Yet the same is not true in practice. In "the [so-called] 'racial democracy,'" Gizêlda Melo Nascimento writes, "there's no need to ask what color a *favela* is, or what is the color of the pain of being poor and discriminated against in this society, which may hold many democratic festivities but meanwhile can't manage to eliminate fully its slavocratic practices" (G. Nascimento 51). In other words, there may not be an equivalent to the "one-drop rule," but racism is still marked visibly on the Brazilian body. Due in part to the complex definitions of race and racism in Brazil and their perceived relationship to the same concepts in the United States (or lack thereof),[5] Afro-Brazilian movements have not simply taken up U.S. parameters for combating prejudice. Rather, scholars and activists strategically employ the notion that race in Brazil has historically been defined as a discursive identity instead of as an innate trait. If race cannot be identified, then people must claim it. Because popular criticism of affirmative action argues that Brazilians are so socially and genetically mixed as to render categorization impossible, activists have begun to encourage people to "out" themselves as black, often whether they identify as such or not.

Therefore, if the discourse of *mestiçagem* (cultural and genetic mixing) has historically conveyed the notion that people could and should whiten themselves, both literally and figuratively (something understood as virtually impossible in the United States), then the same goes for "blackening" or "yellowing" oneself. Genetics does not assign race to you—you *own up to* your race, just like you own up to any other characteristic. Brazilians frequently employ the same Portuguese verb, *assumir*, to lay claim to any identity trait. Whether you're coming out of the closet, admitting to particular religious beliefs, publicly recognizing a biological child, accepting a personality trait, taking on a new responsibility, or openly acknowledging your race (especially if you are identifying as black), you will use the same word to perform all of these actions. One must assumir such elements of identity, meaning that the act of accepting, owning up to, declaring, or taking on an identity is a *choice*, not a biological given. No one else can expose your ancestry and "assume" it for you.[6] For advocates of Afro-Brazilian identity, then, the objective is to encourage people to assumir their blackness. When an individual "assumes" his or her blackness, asserts Elisa Larkin Nascimento, he or she "speaks from a point-of-view that is articulated as a black person who understands him/herself as something that has an inherent value." And this perspective, this "internal gaze . . . makes it such that someone can be Afrocentrist even though s/he is white or Chinese or Japanese or Indian. But this person must *assume* the gaze genuinely" (Duarte and Fonseca 26). For this reason, Maria Nazareth Soares Fonseca points to the example of white Africans who took on black identities and voices during the struggle for independence in African countries: "*eram brancos, mas* ***assumiam****-se como negros*"/ "they were white, but they identified as black" (Duarte and Fonseca 51). Establishing one's black identity as separate from phenotype means taking on a way of seeing that is metaphorical; it means cultivating a worldview that recognizes how race is socially constructed, how racism is embodied, and how sight is both a literal and a figurative capacity. To return again to the title of this chapter, it means, in other words, moving blackness away from the color of one's skin or, in the case of blindness, away from visual impairment, to a shared *social* experience of "the loneliness of darkness" understood as the loneliness of marginalization.

Sight has long served as a metaphor in literature and politics concerning race in the Americas, yet the Brazilian notion of "assuming" an identity is unique, not just in rethinking race but also in rethinking how race and sight intersect. It avers that racial identity is not simply defined by how one is seen by others, but instead that race and sight are mutually constitutive. "Assuming" a black identity requires first adopting the "internal gaze" that Elisa Larkin Nascimento describes. In turn, assuming a black identity also engenders a new vision of the external world. And here is where the Brazilian concept of assuming one's race becomes especially useful for the present analysis of race and sight, because it moves away from ocularcentrism, the notion that "vision is a necessary condition of knowing" (Bolt 541) to suggest that race is not a visible characteristic and sight is not a natural capacity of the eyes alone. With this understanding, then, we are better positioned to understand how Brazilian texts containing blind and/or black characters might be especially suited for contextualizing the transnational trope of blindness and blackness in literary and historical documents.

The title of this section, "Victims of a Physical Darkness," points to the early historical convergence of visual impairment and race's visibility. It comes from a nineteenth-century account by Thomas Nelson, an English medical doctor who boarded an illegal Brazilian slave ship and found that hundreds of the enslaved people had lost their sight during the voyage (Conrad 44). The doctor's words are tellingly abstract. Meant to humiliate and degrade those slave traders (and nations) that still practiced slavery—that is, the aforementioned immoral "physical darkness"—the phrase also betrays the way the doctor himself conflates physical darkness with a supposed physiognomic one. That is, the "darkness" of slavery is akin to the darkness of being blind, for both of which the so-called darkness of skin serves as a visible metaphor. Thus, when the doctor bemoans the fact that, "on the appearance of the negroes, no pen can give an adequate idea," he means that the effects of slavery cannot be articulated in written form, but he also alleges, inadvertently or not, that race cannot be written; it can only be seen (45).

Documentation of the nineteenth-century slave trade is rife with the language of sight: vision's excesses, its role in "enlightened" thought, and the literal and figurative import of its absences. According to abolitionists, one could only comprehend the horrors of slavery by seeing them (i.e., by seeing Africans enslaved), and slavery, at its worst, lay in the figure of the slave whose experience of the Middle Passage had robbed him or her of sight. In the following excerpt, taken from the same medical doctor's records, note his excessive and interchangeable use of the language of vision loss and squalor with respect to enslaved Africans (emphases mine):

> On every side, squalid and sunken ***visages*** were rendered still more hideous by the swollen ***eyelids*** and the puriform discharge

> of a virulent ***ophthalmia*** {a dangerous eye inflammation}, with which the majority ***appeared*** to be afflicted; added to this were figures shriveled to absolute skin and bone, and doubled up in a posture which originally want of space had compelled them to adopt, and which debility and stiffness of the joints compelled them to retain.
>
> On ***looking*** more leisurely around, after the first paroxysm of horror and disgust had subsided. . . . The most of them destitute even of the decency of a rag, and all presenting as woeful a ***spectacle*** of misery as it is possible to conceive. . . .
>
> Not the least distressing ***sight*** on that pest-laden deck was the negroes whom the ***ophthalmia*** had struck ***blind***, and who cowered in seeming apathy to all that was going on around. This was indeed the ultimatum of wretchedness, the last drops in the cup of bitterness. Deprived of liberty, and torn from their native country, there was nothing more left of human misery but to make them the victims of a physical ***darkness*** as deep as they had already been made of a moral one. (44)

Among the many observations one might make about this quotation, two are perhaps most significant. First, the passage clearly corroborates Robert McRuer's argument that "disability (and nonheterosexual identity) must be visibly located elsewhere to allow for" what he calls "the epiphany of heterosexuality" to occur (McRuer 24, 16). In order to normalize heterosexuality and able-bodiedness, and in order for heterosexuals to out themselves as such, disability and nonheterosexuality had to become excessively visible (thereby "safely contained—embodied—in others" [24]). It seems nearly impossible to talk about othering and embodiment without discussing the construction of race and, certainly, this doctor declares his whiteness by declaring his able-bodiedness. "The normalcy of 'the sighted,' " contends David Bolt, "depends on a notion of deviance in 'the blind' " (543). Thus, in contrast to the "squalid and sunken visages" of the "negroes whom the ophthalmia had struck blind," in contrast to their "hideous" appearance, their "swollen eyelids" and the "debility" caused by their excessively cramped quarters, the medical doctor simply "looks around" with "leisure." For the doctor, the "spectacle" is "distressing" and causes "paroxysms of horror and disgust," but, for the Africans he is describing, the reality of that situation has taken their sight. Blindness in enslaved Africans enables the white, European doctor to see, just as their hypervisibility as disabled and black establishes his invisibility as a white man. Indeed, this example gives new meaning to Bolt's assertion that "the metaphorical light in the life of the [sighted]" rests on a "notion of darkness in that of [the blind]" (543).

The next thing one takes away from this passage is a subtle slip in the doctor's discourse; intending to articulate horror at the Africans' loss of sight, he instead expresses horror at the sight of Africans. In other words, what "pest" purportedly ladens the deck of the ship: the illness or the ailing people curled up on it? And why does he suggest that women and children who are "destitute" of clothing present "as woeful a spectacle as it is possible to conceive?" Undoubtedly, the sheer number of people whose health has been mortally compromised must have seemed overwhelming, but surely this medical doctor had seen other people from his own country who were equally sick. Dea Hadley Boster informs us that while "many abolitionists relied on powerful images of disability . . . to represent the institution of slavery," in fact, it was not slavery itself so much as "the fear of disability, defect and helpless reliance that accompanied enslavement" that fanned the flames of their "moral outrage" (67–68). Well-intentioned or not, this doctor drew on the collective fear of so-called physical abnormality to condemn slavery, thereby linking blackness with disability.

The doctor writes that "the sight of negroes . . . struck blind" constitutes the "ultimatum"—the *limit*—"of wretchedness." He rightfully suggests that what leads to the ophthalmia only accentuates the suffering that must have accompanied the enslaved people's illness and loss of vision. Yet his is not a mere expression of sympathy, since his sentimentalist discourse, as focused as it is on reproducing the *sight* of mass blindness, ultimately positions black, disabled bodies at the extremity of squalor. Indeed, he makes this abundantly clear in his earlier description of arriving on the boat, for which the preparation of his "experience, aided by . . . imagination, fell short of the loathsome spectacle which met [his] eyes." The loathsome spectacle in question is not the sight of sick people, but rather the sight of "three hundred and sixty-two negroes, with disease, want, and misery *stamped upon them* with such painful intensity as utterly beggars all powers of description" (43). Meant to act as a synonym for the effects of enslavement, the "painful stamp" is in fact the confluence of disability and blackness, constructed so that the doctor might situate himself at the center of so-called humanity, while enslaved Africans "scarcely retain the form of [it]" (45). Even if abolitionists would later rework the metaphor of blackness in order to cast the trade in human commodities as a "moral darkness," what nevertheless remained was a link between squalor, sightlessness and the construction of blackness mapped onto the slaves thought to embody all three.

## Synesthetic Language and Afro-Brazilian Metaphor

As we have seen, in the nineteenth century, literature inspired by the slave trade tended to pathologize race and disability by articulating one through the other. Even in abolitionist texts that decried the immorality of slavery, the disabled, black body always served as a visual signifier for slavery's deterioration of the moral fabric. By describing the sight of bodies without sight, traders and abolitionists alike attempted to establish their own normativity. In the twentieth century and the beginning of the twenty-first, however, new articulations of blackness and blindness gained popularity—figures that are predicated on supplementing the "lack" attributed to race and disability with the capacity for "magic."

In the United States over the last fifty years, the term "magic/al negro" entered popular discourse as a reference to a specific, stereotyped black figure in film and literature. Nnedi Okorafor-Mbachu describes the "Magical Negro" as a "black character—usually depicted as wiser and spiritually deeper than the white protagonist—whose purpose in the plot was . . . to help the protagonist realize his own faults and overcome them."[7] This character has no interior or separate life of his or her own. His or her wisdom, spirituality, and magical powers exceed the norm, but he or she only uses them for the good of the main (white) character. Although no one has extended this critique of stereotype to blind film or literary characters, there is no doubt that a type of Magical Blind Person[8] often performs a similar function in stories about white protagonists. Alternately dis-abled and super-(dis)abled, the "Magical Blind Person" endeavors to make his peers and the audience see "differently." Like the wisdom of the Magical Negro, the acuity and overly developed senses of super-disability exists only to serve others. In other words, the Magical Blind Person makes possible the "heteronormative epiphanies" that give other characters a "sense of subjective wholeness, however illusory" (McRuer 12).

In Brazil, while contemporary representations of blindness and the stereotype of the blind visionary rely in part on the import of international film and literature, Afro-Brazilian spiritual practices cultivate an alternative representation of human sight and its association with knowledge production. Visual representations of the figures known as *orixás*, deities who are part of the West African/Christian/American syncretic practices called *Umbanda* and *Candomblé*, often show them with their eyes obscured by strings of pearls or other coverings. Claudio Marcio de Carmo, a university professor and *pai-de-santo* (the head of an Umbanda house of worship), explains the depiction of orixás thus: "An *orixá* sees with divine eyes. Furthermore, it sees much more than earthly eyes, which remain closed in order to highlight the earthly limitation that does not affect the *orixás*. As such, aside from a decoration, pearls falling in front of the eyes actually echo and reflect the divine vision that exists beyond human knowledge" (personal communication). That is, human sight makes possible a particular, limited kind of knowledge. Pearls and eye covers suggest that in order to "know" the world more profoundly than humans, the *orixá* must "see" differently. And in that way, Afro-Brazilian syncretic religious practices actually destabilize the presumed link between knowledge production, light and visual ability, and lead to new versions of identity formation and knowledge production that are not predicated on sighting blackness or race, but rather on engaging with the world through blackness.

The depictions of the orixás' sight can be contextualized through Leda Maria Martins's groundbreaking ethnography, *Afrografias da Memória* (Afrographias of Memory). In this text, Martins puts forward the notion that an Afro-Brazilian religious celebration known as a *congado* is characterized by its use of what she calls "synesthetic language." That is, denied the tools to write and record their own histories, Afro-Brazilians created a language based on synesthesia: the intersection and crossing of senses. Although on the one hand a practice of cultural resistance, "synesthetic language" is also an alternative process for producing knowledge about the world, one that notably relies on more than sight alone. She describes this language as blending "together the words, gestures, music and enchantment that are inherent to and present in the signifyin(g) and significant materiality of the *congado's* songs and celebrations; a diction that [doesn't] elide the subject and the object, the breath and the blade, the rhythm and the color" (*Afrografias* 20). Synesthetic language does not posit a kind of supernatural or superhuman site of knowledge; it merely promotes a fuller one. Similarly, the obstruction of human sight in the *orixás* does not mean to attribute "magic" to the visually impaired. It simply moves the social and literary imaginary away from knowledge and, by extension, metaphor as primarily visual phenomena.

The notion that metaphor is mutually and synesthetically constructed is the precise lesson of Miriam Alves's short story, "The Blind Woman and the Black Woman—a fable," published as part of her 2011 collection *Mulher Mat(r)iz*. Upon first examination, it would seem that the story merely uses "the language of disability" as Chris Ewart suggests, "to affirm (an often-subordinate) voice to elucidate agency and figurative empathy for other oppressed and exploited populations" (Ewart, qtd. in Erevelles 39). Actually, there is something more complex going on in Alves's story, based in part on the fact that the relationship between blackness and blindness has its own, unique, historical-materialist manifestation in Brazil.

The story describes the meeting of Cecília, a Brazilian woman of African descent, and Flora (short for Floresta Brasilia), a blind, presumably white woman. It begins in a moment of crisis for Cecília. Due to an unexpected event at the bank, in which a fed-up Cecília refuses to accept the subtle targeting of system(at)ic racism, the two women form a sudden friendship. In the midst of her musings, Cecília recalls how quickly their friendship grew, based in part on a pleasurable sense of mutual benefit. "Cecília," we're told, "interpreted the world of sight for Flora" (34). Meanwhile, Flora literally "opened doors" for Cecília, because as a white, blind woman, she had more privilege than her friend.[9] They had literally met at the door to the bank: a door that had been historically closed to Cecília but subsequently opened for her *when accompanied by Flora*. Their interdependence is not a disabling codependence, but a relationship that gives both of them unprecedented physical access to the world.

One day, at lunch, a casual event tests their relationship. Cecília accompanies Flora to the bathroom, and on the way, a man starts to walk menacingly down their same path. A lifetime of experience tells Cecília that she should make way for this individual, who will not make way for her (as a black woman), but suddenly, the man moves aside. The waiter had caught the man's eye, conveyed that the black woman was leading a blind woman, and the change in his behavior "took place through the subtlety of glances" (35). Cecília suddenly felt alienated from her friend, who, not having witnessed the conversation of glances, didn't perceive what had happened. But Flora has certainly perceived a change in Cecília's temperament, as she withdraws from Flora, and proceeds to immerse herself in her reflections about their relationship.

Later, having spent hours contemplating a spider spinning its web, Cecília has a revelation. She understands that a spider moved between the two women, spinning a "web of life," built of individual strings. And this web is composed of "fragile, beautiful symmetries." Thus the story ends with a black woman's epiphany, brought on by a blind woman. "Beauty. It was this: beauty!" Cecília realizes. "[She] and Flora . . . transformed their painful destiny, the stigmas (just as Flora insisted in reminding her), into the pleasure of sight. It was this: sight!" (36). When Cecília calls Flora to narrate her encounter with the spider, the metaphor of its web, and their shared pleasure in sight, Flora simply tells her friend that she already knew the "web's secret." Once again, the person who is visually impaired seems to function as a person empowered with mystic vision. But unlike typical depictions of blind characters, in this story, the blind individual and the one who has the revelation share a "painful destiny" and the experiences of being stigmatized. This is not an example of what Carrie Sandahl calls the "overcoming narrative," where a "previously whole person adjust[s] to the 'brokenness' of disability by getting over a bad attitude" (584). Nor is it an instance of using a blind character to show a sighted person how to see differently or to be grateful for her sight. The story posits neither of these characters as in need of fixing or rehabilitation.

Instead, Cecília and Flora share a visual understanding of the world. Rather than "focus[ing] on eliminating disability," this story suggests that the characters might "revel" in it, finding in their shared experiences of stigmatization a mutual, imaginative language (Sandahl 584). Certainly, Alves depicts Flora as taking on seeing eyes through her interactions with Cecília—through her friend's descriptions of her surroundings. But that does not mean that Flora needs to sit and watch the spider to understand the metaphor of its web, or that Flora won't describe the web of interracial and interabled friendship as an object that can be seen, using a vocabulary filled with terms pertaining to vision. When Cecília excitedly tells her friend about the invisible web that connects them, Flora's response that she "already knew" does not allude to some kind of superhuman blind omniscience, but simply to the fact that she, too, has read and interpreted the *metaphor* of the web. By the end of the story, we understand that the two women have adopted—assumed—a vision that starts from within. It is an "internal gaze," one made uniquely possible by the meeting of blackness and blindness. Unlike the Magical Negro and the Magical Blind Person—and unlike the "characters" who appeared in the accounts of abolitionists—Cecília and Flora demonstrate a method of knowledge production that neither elides the differences between them nor reduces either one to a mere plot device in the other's transformation.

## Between black and Black in The Black Book of Colors

Another way to approach the notion that the metaphors of race and blindness are written and read through multiple senses is to articulate new understandings of reading and writing. In advancing a concept of "three scripts" (*três escritas*), Vera Godoy has done just that. Based on her research of the work of blind Brazilian author, Elizete Lisbeth, Godoy contends that those books that employ drawn images, text written in Portuguese script, and text written in Braille, offer an expanded kind of reading experience. Meant for blind and sighted children alike, Lisbeth's work makes readers aware that we assimilate metaphors through more than just our eyes. And it accomplishes this by physically changing the way people read. The presence of Braille—which, according to Godoy, both sighted and blind readers use when they read the books—is only the most immediate example of how we experience metaphors through multiple senses. Children who sit and read with adults (blind or sighted), take in the images through the sight, smell, touch, sound, and, in some cases, even the taste of the texts at hand.

If the social and political process of learning racism requires that we forget everything about reading *except* the language of visual characteristics that supposedly identify race, then books utilizing three scripts force us to remember how metaphors develop through more than words and images. Though not written by Lisbeth, *The Black Book of Colors* (*O livro negro das cores*), by Menena Cottin and Rosana Faría, is one such book. Presumably intended for children, this text sets out to define colors. Yet the paper, the Braille, and the images embossed on it are completely black, and the words written in Portuguese are typed in a white font. In the story, a single character—Tomás—describes various colors by associating objects and sensations with them. "Red," for instance, "is a little bit tart, like a strawberry, and sweet like watermelon, but it hurts when it appears on a bruised knee." Yellow "tastes like mustard," green "smells like recently cut grass," and blue "is the color of the sky when the sun heats the tops of our heads." Every definition is illustrated threefold, but ultimately, only in black and white. Both in word and in fact, the book demands an overt interaction with our bodies, through its use of words as well as its three scripts.

Besides reminding readers of how metaphors are created and perceived through our various physical experiences of the world, this particular translation of the book (from Spanish into Portuguese) makes an intriguing statement about race. Portuguese distinguishes between the color "black" and the sociopolitical category "Black"; the first is *preto* and the latter is *negro*. For a Portuguese speaker to refer to a person of African descent as preto is generally considered offensive, whereas negro or *negra* is not. Thus, in using negro rather than preto in the title of *The Black Book of Colors*, the translator, Rafaella Lemos, taps into the potential embodied in three scripts to make blindness talk about race.

There is no doubting the intent behind Lemos's translation. After all, the Portuguese version of the book has been published with Pallas Editora, a respected Brazilian publishing company whose website locates it "in the vanguard of Afro-Brazilian culture." But beyond that official affiliation, the book itself also recognizes the difference between black and Black (preto and negro). When Tomás defines black, "the king of all the colors," he uses the word *preta*, thereby separating the Black (Negro) of the title from the black (preta) of the color spectrum. As a result, readers come to understand "Blackness" as a way of seeing that is intimately and inextricably interwoven with blindness, because the book casts blindness and blackness as non-normative methods of knowing the world. *The Black Book of Colors* establishes itself as an instruction manual for the process of reading vis-à-vis a variety of senses—for the perspective that one cultivates through the act of "assuming" blackness. The book is not necessarily a lesson in seeing past race—though race is undoubtedly one of the metaphors that it seeks to deconstruct. Rather, it posits an internal vision, achieved through the employ of various sensory capacities, where blindness and blackness meet. The intent is neither to do away with color nor to do away with sight, but rather to suggest that both consist of more than visual language would make them seem.

## Coloring the World, Blackly

Nirmala Erevelles's critique of posthumanism sounds an apt, convincing, and timely warning against the overreliance on discursive tools like metaphor in scholarly theorizations of disability and blackness. Her analysis is most pointed when it works within a framework that recognizes how "disability/impairment and race are neither merely biological nor wholly discursive" (48). That said, discourse and biology are not a binary, as the meeting of blindness and blackness repeatedly reminds us. Critics of the social model of disability, which argues that disability is not an innate characteristic but rather emerges through our discursive and physical interactions with the world, contend that this model sometimes overlooks the way that disability is lived and embodied. Along these lines, as Tanya Titchkosky proposes: "our on-going textual encounters with disability are interactive scenes where we can engage and scrutinize the contemporary cultural organization of embodiment" (11). Similarly, works like *The Black Book of Colors* foster embodied, interactive "textual encounters." Indeed, because Brazilian notions of racial identity are not wholly dependent on sighting the raced body but instead on "assuming" blackness in text or speech, discursive portrayals of blackness and blindness in Afro-Brazilian literature often propose a practical use for discourse.

To wit, in an interview about Afro-Brazilian literature, scholar Oswaldo de Camargo elegizes the "unique and metaphorical vision" of Afro-Brazilian writing, a vision that shapes literature, "coloring it blackly" (*colorindo-a negramente*) (Duarte and Fonseca 42). *Colorindo,* which is the gerundive form of the verb *colorir*, has several meanings. On the one hand, it can simply mean to give color to something. But an object that is *colorido* can be either "colorful" or "multicolored." Regardless of how one interprets colorindo, however, the adverb "Blackly" (recall the distinction between preto and negro) nevertheless functions as the most significant word of the phrase. Afro-Brazilian writing is marked not by the skin color of the person penning the text, but rather by the "unique and metaphorical" perspective it adopts of the world. Consider how Conceição Evaristo[10]—writer and longtime collaborator of Alves—echoes Camargo's ideas in a description of her development as a writer:

> I believe that the genesis of my writing came out of the accumulation of everything I heard since my infancy . . . I would close my eyes . . . and then I turned on all of my other senses. My whole body received words, sounds, murmurs, voices that were laced with pleasure or pain. . . . With my eyes closed, I would mould the faces of my characters, real and speaking. It was a game of writing in the dark. In the body of night. (Duarte and Fonseca 390)

Evaristo marks the "beginning" of her writing process with the closing of her eyes and "turning on" of her senses so that her "whole body" might receive the sound-images of her texts. It is no accident that Evaristo draws on the double entendre of writing "in the dark"; like Camargo, she undermines the pejorative associations with vision impairment and black identity to involve the whole of her body in creating a perspective of the world that is colored Blackly.

As we have seen, assuming a black vision necessitates redefining vision itself. In fact, we would do well to take the notion of seeing Blackly as a critical response to the "second sight" of double consciousness so famously elaborated by W.E.B. Du Bois in *The Souls of Black Folk*. For Du Bois, an African American person is "born with a veil and gifted with a second sight"—a double consciousness that gives him or her the "sense of always looking at [his/her] self through the eyes of others" (qtd. in Gilroy 134). According to Paul Gilroy, Du Bois is ambivalent about the implications of that second sight, suggesting variously that it either hinders or empowers black Americans. Gilroy glibly remarks that, "it matters little . . . whether this 'second sight' is a true privilege rather than some sort of disability" (134). Here he too quickly casts the internalization of racist ideologies as a visual impairment, espousing a variant of epistemological ocularcentrism that he perhaps does not intend (i.e., one must "see" one's Self completely in order to know it). Indeed, it matters a great deal whether we interpret second sight as a privilege or a disability, and the choice sets up a false and pejorative dichotomy. The notion of seeing Blackly reminds us that rather than being a convenient or tangential metaphor for conceptualizing blackness, disability is instead fundamental to it.

If we are to move away from the notion that people of African descent are merely "victims of a physical darkness," we must likewise move away from the idea that people with visual impairment are "victims" in the same sense. Following Brent R. Henze, "Outsiders wishing to support the liberatory work of the oppressed,"—and here we might recall that the category "outsiders" may include oppressed individuals depending how the term "oppressed" is defined—"must form responsible and imaginative alliances . . . grounded in appropriate reconceptions of their experiences in relation to others" (qtd. in Sandahl 600). In other words, rather than celebrate texts that make "*imaginary* identifications" that allege a "sameness" between people "without regard for the real differences in [their] experiences and lives," we might take Alves's work and *The Black Book of Colors* as models for how to make "*imaginative* identifications of ourselves with others." These texts encourage us to "interrogate our own experience, seeking points where common ground or empathy might be actively constructed between us while remaining conscious of the real differences" (600). To color something Blackly, to assume blackness, to write and read about the world as if everyone had access to metaphor, regardless of their degree of sightedness: these are practical capacities that encompass the language of vision-as-knowledge without simply depending on it.

## Notes

1. Refer to Editora Nova edition of *Anjo Negro* (2012). Unless otherwise noted, all translations from Portuguese are mine.

2. I limit my discussion of race in this chapter to African descendants in the Americas. As such, the conclusions derived in this chapter may or may not apply to other groups of people in the Americas or elsewhere who do not identify as white.

3. *The Black Book of Colors*, written originally in Spanish by Venezuelan authors Menena Cottin and Rosana Faría, is a children's book that has been translated into various languages, including English. Here I use the Portuguese edition published in Brazil. All translations are my own and may differ from the published English translation of the book.

4. Over the course of the nineteenth century, Brazil sought to consolidate national identity by producing a "new race" (*a raça nova*) that would result in a mixed population. In the twentieth century, the sociologist Gilberto Freyre theorized the history of race relations in Brazil as the foundation for a "racial democracy" (*a democraçia racial*). Despite the horrors of enslavement, Freyre contended that as a result of the conjugal relations and physical proximity endemic to slave labor, Brazil would become a country free of racism. Throughout the twentieth century, leaders, citizens, and foreigners alike claimed that Brazil was a "racial paradise."

5. Discussions of racism and white privilege in Brazil, though present throughout the twentieth century, have increased dramatically over the past decade. As Sales Augosto dos Santos has argued, the notion of Brazil as a "racial democracy" had largely fallen out of favor by the end of the twentieth century. When Afro-Brazilian activist groups began demanding social change in the form of affirmative action policies, the "racial democracy" theory experienced a revival and was attached to particularly vitriolic attacks on the ideas behind affirmative action. Although Brazilians may now be more likely to admit to the existence of racial prejudice and privilege, many resist the idea that races can be neatly divided in the country and suggest that race-based policies are therefore ineffective.

6. To be clear: just because identity traits are "assumed" in Brazil does not mean that people don't try to "out" one another.

7. Okorafor-Mbachu indicates that she takes this definition from a talk given by Steve Barnes at the Clarion East Science Fiction and Fantasy Writers' Workshop in 2001.

8. Kennith Jarnigan and Carrie Sandahl have examined common tropes of blind characters in literature and film. Jarnigan identifies one trope, "blindness as compensatory or miraculous power," that is perhaps closest to the notion of a Magical Blind Person.

9. Though Alves never explicitly states that Flora is white, her privilege makes itself apparent at various points in the story. The title suggests that Flora is not black, or at least that race is not her most prominent feature—a privilege of invisibility consistent with whiteness. Neither the third-person narrator nor the characters intimate that Flora shares Cécilia's experiences of race-based prejudice. If Flora is not white, her blindness effectively renders her so.

10. Evaristo is arguably the most well-known contemporary Afro-Brazilian author. Scholars have yet to examine fully the intersection of disability and Afro-Brazilian identity in her celebrated first novel, *Ponciá Vicêncio* (2003).

## Works Cited

Alves, Miriam. "A Cega e a Negra—Uma Fábula." *Mulher Mat(r)iz*. Belo Horizonte, Brazil: Nandyala, 2011, 32–36.

Bell, Christopher. "Introducing White Disability Studies: A Modest Proposal." In *Disability Studies Reader*, 2nd ed. Edited by Lennard Davis. London: Routledge, 2006, 275–282.

Bolt, David. "From blindness to visual impairment: terminological typology and the Social Model of Disability." *Disability & Society* 20.5 (2006): 539–552.

Boster, Dea Hadley. "Unfit for Bondage: Disability and African American slavery in the United States, 1800–1860." PhD Thesis, University of Michigan, 2010. Proquest.

Carmo, Claudio Marcio de. Personal communication. December 3, 2014.

Conrad, Robert E. *Children of God's Fire: A Documentary History of Black Slavery in Brazil.* University Park: Pennsylvania State UP, 1994.

Cottin, Menena, and Faría, Rosana. *O Livro Negro das Cores*. Translated by Rafaella Lemos. Rio de Janeiro: Pallas Editora, 2011.

De Figueiredo, Fernanda Rodrigues. "A mulher negra nos *Cadernos Negros*: autoria e representçōes." MA thesis Universidade Federal de Minas Gerais, 2006. Web. November 1, 2012.

De Nascimento, Abdias. "Teatro experimental do negro: trajetória e reflexões." *Estudos Avançados* 18.50 (January/April 2004): n.p. Web. November 1, 2012.

Duarte, Eduardo d. A., and Fonseca, Maria N. S. *Literatura e Afrodescendência no Brasil: antologia crítica; Volume 4: História, teoria, polêmica*. Belo Horizonte, Brazil: Editora UFMG, 2011.

Erevelles, Nirmala. *Disability and Difference in Global Contexts: Enabling a Transformative Body Politic*. New York: Palgrave Macmillan, 2011.

Godoy, Vera. "Elizete, um olhar sobre a literature infantil" (presentation, IV Colóquio Mulheres em Letras, Belo Horizonte, May 31, 2012).

Jarnigan, Kenneth. "Blindness: Is Literature Against Us?" National Federation of the Blind Annual Convention. Chicago, July 3, 1974.

Kriegel, Leonard. "Uncle Tom and Tiny Tim: Some Reflections on the Cripple as Negro." *American Scholar* 38.3 (1969): 412–430.

Lemon, Alex. "And Now I See." In *Beauty is a Verb: The New Poetry of Disability*. Edited by Jennifer Bartlett, Sheila Black, and Michael Northen. El Paso, TX: Cinco Puntos Press, 2011, 167–168.

Martins, Leda Maria. *Afrografias da Memória*. Belo Horizonte: Mazza Edições, 1997.

McRuer, Robert. *Crip Theory: Cultural Signs of Queerness and Disability*. New York: New York UP, 2006.

Mitchell, David T., and Sharon L Snyder. *Narrative Prosthesis: Disability and the Dependencies of Discourse*. Ann Arbor: U of Michigan P, 2001.

Nascimento, Gizêlda Melo. "Grandes Mães, Reais Senhoras." In *Guereirras de Natureza: Mulher negra, religiosidade e ambiente*. Edited by E. L. Nascimento. São Paulo: Selo Negro, 2008.

Newman, Adam. "Introducing Black Disability Studies: A Modest Beginning." *Disability Studies Quarterly* 32.2 (2012). n.p. Web. April 14, 2013.

Okorafor-Mbachu, Nnedi. "Stephen King's Super-Duper Magical Negroes." n.p. October 25, 2004. Web. November 1, 2012.

Rodrigues, Nelson. *Anjo Negro*. Rio de Janeiro: Editora Nova Fronteira.: 2012. New edition of 1946 text.

Sandahl, Carrie. "Black Man, Blind Man: Disability Identity Politics and Performance." *Theatre Journal* 56.4 (2004): 579–602.

Tanya Titchkosky. *Reading and Writing Disability Differently: The Textured Life of Embodiment*. Toronto: U of Toronto P, 2007.

Chapter 10

# Mythicizing Disability

## The Life and Opinions of *(what is left of)* Estamira

Nicola Gavioli

### Foreword

*I write about a dead person, Estamira Gomes de Sousa (1941–2011), who would have hardly had access to this essay or been able to engage in conversation with me. Perhaps these notes on ethics and testimony might have sounded lofty to her ears. Estamira's life and opinions—the core of an eponymous Brazilian documentary by Marcos Prado—are now the subject of academic discourse. Questioning the choices by which a filmmaker gives shape to his material does not protect me from criticism: the concern I have about using the portrayal of a real person for academic purposes, abstracting from real-life experience, pervades this study. Although Estamira's voiceover permeates the two-hour documentary, her "voice" remains remote. I hope in this project to honor some of Estamira's lived experience, even as it is dissected in Prado's filmic biography.*

*Recently, a friend who works in the film industry brought to my attention how common it is in Q&A sessions to find hard-core activists in the audience focusing more on the integrity of the director rather than the filmmaking itself. These questions are the favorite domain of the ignoramuses, my friend cynically argued. "They have no clue about the art of the documentary." I could not disagree more with his essentialist perspective (not to mention his trivialization of ethical concerns). What about the real lives of the film subjects, their need for privacy and the imperative to seek consent, a question that becomes especially salient in the case of people with mental disabilities?*

## Introduction

"The doctor asked me if I still hear the voices. I hear the stars, the things, the presentiment of things." The documentary *Estamira* (Brazil, 2004) by Marcos Prado is a repository of poetic intuitions (and enigmas) emphatically delivered in flashes by an old woman who spent many years collecting garbage in the infamous Jardim Gramacho, a dump near Rio de Janeiro, recently closed.[1] Diagnosed as mentally ill, Estamira is regarded by her community as a living question mark. Workers and relatives know all too well that one wrong word can detonate an inflammatory reaction. Estamira's speeches, belligerent monologues addressed to God and nature with frequent and sudden explosions of rage and profanity, touch universal themes—the meaning of life, the fall from grace of humankind, the existence of hidden truths behind appearances in the natural environment—but they also engage in secular matters, such as how psychiatry sedates patients through the consumption of pharmaceuticals. The index of her biography displays unhealed guilt over her mother's internment in a squalid mental institution, a gallery of turbulent encounters with men, episodes of abuse, betrayals by her husband, and the experience of a painful mental condition.

After its theatrical distribution, *Estamira* was commercialized in a package of two DVDs, containing interviews with the director, the crew, a second complementary film, *Estamira para Todos e para Ninguém*, and unusual extras, like a collection of Estamira's best roaring laughs ("Gargalhadas Estamirais"). The mythopoetic operation by Marcos Prado and producer José Padilha gave rise to an award-winning play, *Estamira-Beira do Mundo*, directed by Beatriz Sayad, interpreted by actress Dani Barros. These manufactured representations of Estamira, a person both culturally and physically dislocated from the edit rooms of the entertainment industry, strive to mold the life of a human being into a mythical form. This chapter reflects on the ethical issues inherent in filmmaking disability through the contradictions, problematic aesthetic choices and incoherencies among materials. The core issue explores what is left of Estamira, a witness of her own mental and material conditions. Is the act of exposing oneself on camera sufficient to meaningfully bear testimony? Is her consent merely implied? Finally, does her filmic representation reinforce, subvert, or vacillate between stereotypes of disability?

## Ethical Criticism and Documentary: Is the Implied Author of Estamira Going Solo?

Literary critic Wayne C. Booth has observed the fundamental misconception about ethical criticism in his essay "Why Ethical Criticism Can Never Be

Simple:" *in pectore*, ethical critics are would-be censors of true art. Notoriously, Oscar Wilde could not tolerate this category of judgmental readers. Nevertheless, this is a simple-minded notion of what it means to engage in an ethical reading of a text. As Booth explains, "Of all the mistakes made by the enemies of ethical criticism, the most absurd is failing to recognize that a great proportion of what we call literary works are not only implicitly ethical . . . but explicitly designed to elicit ethical responses" (30). Not all works of literature ask readers to prioritize ethical inquiry with the same intensity. Nevertheless, ignoring the political message in George Orwell's *1984* or the solicitation to listen and react to Toni Morrison's *Beloved*'s "ever-present penetrating thought" would be "offensive to the author–at least to the implied author" (31). Resisting the invitation to focus on ethical matters is akin to amputating these texts at their core. It is unlikely that neutrality inhabits a text, even one considered "above morality or immune to ethical criticism" (33). How can the author's gaze be neutral? Or: How and why should we avoid recognizing a peculiarity of tone, an idea about the world, expressed at least in the phantasmatic implied author? Even though Booth refers to literature, we can extend his reflections to the art of film and, more particularly, to the domain of documentaries in which understanding the director's intentions is indeed relevant to shaping the critical debate and positioning the audience. The focus on the narrator and author(s)' intentions and responsibility is intensified in the art of the documentary, in which the protagonists not only evoke, obliquely and metonymically, real people but are recognizable individuals (although documentary filmmaking also embraces fictional elements as a tool for narrative). Subaltern people, minorities, struggling individuals are often chosen as privileged subjects in contemporary documentaries (Oscar-winner short *Inocente*, 2012; *To Be Heard*, 2010; and *Dzi Croquettes*, 2009 are three recent and notable examples). They may tell incisive, inspiring, and surprising stories. Their points of view are unusual and sometimes underrepresented in society and other media. Disability is one of these categories.[2] How might one address the representation of disabled people in documentary through an ethical reading approach? And who practices this form of criticism in Brazil? In recent years, the preoccupation with ethical issues in literature, cinema, and other arts has gradually grown in Brazil. The society finds itself at a political juncture in which the demand for shedding light on the years of military dictatorship has allowed for the appearance of forms of criticism concerned with human rights and the representation of silenced and abused individuals. Paradigmatic in this sense is the collective work *Escritas da Violência (Projeto Temático* FAPESP 2006–2010), coordinated by Márcio Seligmann-Silva, Francisco Foot Hardman, and Jaime Ginzburg, which originated two edited volumes in 2012. The scholarly work of Jaime Ginzburg, in particular, has given emphasis to the enduring authoritarian tendencies subtly or proudly displayed in Brazilian culture, from the poetry by José de Anchieta to popular movies by contemporary filmmakers. The recent debate over Monteiro Lobato, a beloved children's storyteller for generations, and his "Negrinha" and *Caçadas do Pedrinho*, stories that are embedded in racial prejudice, gained new weight after the publication of Monteiro Lobato's correspondence displaying sympathies for racist organizations and approval for eugenic theories.[3] From now on, approaching "Negrinha" without considering the agenda of its historical creator looks like a hypocritical omission and an ideological gesture. In "Negrinha" we can trace a coherent continuity between the author's ideas and the text. The focus on hidden meanings, ideology, and values in the text by an "implied author" appears to us as irrevocably and rightly conditioned by what we know through historical documentation. More interesting is to consider works of literature and cinema in which this extra-textual information (in this case, Marcos Prado's interview) seems to collide with aspects of the work itself. This is particularly relevant in social-issue documentaries.

In this chapter, after revealing incoherencies between Marcos Prado's verbal statements and the implied author's fluid purposes through the film, I focus on Estamira's self-expression through personal and enigmatic codes of communication, both verbal and nonverbal, which I read as testimonial acts by a socially subaltern, physically abused, and mentally ill woman. In particular, through a disability studies reading, I question whether capturing on camera and technically highlighting the subject's moments of secret communication replicates and reinforces negative stereotypes about disability or contributes to a new approach entirely. With *Estamira*, Marcos Prado offers strong material for reflecting on the intersecting dilemmas of authorship, ethics, and disability representation.

Marcos Prado began documenting the biggest dump in Brazil in the photographic volume *Jardim Gramacho* (2004). During the preparation for this volume, completed over an entire decade, Prado met Estamira. On the official website of the movie, Prado recalls this encounter in a written statement (in English) about the origin of his documentary: "I approached her asking if I could take her portrait. She consented and told me she had lots of 'things' to say to me: 'my mission is to reveal and reclaim the truth,' 'you are common, I am not.' . . ." Prado describes his serendipitous encounter with Estamira as giving insight to his initial conception: "The first motivation I had on doing this film was Estamira's life and existence. Living like a *prophet* of the dump, screaming out the values lost in our society, fighting against religion, sanity, hypocrisy, creating neologism and poetic philosophical metaphors to express herself" (my emphasis). In this short description, the emphasis on the subject's linguistic creativity and the choice of the word "prophet" are significant. Representing the mentally ill as individuals speaking in strange and unconventional ways is a stereotype and a recurring artistic trope. Sander L. Gilman writes about the persistent stigmatization of different "Others" through history on the basis of the general perception of a different way of speaking. The mentally ill have been represented for centuries as individuals who express bizarre and at times prophetic utterances in odd languages (242). Whether consciously or not, Marcos Prado followed in his documentary a stereotypical association between disability and prophecy, although he claimed that what he saw in Estamira was primarily an inspired creative mind, and secondarily a woman with a mental disorder.

Prado's written statement reveals his vision for this project: a character-driven documentary wrapped up in a mystical atmosphere. Nevertheless, the direction of the film changed course, as Prado suggests: "In the beginning of the shootings I discovered Estamira was starting a public psychiatric treatment with medicines for the first time in her life. That was one of the reasons that made me believe I had to spend a long time following her. *I wanted to see the results of the medicine in someone living in such conditions as Estamira*" (my emphasis). The character-driven portraiture is gradually replaced by another vision. Estamira becomes the vehicle for addressing broader issues: mental health, medicine, poverty, and marginality.

The long interview with Marcos Prado demonstrates the director's high level of awareness about possible critiques of *Estamira.* He systematically anticipates questions and concerns related to the ethics of his filmmaking. Prado emphatically addresses an unseen interviewer saying "Don't even ask me" about ethics, as if this aspect were an obvious imperative for him since the very start. This staged Q&A is a strategically crafted *captatio benevolentiae*, an archive of good intentions, aiming to reinforce the idea of Estamira's resolute agency through the project and to explain the coherence between aesthetic choices and content of the film. These are Prado's words on these two delicate aspects:

A. Aesthetic "excess"

> The narrative of the film is entirely poetic, philosophical. For this reason, any excess of beauty, of beautification, of aesthetics, of perfection would be allowed. Of course if it was a film with no parallel narrative in contact with the excess of aesthetics, I think

> it would be bothersome. But the film largely follows Estamira's magic, poetic speeches, with her cosmology of life . . .

As Prado has also remarked, the opening song, "Janela de apartamento," by Décio Rocha, evocative and unsettling, is considered "a metaphor for the entire film . . . all this juncture of beautiful images, intense songs and Estamira's anthologic and magic narrative, all that makes up this film that leads you, if you give yourself to it, to unknown places." Marcos Prado defends his artistic choices as a faithful representation of Estamira's cosmology. Vortexes of clouds, flames of fires, dramatic skies and landscapes, black and white grainy shots, a pseudo-archaic preverbal litany all contribute to re-create Estamira's perception of the world. For Prado, the truth of the film resides precisely in the baroque display of its larger-than-life artificiality that endeavors to evoke Estamira's inner world. At moments, the operation verges on romanticizing mental illness as an overwhelming poetic furor engaged in a struggle against the universe. Prado's poetics seem close to the ideas of German director Werner Herzog, who wrote on the art of documentary filmmaking that "There are deeper strata of truth in cinema, and there is such a thing as poetic, ecstatic truth. It is mysterious and elusive, and can be reached only through fabrication and imagination and stylization."[4] However, if we compare Prado's vision and words with the final film, we hardly find coherence. At moments, the search for beauty—which Prado locates in the orchestration of larger-than-life visual effects and poetic metaphors—goes astray, displaying a taste for abjection and the representation of repulsive details, such as the focus on trash as nutrition and sustenance for Estamira and her family.[5] As a result, the film suffers an identity crisis, as it follows diverging aesthetic paths. The implied author's purposes (and values) inscribed in this project look fluid, unstable, and contradictory if confronted with the statements by Marcos Prado. As noted earlier, a second crucial aspect is addressed in the interview. The director reiterates that the genesis of his artistic project is legitimated by the approval (and "predisposition") of the film subject.

B. Estamira's agency

> In 2000, I realized that there were photos that could tell the story. What was lacking was getting a bit closer to the people. And during that visit in 2000, with this goal in mind, I found a lady sitting in her campsite. I asked her permission to take a picture of her. She gladly consented and said: "Sure you can,

> but then you sit here by my side because I wanna talk to you."
> This lady was D. Estamira.

In the straightforward recollection of their first encounter, the director introduces elements of a fairy-tale narrative ("She told me she lived in a castle all decorated with things taken from the trash"). He characterizes Estamira as the possessor of a mysterious wisdom ("She began to sound more metaphysical"). For Prado, Estamira is *constantly* extraordinary. Sometime later, Marcos Prado visits Estamira at her *barraquinho*:

> I kept D. Estamira in my mind for more or less than a month thinking what a fantastic woman she was. I wanted to make a documentary about her. I started looking for her. . . . Finally I arrived at her home. . . . D. Estamira turned and said to me: "You came late but you don't fail." I told her "I came here to ask for your permission to make a movie about your life." She said: "I have been waiting for this for a long time." . . . There was a predisposition in D. Estamira in wanting to tell her story.

Estamira's serendipitous willingness to participate in the project, a long-awaited occasion by her as Prado describes it, is presented as a sign of destiny. Between the lines it is suggested that Estamira welcomed both Prado *and* his vision for the film. Nevertheless, Prado's relaxed and seemingly unproblematic recollection of the spontaneous approval by Estamira raises the fundamental question of informed consent in documentary filmmaking.

## Informed Consent, Documentary, Disability: Estamira on the Phone

The debate on the ethics of documentary filmmaking is complex. The 2009 study "Honest Truth: Documentary Filmmakers on Ethical Challenges in Their Work" by eminent documentary scholars Patrícia Aufderhaide, Peter Jaszi, and Mridu Chandra presents the results of forty-five interviews with documentary professionals. According to the authors of the study, many filmmakers share a common uncertainty: "They daily felt the lack of clarity and standards in ethical practice. They also lacked support for ethical deliberation under typical work pressures" (2). This fascinating study offers examples of critical moments in which directors had to choose whether to shoot a great scene or protect their subjects. Some filmmakers confess experiencing regret over such decisions (3).

In the relationship between filmmaker and subjects there are crucial variables involving power and mutual trust. To what degree is a filmmaker responsible for respecting the people who provide the stories she or he needs? Informed consent is the backbone of this relationship: subjects must be informed of the purposes of a project and consciously and autonomously decide to be on camera. According to scholar Kate Nash, "While there is a growing body of research focused on the documentary maker, relatively little is known about the participant's experience of documentary production or the interpersonal relationships on which documentary depends" (2). The issue of informed consent is essential but not simple. In *Introduction to Documentary*, film professor Bill Nichols shows the inherent complexities of this principle: "Of exactly what consequences or risks should filmmakers inform their subjects? To what extent can the filmmaker honestly reveal his or her intentions or foretell the actual effects of a film when some intentions are unconscious and many effects are unpredictable?" (54). These already challenging questions get exponentially more complicated when the participants are diagnosed as mentally ill individuals. How properly *informed* is this category of subjects? How do they process and understand this information? Is there real intention in the consent they give? How does the filmmaker perceive the participants' ability to give consent?

Insisting on Estamira's agency in the already mentioned interview, director Marcos Prado asks: "Is it unethical to film a person who has no self-control? D. Estamira was completely free to come, go and do whatever she wanted, by herself. . . . Although diagnosed mad, D. Estamira is not mad. She has a very lucid mind." In two moments in the film, Estamira affirms that "I can distinguish mental disturbance" and "mental disturbance is not a disability, right?" Estamira's disability does not cut her off completely from conventional reality. She demonstrates awareness and insight about her condition. She shows the urgency of delivering an important message. The director is not stealing her story: Estamira is present, engaged in conversation, looking straight at the camera. In this instance, then, informed consent is a more nuanced matter than, say, in Werner Herzog's *Land of Silence and Darkness* (1971), a gripping documentary on different forms of physical and mental disability. A long scene in Herzog's movie captures a moment in the life of Vladimir Kokol, a twenty-two-year-old deaf and blind boy who received no special training to adapt to his disabilities. "It was never tried to awaken him," the director informs us. Vladimir cannot walk and cannot communicate with the external world. He lies on the floor, stands up, produces unarticulated sounds with his lips, picks up a ball and beats himself with it. All of Vladimir's gestures respond to solicitations from his inaccessible inner world. Herzog gives us an extreme example in which informed consent by a subject is unattainable. Originating from a fundamental lack, Herzog's decision to keep the scene blurs boundaries: it is both an act of exclusion and a call for exception in the name of a higher educational cause. The issue of informed consent is problematic in *Estamira*. Some scenes show disruption of the pact between Marcos Prado and Estamira:

A. In a moment of anger, Estamira shows her lower back in front of the camera. Although the gesture has no shock value per se, and the nudity revealed is motivated by the protagonist's dramatic memories of a medical surgery, questions are raised about whether Estamira *wanted* this moment immortalized on camera.

B. Several members of Estamira's family are interviewed on camera. They broaden the audience's understanding of the documentary subject, presenting anecdotes about her life *before and beyond* her disability. Nevertheless, as Marcos Prado disclosed ("Entrevista com o diretor"), Estamira was not initially aware of her family's participation in the project and, as a consequence, she became deeply disappointed with Prado. She was not estranged from her family, but she resented the lack of information. How did Prado convince the subject's family to participate? Was there monetary contribution involved? Are the words of relatives necessarily reliable and accurate in telling Estamira's stories?

C. Several scenes in the film reveal Estamira losing control. This happens whenever people in her family mention the name God or Jesus. She screams aloud and insults anybody who dares to contradict her about religious matters. These private moments seem less problematic, however, than the scene in which Estamira appears totally disconnected from reality, captured in a trance, with her eyes searching for an indefinite object. The camera meticulously captures this moment through extreme close-ups of her face and mouth. In the following scene, she is "visited" by an invisible presence calling for her attention. She pieces together a phone from the surrounding trash and starts communicating out loud in an unintelligible private code. The phone call lasts for nearly two minutes in which Estamira's mood transitions from aggressive

> to surprised and finally content. The communication with the director is abruptly broken. During this time, it appears that Estamira is not the same individual who made a pact with Marcos Prado. The director focuses on her delirium, offering a shocking and memorable scene for the audience at the expense of Estamira's consent. Prado claimed that Estamira was the first person to watch the final version of the film. She was invited for a private screening and left alone in the room. Interestingly, she claimed she did not remember being in some of the scenes shown to her ("Entrevista com o diretor").

Editing material for a documentary project is often focused on the construction of a narrative. The editor is a storyteller who selects and re-creates stories and characters according to various factors: personal aesthetics, sensitivity, ideology, and even marketing strategies. In this laboratory of manipulation, the subjects of a documentary may be particularly affected by choices that escape their control. As G. Thomas Couser writes, in reference to the related context of life writing, "Co-authoring another's life can be a creative or a destructive act, a service or a disservice, an homage or an appropriation" (36). Couser emphasizes how the vulnerability of the subjects can be the result of different levels of imbalance: "in race, culture, gender, class, age, or (in the case of narratives of illness or disability) somatic, intellectual, or emotional . . ." (37). Filmmakers know that there are risks involved. After the release of a documentary film, subjects can express their complaint through the media: frustration, disappointment, and resentment. They can denounce on TV, or write letters to newspapers claiming they were betrayed. In the majority of cases, the documentary continues its commercial life without being touched by these polemics: it is in fact common practice for the director, before or after shooting interviews, to ask subjects to sign a release form that authorizes free artistic work based on their stories. What we know about Estamira's reactions to the film is a collection of quotes and anecdotes that Prado reported. Disapproval of the final project by Estamira is entirely hypothetical. Even so, we might wonder whether the media would have treated her as capable of expressing criticism based on factual experience or rather as a fundamentally unreliable individual living in a fantasy world. If the goal of *Estamira* was to present a portrait of an extraordinary individual, it achieved this through radically alienating the subject from her own image on screen. This scission is an example of what German philosopher Günther Anders described as a "phantom" relation. Anders's study focused on the effects of television and radio on mass consumers and is a precursor to contemporary debates on the effects of visual arts and the Internet on their audiences. Anders's commentary on the media's influence on the individual is prophetic: "When the world is perceivable, but no more than that, i.e. not subject to our action, we are transformed into eavesdroppers and Peeping Toms" (20). Estamira and her disability emerge as an exception, a freak show, a curiosity, a possibility of life from which the majority of viewers was spared, a dark fairy tale with an opaque agenda that does not call for real intervention. Did Estamira herself, alone in her private screening room, perceive the film as an *interesting* and *unusual* product with special visual effects and some fascinating lines? For Anders,

> —When the event is no longer attached to a specific location and can be reproduced virtually any number of times, it acquires the characteristics of an assembly-line product; and when we pay for having it delivered to our homes, it is a commodity.
>
> —When the actual event is socially important only in its reproduced form, i.e., as a spectacle, the difference between being and appearance, between reality and image of reality, is abolished. (20)

The metamorphosis of Estamira into a character is apparent in the extra "Gargalhadas Estamirais," a collection of the very "best moments" of Estamira's laughs. Close-ups of her face, de-contextualized repetitions, and funny sympathy-seeking sketches are all utterly disembodied. The documentary subject disintegrates into abstraction. She is even molded into an adjective: *Estamiral.*

Anders's notes on media are further relevant to Estamira's story. The adaptation of *Estamira* into a stage play by Beatriz Sayad is a predictable follow-up to Marcos Prado's documentary. Not the repetition by media, but the representations on stage turn Estamira's story into a commodity. When the stage curtain drops, is it the words or the human experience of Estamira (the poverty, the disease) that resonate in the audience's memory? After *Medea, King Lear*, and Beckett's Winnie: the memorable drama of Estamira in the events calendar.

## Testimony: The Eloquence in the Hand

*Estamira* also endeavors to be a film of testimony, akin to Spanish American *testimonio* narratives. Focusing on an exceptional character is an occasion to address the larger issues of poverty, marginalization, and mental disorder in contemporary Brazil. This programmatic choice by Prado is what I would call the first level of testimony present in the film: a *filtered* or *manufactured* testimony. Prado's film finds its own justification in addressing urgent matters through beautiful shot-making. Estamira's speeches denounce various forms of abuse. The most salient is violence against women perpetrated by men, and especially fathers and husbands. During several periods in her life, Estamira experienced episodes of sexual exploitation and betrayal. Vivid memories of these abuses shape her visceral attacks against male domination and, in particular, against God, the quintessential representative of patriarchy.

Estamira complains about the devastating effects that capitalist consumerism has on the environment and on human beings. Urban populations waste goods and resources that eventually find their way to Jardim Gramacho, where "invisible" workers risk their health picking through mounds of trash. The social dimension of the documentary is amplified in a second video created by Marcos Prado and included in the extra of the film: *Estamira Para Todos e Para Ninguém.* Estamira is presented here as a more down-to-earth individual, able to articulate coherently and express political messages. For example, she recalls having sent a letter to former president José Sarney inquiring about why the majority of Brazilian citizens were living less freely than the military minority. This video juxtaposes the voice of Estamira with that of other workers and subalterns of society. The result is a collection of micro-portraits in which the themes of social injustice, race-based discrimination, and unemployment emerge. *Estamira Para Todos e Para Ninguém* focuses on the material aspects of working in Jardim Gramacho, on the heavy chores and the miserable remuneration. There is no future here, says one of the youngsters. The video emphasizes practical challenges such as eating trash for survival and avoiding contact with health-threatening hospital waste.

*Estamira* and *Estamira Para Todos e Para Ninguém* dramatically address the issue of mental illness in Brazilian society. One psychiatric patient shares her overwhelming anxiety in relation to hospitals and doctors. She fears her family will ultimately relocate her to a mental institution. "Illness can reach anybody," she complains. She believes a malignant red flower in the house is responsible for her disgrace. This subject plays as counterpoint to Estamira, who expresses her rage against the drugs that her doctor prescribes. After a visit with her psychiatrist at the José Miller Psychosocial Clinic, Estamira shows the pills that are prescribed to her. These pills, Estamira claims, do not help. On the contrary, they make her feel worse. "I am not a robot of blood, I am not a robot." This is one of the strongest scenes in the film: Estamira's speech resembles a political attack on pharmaceutical cures and the lack of true empathy among health care providers. Estamira's distrust grows, exploding in the scene:

> My doctor prescribed the remedy for anger (*laughs*). I was very disappointed, very sad. Very deeply angry at her for saying such a thing. And you know what she said? . . . That it is magic, telepathy, media and the fuck. . . . She offended me way too much. . . . I know doctors, doctors, doctors . . . good ones. She is a copycat. I am her friend, I like her. I like everybody, but she is a copycat. They are, you know, doing what? Doping whoever, with only one drug. They cannot do it. The remedy wants to know more than Estamira? Pay attention. About the remedy I say: Do you feel well? Then stop it. Give it a break. If it hurts, go there to complain, as I did three times. At the fourth time they received me . . . they create addictions, doping . . . the amount of medication, all has a limit . . . dope to blind people.

In Estamira's account, Doctor Alice mixes science with irrational references to magic. Alice is called a copycat: her speech and her cures are unoriginal and predictable. The visit and subsequent prescription are perceived as a violent imposition. Estamira refuses to be explained by and reduced to a category taken from the psychiatry manual. This scene works to differentiate this documentary from many "impairment-oriented films" in which "the individual with an impairment becomes circumscribed by his or her body" (Darke 103). Prado leaves a space for his subject to express doubts about the nature of her mental condition and about the efficacy of standard medical prescriptions. Estamira's complaint might be seen as a reaction against the passive acceptance of an essentialist definition of herself molded by the medical and the social discourses. Doctor Alice is considered a copycat by her patient because she seems to repeat a script. The patient's critique against standard cures (or "doping") leads the viewers to pay attention to the problematic line between *being* and *being perceived* mentally incapable. If Estamira can articulate her precise critique, whereas medicine classifies her as insane, the audience is asked to reflect on and contest the limits of "shared cultural scripts of disability" (Snyder, Mitchell 186) that often equate mental illness with utter passivity. Prado's film suggests that there are variations within the generic category of madness, challenging the cultural binary between sanity and insanity. As Shayda Kafai efficaciously illuminates there is a fluidity in madness that is often obscured by the repetition of stereotypes and by self-censorship: "The stigmas of madness, the falsity of the sane/

mad binary and the assumption that one cannot exist simultaneously in the border spaces of sanity and madness are all perpetuated by silence . . ." (9). Estamira exemplifies the concept of "mad border body" (Kafai 1): although ill, she is a vital character, opinionated, fighting to be treated with respect, content at times, and capable of work. In addition, her mix of metaphors, virulent and abrupt verbal attacks, colorful expressions, syncopated sounds and neologisms give shape to a rich language: a fascinating, strange and irreproducible form of communication. As Tobin Siebers puts it, "disability aesthetics embraces beauty that seems by traditional standards to be broken, and yet it is not less beautiful . . . disability enlarges our vision of human variation and difference" (3). The film does not suggest that death would liberate Estamira from the burden of living, as if she were irremediably damaged by illness, a message that other films on disabilities convey (Darke). Although the film does not seem to advocate demedicalization of mentally ill patients, Estamira's blast against doctors is also accompanied by black and white images showing queues of people waiting to be treated outside the José Miller clinic. Emphasizing the slow movement of a multitude of patients asking to be heard and *saved* by doctors, as if on a pilgrimage, the director raises interesting questions: how much attention and time does each patient receive? Are psycho-pharmaceuticals prescribed after accurate diagnoses? What happens in the doctor-patient relationship when patients refuse to follow the medical prescriptions?

The film touches on a variety of relevant issues; nevertheless, the lack of focus weakens its testimonial power. Estamira is invested by her biographer in too many endeavors: she is a prophetess and an oral poet, the denouncer of different human wrongdoings and the communicator of the experience of her mental condition all together. Nevertheless, the film raises even more questions about a genuine act of testimony when Estamira is able to communicate the experience of illness. This channel of personal expression escapes even the director's control and is located in the mysterious gestures of Estamira's right hand and in the articulation of the sounds of an imaginary language (in which a few Portuguese words are discernible). Only she owns this space. "I have a computer in my finger," she explains, tracing invisible signs in the air. This form of nonverbal communication remains unexplored by the director. He scans Estamira's gestures in a few moments but it is apparent that he does not know how to incorporate them into his narrative(s). They are left as sporadic tics.

As philosopher Giorgio Agamben describes there are levels of testimony that camp survivors located in disorganized, unintelligible forms of expression. Agamben recalls the obscurity that Auschwitz survivor Primo Levi found in the poetry of Paul Celan, compared by him to "an inarticulate babble or the gasps of a dying man" (37). Later on: "In Auschwitz, Levi had already attempted to listen to and interpret an inarticulate babble, something like a non-language or a dark and maimed language" spoken by Hurbinek, a young child prisoner in the concentration camp. Agamben quotes from Levi's writings: "Hurbinek . . . was paralyzed from the waist down, with atrophied legs, as thin as sticks; but his eyes, lost in his triangular and wasted face, flashed terribly alive, full of demand, assertion, of the will to break loose, to shatter the tomb of his dumbness" (37). The passage from Levi talks about the double lacuna of testimony: while Hurbinek passed through mental and physical annihilation without a recognizably human language with which to communicate, Levi survived, and possessed a language (but lacked the full experience of destruction in the camp). Bearing witness must acknowledge the fundamental impossibility of bearing complete witness. Still, part of that experience can be communicated. Levi writes that Hurbinek "bears witness through these words of mine" (38). For Levi, it is by proxy that witnessing can occur, while Agamben further problematizes this issue, arguing that "whoever assumes the charge of bearing witness" in the name of *the drowned*, "knows that he or she must bear witness in the name of the impossibility of bearing witness" (34).

Marcos Prado cannot represent Estamira's experience by proxy: his film displays a confused agenda, meanders in too many directions, aims to produce wonder, often distracting from the testimony of Estamira's story of mistreatment and mental condition. In spite of that, whenever Estamira speaks her invented language or whenever she draws signs in the air, she seems to delineate a margin of freedom that eludes Prado's agenda and his supposed pact with her. The already mentioned phone call scene, presented by the filmmaker as shock-inducing, provides Estamira real space in the film to communicate freely, although in enigmatic and unconventional ways. Perhaps the imperfect translatability of Estamira's mental world into common language *is* the legacy that she leaves for the viewers of the film. Paradoxically, we may ask what is left intact of the "authentic" Estamira if not those impenetrable writing and speaking acts?

On the other hand, it would be disingenuous to consider this relative freedom of the documentary subject as untouched by the editing process. The director orchestrates all the elements of his film. What he cannot control and subvert are the articulation and the meaning of the sounds produced by his protagonist. The close-up of the face and mouth of Estamira while delivering her speech on the phone is also a problematic choice: invasive as it is, it gives preeminence to the character's secret code, directing the concentration of viewers exclusively on it. Prado determines both the inclusion and the long duration of this scene. The audience cannot deduce how often Estamira experiences similar episodes, but given the duration of the scene, common recurrence is implied. A disability studies–informed focus on cinema, as exemplified by the contributors to the volume *The Problem Body: Projecting Disability on Film*, refines our attention to the ambivalence of such a scene. The image of a woman speaking differently and in vehement tones with a nonexistent interlocutor might reinforce the association of Estamira with unintelligible or frightening alterity. On the other hand, the duration of the scene and the close-ups produce a counter-effect, gradually accompanying and disclosing a variety of emotional reactions by Estamira. The expressivity of her face and the changing tones of her voice appear to make her more familiar: she is recognizably a member of our community. Marcos Prado's *Estamira* offers much food for thought on the practice of documenting disability in contemporary Brazil. Prado's film is also paradigmatic of the possible contradictions between aesthetic aspirations of a director and the urgency of communication by a subject with disability. Crucial issues of power and trust between director and participants become more complex when the primary subject has been diagnosed as mentally disabled. Informed consent is, in these cases, an opaque territory that is difficult to delimit. This reading also reveals the complexity of determining whether *Estamira* contributes to the perpetuation of stereotypes, fears, and distortions about mental illness or to the presentation of disability as a human experience in which creativity and social commitment are kept alive.

## Notes

I would like to thank Thomas C. Shepard, Dante Noto, and Meg Moritz for their suggestions. All translations from the film and the extras are mine.

1. Jardim Gramacho was officially closed in June 2012.

2. Some notable examples of documentaries on disability are: *Twitch and Shout* (1993) by Laurel Chiten; *Freedom Machines* (2004) by Richard Cox, Janet Cole, and Jamie Stobie; *Murderball* (2005) by Henry Alex Rubin and Dana Adam Shapiro; *The Key of G* (2007) by Robert Arnold; *Praying with Lior* (2008) by Ilana Trachtman. Recent Brazilian documentaries on disability include: *Clarita* (2007) and *Dois Mundos* (2009) by Thereza Jessouroun; *Além da luz* (2010) by Yves Goulart; *Arte na Deficiência* (2010) by Carolina Pessôa. A good source for Brazilian short documentaries and feature films telling stories about disabilities is the website *Porta Curtas* (portacurtas.org.br).

3. Brazilian writer Ana Maria Gonçalves wrote a powerful piece on racism in the works of Monteiro Lobato and on the disingenuous attempts to defend Monteiro Lobato from criticism in "Carta Aberta ao Ziraldo" (www.idelberavelar.com/archives/2011/02/carta_aberta_ao_ziraldo_por_ana_maria_goncalves.php).

4. Serbian director Goran Radovanovič, *auteur provocateur*, represents the extremes of this search for a poetic truth in documentary filmmaking. In the 2009 interview "Art is a lie that makes us realize the truth" available online (*Doc online* website), Jeanete de Novais Rocha asked Mr. Radovanovič: "What kind of ethical problems could the use of reality cause as a background to construct your films?" He assertively replied: "Since I am an artist who wants to tell my artistic truth, there are no ethical problems. In my documentary films I am not trying to tell any other truth but artistic one. That is why I am not afraid to reconstruct and recreate the reality which is far away from the rough reality! In this sense there are no ethical problems that could appear during the process of documentary filmmaking. Ethical problems could only appear if my artistic manipulation of the reality is bad aesthetic" (138). The open question is why the documentary (and not the feature film) should be the ideal form for artistic manipulation of reality.

5. The Brazilian short documentary *Vidas no Lixo* by Alexandre Stockler (2008), available on the *Porta Curtas* website (portacurtas.org.br) presents the same problematic choice. The first scene of the film focuses on a young worker selecting and eating pieces of trash. It is unclear if the scene was filmed with the consent of the subject.

## Works Cited

Agamben, Giorgio. *Remnants of Auschwitz: The Witness and the Archive.* Translated by Daniel Heller-Roazen. New York: Zone Books, 1999.

Anders, Günther. "The World as Phantom and as Matrix." Translated by Norbert Guterman. *Dissent* 3 (1956): 14–24.

Aufderheide, Patricia, Peter Jaszi, and Mridu Chandra. "Honest Truths: Documentary Filmmakers on Ethical Challenges in Their Work." *Center for Social Media* (2009). Web. June 22, 2013.

Booth, Wayne C. "Why Ethical Criticism Can Never Be Simple." In *Ethics, Literature, Theory: An Introductory Reader*. Edited by Stephen K. George. Lanham: Rowman & Littlefield, 2005, 23–34.

———. "Who is Responsible in Ethical Criticism?" In *Ethics, Literature, Theory: An Introductory Reader*. Edited by Stephen K. George. Lanham: Rowman & Littlefield, 2005, 79–97.

Couser, Thomas G. *Vulnerable Subjects: Ethics and Life Writing.* Ithaca: Cornell UP, 2004.

Darke, Paul. "No Life Anyway: Pathologizing Disability on Film." In *The Problem Body: Projecting Disability on Film*. Edited by Sally Chivers and Nicole Markotić. Columbus: Ohio State UP, 2010.

Gilman, Sander L. *Disease and Representation. Images of Illness from Madness to AIDS.* Ithaca: Cornell UP, 1988.

Gonçalves, Ana Maria. "Carta Aberta ao Ziraldo." *O biscoito fino e a massa.* Web. June 22, 2013.

Herzog, Werner. "Minnesota Declaration: Truth and Fact in Documentary Cinema *Lessons of Darkness.*" Translated by Moira Weigel. *Werner Herzog Film: Home.* Web. June 22, 2013.

Kafai, Shayda. "The Mad Border Body: A Political In-betweeness." *Disability Studies Quarterly* 33.1 (2013): n.p. Web. June 22, 2013.

Nash, Kate. "Telling Stories: The Narrative Study of Documentary Ethics." *New Review of Film and Television Studies* 10 (2012): 1–14. *Taylor & Francis.* Web. June 22, 2013.

Nichols, Bill. *Introduction to Documentary.* Bloomington: Indiana UP, 2010.

Prado, Marcos. "Director-Statement." *Estamira* official film website. Web. June 21, 2013.

Rocha, Jeanete de Novais. " 'Art is a lie that makes us realize the truth:' An Interview with Goran Radovanovič." *DOC-online: Revista Digital de Cinema Documentário.* ("Dossier Documentário e Ética"). Web. June 22, 2013.

Seligmann-Silva, Márcio, Jaime Ginzburg, and Francisco Foot Hardman, eds. *Escritas da Violência. Vol. I: O Testemunho.* Rio de Janeiro: 7 Letras, 2012.

———, Márcio, Jaime Ginzburg, and Francisco Foot Hardman, eds. *Escritas da Violência. Vol. II: Representações da Violência na História e na Cultura Contemporâneas da América Latina.* Rio de Janeiro: 7 Letras, 2012.

Siebers, Tobin. *Disability Aesthetics.* Ann Arbor: U of Michigan P, 2010.

Snyder, Sharon L., and David T. Mitchell. "Body Genres: An Anatomy of Disability in Film." In *The Problem Body: Projecting Disability on Film.* Edited by Sally Chivers and Nicole Markotić. Columbus: Ohio State UP, 2010.

## Filmography

*Dzi Croquettes.* Directed by Tatiana Issa and Raphael Alvarez. Canal Brasil, 2009.

"Entrevista com o diretor." Extras. *Estamira Para Todos e Para Ninguém.* DVD. Zazen Produções, 2007.

*Estamira.* Directed by Marcos Prado. Zazen Produções, 2004.

*Estamira Para Todos e Para Ninguém.* Directed by Marcos Prado. Zazen Produções, 2007.

*Inocente.* Directed by Sean Fine and Andrea Nix Fine. Salty Features, Shine Global, Fine Films, 2012.

*Land of Silence and Darkness.* Directed by Werner Herzog. Werner Herzog Filmproduktion, 1971.

*To Be Heard.* Directed by Amy Sultan, Roland Legiardi-Laura, Edwin Martinez, and Deborah Shaffer. Dialogue Pictures, 2010.

Chapter 11

# "En ninguna parte"

## Narrative Performances of Mental Illness in *El portero* by Reinaldo Arenas and *Corazón de skitalietz* by Antonio José Ponte

LAURA KANOST

In the 1980s and 1990s, at the same time that mental health care reform was gathering momentum in Latin America[1] and disability studies was developing as a discipline in the United States and Britain, Cubans identified as mentally ill were exiled to the United States in the Mariel Boatlift along with criminals and political dissidents, and the post-Soviet political and economic crisis known as the "Special Period" exacerbated experiences of mental illness on the island.[2] These Cuban crises help to illustrate how the very real—and mutable—relationship between the political and the personal can destabilize clichéd metaphors of mental illness: as exile, as homelessness, as dictatorship. In late twentieth-century Latin American literature and society, the physical and conceptual spaces accessible to persons with mental illness were shifting: asylums and large psychiatric hospitals were being replaced with community-based mental health care, and fixed categories of difference were opening to more dynamic models.[3]

To consider this state of flux, I borrow the concept of liminality, used by Jeffrey Willett and Mary Jo Deegan to describe the social position of disability as a space with the potential to reconceptualize the physical and sociocultural barriers that serve to "other" people with disabilities. Willett and Deegan argue that, similar to the liminal stage of a rite of passage originally postulated by anthropologist Victor Turner, people with disabilities often experience a lack of a clear social or gender role, social invisibility or literal seclusion, symbolic association with death and contamination, and socioeconomic outsiderhood. Despite this multitude of hardships, Willet and Deegan make the case that the liminal position has a transformative power because, from the unique vantage point of liminality, a person "is forced to think about the established social structure as they prepare to re-enter that structure" (n.p.).

Within this context, this chapter discusses *El portero* (1989)[4] by Reinaldo Arenas and *Corazón de skitalietz* (1998) by Antonio José Ponte, Cuban narratives that both represent and perform the sociocultural liminality of mentally ill characters. By foregrounding diverse ways of perceiving, understanding, and feeling, these texts compel readers to occupy an uncomfortable but potentially transformative parallel space of indeterminacy, creating an opportunity to rethink what it means to be mentally ill, and by extension, what it means to be disabled. The protagonists' atypical perceptions and thought processes—what would be considered "impairments" under the social model of disability—are not easily separated from their sociopolitical contexts, where the social model would point to the emergence of "disability." Dichotomies such as impairment/disability, mind/body, "normal"/disabled fall apart, recalling Lennard Davis's concept of dismodernism, Ato Quayson's aesthetic nervousness, and what Fiona Kumari Campbell calls "decentering abledness."

## On the Threshold

Wandering, placelessness, and liminality have long been tropes associated with the spatial and rhetorical othering of mental illness, both—paradoxically—as a lack of subjectivity and as an unparalleled form of creativity and subversiveness.[5] The liminal states of exile and mental illness have been conceptually linked for centuries, most extensively through the medieval motif of the ship of fools, which Michel Foucault discusses in *Madness and Civilization.* Confined to the ship, from which there is no escape, the "madman is delivered to the river with its thousand arms, the sea with its thousand roads, to that great uncertainty external to everything. He is a prisoner in the midst of what is the freest, the openest of routes" (Foucault 11). Always adrift, not belonging to any place, the ship of fools keeps "mad" others away from "normal" society. In *El portero* and *Corazón de skitalietz,* the mentally ill protagonists experience this liminal social and political position as tremendously isolating, but simultaneously, as a space of agency and possibility. The use of narrative focalization in both texts requires readers to drift along with the protagonists.[6] The Mariel Boatlift of 1980, a key contextual element for *El portero*, mirrors the ship of fools icon: among this exodus of 124,776 Cuban dissidents and criminals (García 46) were a number of patients from psychiatric hospitals, making literal the long-standing metaphorical association between mental illness and exile. In fact, according to María Cristina García, the port of Mariel became known as the "Bay of Fools" (60). García discusses the intensely negative response in the United States to the perception that the Cuban government had used the boatlift as a way of purging the island of criminals and people with developmental and psychiatric disabilities.[7] Compounding the liminal status of these disabled immigrants was what García calls a "state of limbo" (75) that resulted because the United States denied the Mariel Cubans the official refugee status long awarded to Cubans arriving on U.S. shores and housed them in processing camps; "the government labeled the Cubans with the rather ambiguous term 'entrant,' which allowed them to remain temporarily in the United States until a more permanent status—if any—could be defined" (García 69). Long after setting foot on U.S. soil, the "marielitos" remained adrift in terms of political and social status, and the public widely perceived them as morally, physically, and mentally defective.

It is against this sociopolitical backdrop that Reinaldo Arenas (1943–1990), a Mariel exile himself, constructs the tale of *El portero*. The eponymous doorman, Juan, is a liminal figure in terms of his occupation—which literally places him on a threshold—his Mariel exile identity, and his apparent mental health problems. The plot of the first half of the novel revolves around Juan's failed attempts to show his New York apartment building's quirky tenants to a mysterious other door, one that he believes leads to another plane of existence. In the second half, Juan suddenly is able to converse with the tenants' various pets, and together they plan to escape the building and go in search of utopia. When the tenants have Juan committed to a psychiatric hospital, the animals rescue him and, apparently, they succeed in carrying out their planned exodus.

Just as Juan is constantly relegated to various thresholds throughout the novel, the reader of this text is caught between psychological and supernatural explanations for Juan's extraordinary perceptions of the world, placing the novel within the fantastic genre as defined by Tzvetan Todorov.[8] In his memoir, *Antes que anochezca*, Arenas describes Cuban identity as an experience of liminality:

> And for Cubans who, like us, have suffered persecution for twenty years in that terrible world, *there is really no solace anywhere.*

> Suffering has marked us forever, and only with people who have gone through a similar experience can we perhaps find some level of understanding. (308, emphasis added)[9]

Through its fantastic elements, *El portero* creates a space for communication by compelling its readers to inhabit, albeit only indirectly and temporarily, the thresholds that Juan occupies both as a Mariel exile and as a person who is perceived as mentally ill. The trope of uncertainty pervading the novel's narration, plot, and genre extends to its readers, who may temporarily inhabit a liminal space of fantastic vacillation.

The limitations and potential of Juan's liminal status are suggested by his relationship to the text's narrators and his interactions with in-between spaces. *El portero* is narrated with a peculiar mix of omnipresent surveillance and persistent uncertainty, implying that the reader, who performs a secondary sort of surveillance over the world of the novel, is likewise limited in the ability to make Juan an object of knowledge. The narration is told in anglicized Spanish through the collective narrative voice of the local pre-Mariel Cuban exile community, already successfully assimilated into U.S. society. This "we" presents its narration as testimony about Juan's failure to integrate. The testimony, situated in the year 1992 (postdating the novel itself), claims to be based on evidence gathered through a comprehensive system of surveillance, as well as Juan's own writings. Although the narrating "we" cannot have immediate access to Juan's perceptions and thoughts, the focalization sometimes seems to do just that: the narrating agent usually highlights its inability to know Juan's inner life, but at other points it seems that Juan has become the focalizer, ostensibly due to the work of psychologists who the narrators say have been hired to reconstruct Juan's psychological states (106). Juan is initially introduced as "a young man who was dying of grief"—a condition that the narrating agent cannot explain or even adequately describe—and immediately thereafter as a Cuban exile living in the United States, thus establishing from the very beginning of the novel an association between the state of psychiatric distress and that of exile from Cuba (3).

The panoptical presence of the narrators recalls Arenas's accounts in his memoir, *Antes que anochezca*, of the Castro regime's omnipresent surveillance network. Juan is subjected first to the narrators' watchful eye, and later to confinement in the physical structure of a psychiatric hospital. Yet, although the narrators—and in turn, the reader—see and hear all, they are ultimately unable to make any firm conclusions about Juan. Likewise, Juan soon escapes from the hospital, in spite of all the obstacles meant to control him. This indirect association between government surveillance and mental health care facilities has direct referents in the context of Cuban politics. While vast improvements in La Mazorra, then the country's only public psychiatric hospital, were a triumph of the Revolution, Marxist ideology infuses the Cuban mental health care system's approach to mental illness and its treatment (Collinson and Turner). The Cuban government has been accused of using its psychiatric facilities to confine and torture political dissidents (Brown and Lago), and under the Castro government it has become a commonplace for critics to liken the entire island to an insane asylum that holds its occupants by force.[10] Ever on the threshold, the doorman cannot be confined by the Cuban government, the Cuban exile community, or the New York psychiatric hospital. His social liminality brings him great loneliness, but it also allows him to slip between the cracks of oppressive apparatuses.

Further underscoring Juan's liminality is the fact that he constantly occupies liminal physical spaces—the boat, doorways, the psychiatric hospital, and the unresolved final journey—and, not coincidentally, also experiences liminal mental states and social positions. The narrators present him as a person who, "unlike us, could not or would not adjust to this practical world. On the contrary: he explored absurd and desperate paths." Worse yet, the narrators say, Juan attempted to take everyone he met along with him (4). Having had difficulty holding down previous jobs due to spells that the narrators call "illumination or madness" (5), as a doorman, Juan feels called to show the tenants the way through another sort of door, a door leading out of the constricted spaces of everyday life to another plane of existence, to what he calls "timeless regions with no material limits" (7).

After establishing this situation, the first half of the novel focuses on Juan's attempts to gain the tenants' trust so that he can steer them toward this special door. As the tenants are introduced one by one, it becomes apparent that this apartment building is home to an unusual number of liminal people: many of the tenants are Cuban exiles, and all of them are quirky if not disturbed: obsessive, addictive, delusional, suicidal. In fact, the narrators refer to almost all the tenants as mad at one point or another, and throughout the first part of the novel, Juan does not stand out as any more unconventional than anyone else in the building. Like Juan, the tenants each have latched onto an ideology or metanarrative through which to navigate life, and many of them are obsessed with converting others. Thus, Juan is unsuccessful in his proselytizing, but just as he sinks into despair, the pets that live in the building begin to speak to him, and the second half of the novel deals with their democratic discussions of how to escape from the tenants and set out on a journey.

The tenants spy on Juan's now increasingly bizarre behavior, and decide to have him committed to a psychiatric hospital. Ironically, Juan's interactions with the other patients parallel his previous interactions with the tenants. In the hospital, each patient is known by a number instead of a name, and drugs often impede interaction, but, like the tenants, the patients are a series of obsessive, quirky personalities who won't listen to Juan. One by one, the narrative characterizes each patient through a defining mania, perhaps the most striking being "el profesor," who believes that the hospital is actually a ship that has run aground, conjuring the image of a stationary ship of fools. This catalog of sorts is contained, in the Spanish text, within one extraordinarily long paragraph (three and one-half pages), suggesting the group living conditions in the psychiatric institution. Indeed, the hospital is unequivocally portrayed as a Goffmanian total institution, where the patients are expected to surrender all control over their bodies, minds, and identities: they are physically restrained, given large doses of sedatives, and renamed with numbers like prisoners.[11]

Although the novel portrays the psychiatric hospital as an oppressive institution, it also seems to suggest that Juan's very liminality allows him to escape its clutches. His unique ability to communicate with the animals from the apartment building becomes his way out. The pets rescue Juan, and they all set off on a journey. Thus, the end of the novel finds Juan yet again in a liminal position, in search of his destination, an idyllic mountain. The group travels across the United States, arriving at the Pacific coast. As they continue south along the coastline, searching for the mountain, the travelers are joined by more and more animals. The narrators continue their surveillance, using a telescope to observe from afar, until the group reaches the equator (187). There, they shrewdly break off the narration, announcing that Juan is their secret weapon, because "a people forced out of their country and persecuted, a people in exile and who consequently suffer humiliation and discrimination, live for their day of revenge" (189). The narrators' menacing conclusion thus leaves Juan stranded in a state of potentiality at an imprecise geographical location.

Yet *El portero* extends two pages beyond the ending of the official testimony. Immediately following the narrators' conclusion is a section titled "La puerta," "The Door," which apparently is narrated by Juan himself—the only time in the novel that Juan speaks directly without his words being italicized or placed within quotation marks. A paragraph narrated entirely in the conditional tense describes how each of the animals would pass through a door to a perfect habitat, a place where "nobody could spy on them through telescopes, or have them followed by undercover agents" (156 in the Spanish, my translation). Following this paragraph is a single sentence, now in the future tense: "That is, all except me, the doorman, who on the outside will watch them disappear forever" (190). These verb tenses underscore the sense of potentiality surrounding Juan's fate, and since he remains forever waiting for his turn to go through the door and thus reach some kind of conclusion, the novel is suspended, even at its conclusion, in the liminal realm of the fantastic. The last page of the novel presents a lost dog ad that seems to confirm that, at the very least, the dog Cleopatra has disappeared without a trace.

Thus, even at its conclusion, *El portero* refuses to release the reader from fantastic suspension; consistently indeterminate narration and focalization rule out any coherent psychological, supernatural, or allegorical interpretation of Juan's experiences. Although the narrators somehow manage to observe Juan's every move, they also highlight their own inability (or refusal) to interpret the cause of the phenomena. The narrators claim, for example, to know that on the liminal night of New Year's Eve, Juan concluded that his life was meaningless and he needed to abandon the universe, but they explicitly do not decide whether this was a moment of lucidity or insanity (104–105). Similarly, when the dog Cleopatra first speaks to Juan, the narrators interrupt to tell the reader directly not to expect a neat explanation of any kind (105–106).

At the same time, the novel's narration maintains fantastic vacillation on a more subtle level, using focalization to limit the reader's access to evidence that would explain away Juan's adventures. Although the narrators seem to watch Juan's every move, most of the novel seems to be focalized through Juan himself, often without outside perspectives that might corroborate or contradict his perceptions. Even when the narrators do present an outside perspective or quote his unconventional speeches, it is not clear whether Juan's behavior can be considered pathological. The crux of the fantastic vacillation in *El portero* is the question of whether Juan's interactions with the animals can be attributed to mental illness. Excluding the narrators, the other characters in the book seem never to entertain any other explanation. Clearly, the tenants decide that Juan requires urgent mental health care, because they call an ambulance to take him to a psychiatric hospital. Confronted with surveillance video of the conversations between Juan and the animals—which has picked up the various voices—the psychiatrists go to the extreme of diagnosing Juan with a brand new disease, "magnetic ventriloquism" (164). This diagnosis is later changed to schizophrenia because the original symptoms do not reappear once Juan is in the hospital, separated from the animals (170). If the change in Juan's "symptoms" in the absence of the animals is not enough evidence for a supernatural explanation, magic certainly seems to be at work when the animals rescue Juan from the hospital. The narrators state that, through their "discreet surveillance," they know how Juan was able to escape (176). High above the city streets, a throng of animals work together to remove the bars from Juan's hospital window, and they all escape through it, the orangutan carrying Juan as though he were its baby (177).[12]

*El portero* defies rigid classifications and compels its reader to do the same by exploring liminality on various levels. The doorman, keeper of the threshold, also occupies a liminal sociopolitical space as an exile and as a person with unconventional thought processes and behavior. The complex nature of Juan's liminality is encapsulated in his confinement to the psychiatric hospital; his liminality causes him to be placed in a dehumanizing total institution, but it is also the reason why Juan ultimately cannot be restrained. The reader, too, experiences a sort of liminality through the novel's unwavering fantastic uncertainty. Unable to know for certain whether Juan's experiences can be explained by psychology or magic, or perhaps a little of both, the reader may feel uncomfortably powerless, but may also open up to more complex perspectives on the experiences of mental illness and exile. Thus, the fantastic genre may be effective in representing a character's mental illness as a fluctuating or transitory experience rather than a fixed otherness, precisely because it does not allow for an easy categorization of people as either "normal" or "mad."

## "En ninguna parte"

Antonio José Ponte (b. 1964) wrote his 1998 novella *Corazón de skitalietz* years before being exiled, and his representation of an experience identified as mental illness reflects both the physical and emotional stress of scarcity that took place in post-Soviet Cuba and the island's leading role in the community-based restructuring of mental health care services in the late twentieth century. In Ponte's novella, an unemployed historian known as Escorpión and an astrologer named Veranda bond while wandering their native Havana, displaced within a once-familiar space due to recurring Special Period blackouts and shortages as well as to their personal marginality. The word *skitalietz* in the title refers to this state of being displaced within one's own homeland, which here represents not only the experience of living in Special Period Cuba,[13] but also the vicissitudes of the body: Veranda is dying of cancer, and Escorpión is receiving treatment for a mental illness at a day clinic.

The narrative, focalized almost entirely through Escorpión, is itself disorienting. The protagonist's often unconventional perceptions wander in and out of dreams, medicated states, and critical contemplation of his situation. In his first meeting with Veranda, for example, they are having an unremarkable conversation when suddenly "[e]yes opened in the cushion his elbow was resting on and the cushion turned into a cat. 'Historian?,' asked the cat in a very clear voice," at which point Escorpión tries to remember how many pills he has taken, and when (83). Here and when he returns to his apartment to take a pill, the focalization does not allow an external viewpoint to clarify what is happening. Readers perceive the world of the novella as Escorpión does, including a sense of uncertainty about whether these perceptions can be trusted. Escorpión similarly reflects on the reliability of his own thought processes in a conversation with his supervisor at work: "Scorpio admitted to himself that he must have been in a very bad state to repeat the words of a dream to his boss" (87). The boss's reaction—asking Escorpión to go on vacation—suggests that he, too, thinks Escorpión's behavior is unusual, a symptom of stress that could be alleviated by rest (87). By filtering the narrative through Escorpión's unstable perceptions, Ponte foregrounds the experience of wandering at home, of reflecting on one's own inner space as though foreign. Blackouts, scarcity, physical and mental instability, and reading all entail a defamiliarizing impulse that brings varying degrees of confusion, discomfort, innovation, and wisdom. "La ficción ocurre en ninguna parte," (fiction occurs in no place), Ponte writes in the "epilogue" that precedes the narration (viii in the Spanish): placelessness, liminality, and crisis form spaces of both distress and potentiality.

The physical spaces through which Escorpión wanders correspond, then, to this very human experience of skitalietz, which the protagonist himself comes to identify as his professional occupation (118). By naming his crisis, Escorpión strongly affirms his own subjectivity. His range of possible actions is limited by the geography of the island, the availability of resources, and the community's perceptions of him as mentally ill, and contrary to the conventional discourse that excludes the "mad" from the position of subject, Escorpión is undeniably a thinking and speaking subject. In *The Practice of Everyday Life*, Michel de Certeau describes a similar tactic by which individuals negotiate apparently fixed systems: "without leaving the place where [the consumer] has no choice but to live and which lays down its law for him, he establishes within it a degree of plurality and creativity. By an art of being in between, he draws unexpected results from his situation" (30).

Such a creative appropriation of space occurs in Escorpión's visits to the day hospital, where he and the other clients engage mental health discourse to discuss their own diagnoses and treatment options, demonstrating a well-developed knowledge of medications (89–90). The doctors are intentionally excluded from these conversations because they lack the embodied experience necessary to understand the issue: "It was understood that their knowledge was only theoretical. Not one of those white coats had gone to bed with medication" (18 in the Spanish, my translation). When Escorpión asks one of the most experienced patients if anyone there ever got well, he answers by contrasting his personal experience with a reference to Thomas Mann: "Of course. What did you think? This is not the sanitarium of *The Magic Mountain*" (90). In this prerevolution mansion converted into a day hospital, the patients analyze the relationship between Cuban politics and their personal crises: in group therapy, Escorpión complains of lack of interest in his job, and a fellow patient, "one of the experts," diagnoses him with "professional anemia," a condition that could surely be remedied by reviving his identity as a worker (18 in the Spanish, my translation). One patient links his own feeling of fragmentation to recurring Special Period blackouts: "When there's no electric light in the darkened house, I've had the security of knowing that another someone like me, another me in some illuminated part of this same city does things for me, lives my life" (91); Escorpión, however, is uncertain whether this is "the true language of wisdom" or just the paranoid discourse of "un loco" (92). When Escorpión is informed that he has been laid off of his job, and is offered "the chance to go live in an agricultural camp," he surmises that this "wouldn't be very different from a day clinic. More sweat, fewer pills. More confidence in the therapeutic virtues of work" (95).

Veranda and Escorpión rewrite these sociopolitical expectations by not working, not following an expected path or remaining within an enclosed space. The unpredictability of their movements becomes an art: they show one another the most beautiful places they know, and they curate a "revista de la calle" or "street journal" made up of found papers (36 in the Spanish, my translation). As Veranda and Escorpión wander the city together, having synchronized their medication schedules, they grow to resemble "locos" more and more, both in their own self-assessment and in the reactions of others (111–115). Escorpión draws a distinction between physically wandering and mentally wandering, demonstrating what seems by now to be an uncharacteristic lack of self-awareness: "Scorpio could live in the street, stop shaving, but he knew that the moment his ideas began to wander he would be on the road toward stupidity or madness" (115). Readers can only follow along on this errant narrative path.

The limits on Escorpión's wanderings become much tighter when the rest of society decides that such unconventional trajectories are the symptom of an ill that must be treated. The police and a social worker attempt to bring Escorpión back into line by taking him to a homeless shelter; there he gives his occupation as *skitalietz*, and when they ask if he is Russian, he critically assesses their perception of him: "they want to make a nut out of me" (118). This is a temporary shelter for various types of wanderers who will then be sent on their respective ways back to socially acceptable spaces and behaviors: "Passage through the ambulant home ended in detox centers, old people's homes, psychiatric hospitals, return to families. As for him, they'd dispatch him off to a madhouse, he was almost sure" (119). While Veranda is in the hospital near the end of her life, she and Escorpión observe flies buzzing around the room, and reflect on the meaning of freedom within a limited space: "Freedom can consist of a closed space that's a little larger" (122). Escorpión and Veranda are able to—and obliged to—move in and out of the spaces of the hospitals as a function of their socioeconomic marginality. Their ability to contemplate this condition is in itself an appropriation of the subjectivity that is implicitly denied by the authorities who treat Escorpión like a homeless *loco* who needs someone else to impose limits.

Through the experience of displacement, Escorpión and Veranda consciously and painfully occupy the bodies and identities that have become their only home. When Escorpión finally leaves the city limits after Veranda's death, he does not find freedom, but rather, the discomfort of liminality. He is well aware that his placelessness in society is related to his unconventional thought processes—and this experience is self-aware and utterly corporeal: "Opposite the shore most of the liquid residues of the city were emptied out. Sweat, saliva, blood, urine, semen, shit, all mixed there with the salt water. At that point Havana life ended" (127). This tragic final scene reaches out to its readers, the spectators whose eye Escorpión feels watching him: "He had the feeling that someone was watching him, that he was part of an exterior shot on a film set. He didn't know what to do before God or the camera" (49 in the Spanish, my translation). The anguish of liminal subjectivity carries with it a unique perspective from which to envision and catalyze otherwise unfathomable social and cultural change (Willett and Deegan). The conclusion of Ponte's text, however, emphasizes the anguish.

With narratives focalized through characters considered to be mentally ill, both *El portero* and *Corazón de skitalietz* ask their readers to temporarily inhabit their placelessness, to imagine the defamiliarizing vantage point of a ship adrift. This mechanism affords an opportunity to perceive ways that mental illnesses exist as a complex relationship between bodies, minds, discourses, cultures, and sociopolitical structures. Like a photograph of an outwardly visible disability, these narrative performances of psychological, emotional, and physical wandering ask readers to become aware of their own relationship to and assumptions about mental illness. As Michael Berubé points out, a disability perspective can open new views on narrative itself: "rereading narrative from the perspective of disability studies, [. . .] leads us to reread the role of temporality, causality, and self-reflexivity in narrative and to reread the implications of characters' self-awareness, particularly in narratives whose textual self-awareness is predicated on the portrayal of cognitive disability" (576).

By reading narratives like *El portero* and *Corazón de skitalietz*, we are also led to rewrite existing models of disability. Mental illnesses have themselves occupied a liminal position within the field of disability studies, since these conditions do not easily fit the influential social model of disability. As Anna Mollow has convincingly argued in her study of depression,

> [. . .] the strategy of maintaining a focus on social oppression rather than personal suffering—or on "disability" as opposed to "impairment"—risks reifying a dichotomy that does not easily apply to disorders like depression [. . .] Moreover, analyses that privilege disability over impairment deflect attention from the political nature of impairment itself [. . .] the oppression of disabled people is not merely "something imposed on top of" a pre-existing impairment; rather, the production of some impairments is itself a political process. (76–78)

Inclusion of mental illness is vital in disability studies precisely because it complicates models that are too simple to be inclusive of a wide range of experiences of bodily difference taking place in a wide range of cultural and political contexts.

Mental illness is especially critical to the development of Latin American disability studies because of the prevalence of these experiences in the region and the way that they intertwine physical, social, and political factors. Robert Kohn and coauthors explain that the percentage of disabilities identified as mental illnesses more than doubled in Latin America and the Caribbean from 1990 to 2002: "it was estimated in 1990 that psychiatric and neurological conditions accounted for 8.8% of the disability-adjusted life-years (DALY) observed in Latin America and the Caribbean. In 2002, that burden had increased to more than double, 22.2%" (my translation). That study states that this shift might be due to a transition from communicable to chronic illnesses, greater attention given to emergent disorders, and a population shift that has meant that greater numbers of people reach the age that puts them at risk of developing adult mental disorders (230). Going on to provide detailed numbers on how people are affected by different disorders in the region, the study finds that in many, perhaps most cases, the majority of people affected by mental illness in Latin America and the Caribbean are not served by a mental health care system.

Cultural narratives of mental illness represent, and have an effect on, ways of understanding these experiences, and are an important part of the ongoing change in how people with mental illnesses are perceived and the spaces they are able to occupy. Disability rights are far from equal in Latin America, and contemporary Latin American popular and literary culture still includes essentializing, clichéd representations of mental illness and other disabilities. At the same time, however, accessibility is gaining momentum, and texts like *El portero* and *Corazón de skitalietz* align with Fiona Kumari Campbell's call for cultural producers to "recover and apprehend the life-worlds of humans living peripherally," forming "disability imaginaries":

> Ontological differences, be that on the basis of problematical signifiers of race, sex, sexuality and dis/ability, need to be unhinged from evaluative ranking and be re-cognised in their various nuances and complexities without being represented in fixed absolute terms. It is only then, in this release that we can find possibilities in ambiguity and resistance in marginality. (14–15)

*El portero* and *Corazón de skitalietz* contribute to a Cuban disability imaginary the anguished potential for creativity in a state of physical and cognitive-emotional disorientation.

## Notes

1. Cuba has been a leader in the process of reformulating national mental health care systems that took place beginning in the 1990s to respond to international recommendations for protecting human rights of mentally ill people. These reforms, which in many countries coincided with a renewed emphasis on human rights following the fall of dictatorial regimes, involve restructuring the mental health care system with a new emphasis on community-based and preventive care rather than large in-patient institutions (Caldas de Almeida and Horvitz-Lennon 219). Throughout Latin America, however, policy reforms were not always reflected in real infrastructure: "available information indicates generally low levels of implementation of mental health plans. [. . .] In most countries the majority of mental health care resources continue to be allocated to psychiatric hospitals, and community-based services are insufficiently developed" (Caldas de Almeida and Horvitz-Lennon 220).

2. Margaret Price maps the usage, connotations, and overlap of various terms (e.g., mad, survivor, mental illness, neurodiverse, psychosocial disability), ultimately preferring "mental disability," which groups together intellectual, cognitive, and psychiatric differences. I agree with Price that "psychosocial disability" is a more accurate

and less medicalizing term than "mental illness," but like her, I believe it is not in wide enough use to be commonly understood. For lack of a succinct and broadly recognizable alternative, I consider "mental illness" acceptable because many people who experience differences in cognitive and emotional functioning do feel great relief when they learn to cope with them through therapy, medication, and the like.

3. I have argued elsewhere that late twentieth-century Latin American literature often represents the asylum or psychiatric hospital as a problematic and contested space, signaling a crisis in the concept of mental illness. If the function of the asylum is to partition mentally ill people off from the rest of society, thereby emphasizing their otherness, a literary or real-life crisis in the structure or role of the asylum denotes a crisis in that society's conception of mental illness; an asylum that is permeable or crumbling is a structure that does not neatly contain mental illness as a mark of inherent otherness. This change is part of a shift in the concept of the self, an ongoing transition from a model of subjectivity founded on a myth of bodily perfection, to a subjectivity relying on a concept of the body as constantly changing, adapting, and interacting with its surroundings in complex ways.

4. *El portero* was written in New York from 1984 to 1986, was published first in French in 1988, and was subsequently published in Spanish in Barcelona in 1989 and in Miami in 1990. I refer to the 1990 Universal edition, and to the 1991 English translation by Dolores M. Koch.

5. For in-depth criticism of the madness-as-subversive cliché in the context of gender studies, see Caminero-Santangelo and Kanost "Re-Placing."

6. The concept of focalization, first proposed by Gérard Genette in 1972, allows for a distinction between the narrating voice that tells the story and the agent(s) whose perceptions act as a filter determining what information is available to that voice.

7. Twenty-six thousand of the refugees were labeled as criminals, while "an estimated fifteen hundred had mental health problems or were mentally retarded"—a telling lack of distinction—and another "sixteen hundred had chronic medical problems such as drug and alcohol abuse, tuberculosis, or cardiovascular disease" (García 64). Approximately 2.5 percent of the Mariel immigrants had disabilities, then, and about half of these were developmental or psychiatric disabilities.

8. My discussion of the fantastic is informed by Tzvetan Todorov's model, which hinges on the reader's projected response to the imaginary world of the text, for a fantastic text "must oblige the reader to consider the world of the characters as a world of living persons and to hesitate between a natural and a supernatural explanation of the events described" (33). Todorov stipulates that if the "laws of reality" can explain the phenomena, then the work is classified in the uncanny genre, whereas if "new laws of nature" must be adopted, the work belongs to the marvelous (41). Because the fantastic exists on the border between the uncanny and the marvelous, it has an affinity for themes of liminality.

9. Unless otherwise indicated, all English quotations of works originally written in Spanish are from the published English translations.

10. An Internet search of the terms "Cuba" and "manicomio" or "madhouse" turns up pages of examples of this rhetoric. An early instance comes from a 1963

*Time* magazine article: "Last week a new boatload of 750 refugees landed in Miami with reports of ever higher prices, tighter rations and lower wages. 'Cuba is a madhouse,' said one bitter arrival" ("Becoming Destructive"). More recently, during Castro's severe illness in late 2006 and early 2007, reflections on the legacy and future of the revolution have reiterated the madhouse imagery. For *BBC Mundo*, Carlos Alberto Montaner suggests that "such a crazy, excentric guy remained in power for so long" because Castro "created a hermetic institutional cage with no way out," and speculates that when Castro dies, reformers and opposition democrats "will begin an organized and peaceful process of dismantling that anachronistic madhouse" ("Fidel Castro: Palabras mayores," my translation).

11. Arenas writes in his memoir that Juan's character is based on his good friend, fellow Mariel exile Lázaro Gómez Carriles. *Antes que anochezca* is thus a key intertext for *El portero*: "Lázaro finally had to enter the psychiatric ward of a city public hospital, where he stayed several months. I went to see him every week during visiting hours. The ward atmosphere was Dantesque in the worst sense; all possible types of insane people were screaming all the time, day and night. When I entered that building I had an overpowering feeling of bewilderment and anxiety" (307–308). Arenas continues, "He was unemployed for a while and then landed a job as a doorman. We were no longer the same; we had witnessed the horror of a New York mental hospital, the craziness, the misery, the mistreatment, the discrimination." (308). *El portero* is dedicated to Lázaro.

12. Other critics have not focused on issues of mental illness, the fantastic, or disability in *El portero*, but many have discussed the book's genre and relate it to the political context of Arenas's life (Soto, Álvarez Borland, Luis, Cacheiro). Alina Camacho-Gingerich suggests a psychological explanation, pointing out that Juan escapes from the psychiatric hospital immediately after falling into a deep, medication-induced sleep, and therefore his subsequent waking and escape may be read as only a dream (84). However, the narrators consistently limit their observations to information that could be gleaned from omnipresent surveillance.

13. Loss situates the novella and the Russian term *skitalietz* within the Special Period context, culturally, politically, and economically. Lygia Navarro's article "Tropical Depression" chronicles widespread suicide and self-medication in contemporary Cuba: "After the fall of the Soviet Union, the island fell into its own Great Depression, which Castro euphemistically dubbed "the Special Period in Times of Peace," and suicides spiked to more than double the already-high rate of 1959, becoming the second-leading cause of death for Cubans ages fifteen to forty-nine. [. . .] Official numbers do show that, in a country of 11 million people, annual consumption of only three sedatives [. . .] is 127 million tablets."

## Works Cited

Alarcón, R.D., and S.A. Aguilar-Gaxiola. "Mental Health Policy Developments in Latin America." *Bulletin of the World Health Organization* 78.4: 2000. 483–490. Web. February 26, 2013.

Arenas, Reinaldo. *El portero.* Miami: Universal, 1990.

———. *The Doorman.* Translated by Dolores M. Koch. New York: Grove, 1991.

———. *Antes que anochezca.* Barcelona: Tusquets, 1992.

———. *Before Night Falls.* Translated by Dolores M. Koch. London: Serpent's Tail, 1993.

"Becoming Destructive." *Time* May 31, 1963. Web. February 3, 2007.

Bérubé, Michael. "Disability and Narrative." *PMLA* 120. 2 (March 2005): 568–576. Web. October 8, 2012.

Brown, Charles J., and Armando M. Lago. *The Politics of Psychiatry in Revolutionary Cuba.* New York: Freedom House, 1991.

Caminero-Santangelo, Marta. *The Madwoman Can't Speak, Or Why Insanity Is Not Subversive.* Ithaca: Cornell UP, 1998.

Campbell, Fiona Kumari. *Contours of Ableism: The Production of Disability and Abledness.* New York: Palgrave Macmillan, 2009.

Certeau, Michel de. *The Practice of Everyday Life.* Translated by Steven F. Rendall. Berkeley: U of California P, 1984.

Collinson, S.R., and T.H. Turner. "Not Just Salsa and Cigars: Mental Health Care in Cuba." *The Psychiatrist* 26 (2002): 185–188. Web. February 21, 2013.

Davis, Lennard. *Bending over Backwards: Disability, Dismodernism and Other Difficult Positions.* New York: New York UP, 2002.

Foucault, Michel. *Madness and Civilization: A History of Insanity in the Age of Reason.* Translated by Richard Howard. New York: Vintage, 1988.

García, Cristina María. *Havana USA: Cuban Exiles and Cuban Americans in South Florida, 1959–1994.* Berkeley: U of California P, 1996.

Genette, Gérard E. *Narrative Discourse: An Essay in Method.* Translated by Jane E. Lewin. Ithaca: Cornell UP, 1983.

Goffman, Erving. *Asylums: Essays on the Social Situation of Mental Patients and Other Inmates.* New York: Anchor, 1961.

Kanost, Laura. "Political Asylums: Locating Mental Illness in Latin American Literature (1980–2000)." Diss. University of Kansas, 2007.

———. "*Pasillos sin luz*: Reading the Asylum in *Nadie me verá llorar* by Cristina Rivera Garza." *Hispanic Review* 76.3 (2008): 299–316.

———. "Re-Placing the Madwoman: Irene Vilar's *The Ladies' Gallery.*" *Frontiers: A Journal of Women Studies* 31.3 (2010): 103–115.

Kohn, Robert, Itzhak Levav, José Miguel Caldas de Almeida, Benjamín Vicente, Laura Andrade, Jorge J. Caraveo-Anduaga, Shekhar Saxena and Benedetto Saraceno. "Los trastornos mentales en América Latina y el Caribe: asunto prioritario para la salud pública." *Revista Panamericana de Salud Pública* 18.4/5 (2005): 229–240. Web. February 26, 2013.

Loss, Jacqueline. "Skitalietz: Traducciones y vestigios de un imperio caduco." In *La vigilia cubana: Sobre Antonio José Ponte.* Edited by Teresa Basile. Rosario, Argentina: Beatriz Viterbo, 2009, 95–109.

Mollow, Anna. "'When Black Women Start Going on Prozac': Race, Gender, and Mental Illness in Meri Nana-Ama Danquah's 'Willow Weep for Me.'" *MELUS* 31.3 (Fall 2006): 67–99. Web. February 26, 2013.

Montaner, Carlos Alberto. "Fidel Castro: Palabras mayores." *BBC Mundo*. Web. February 3, 2007.

Navarro, Lygia. "Tropical Depression." *Virginia Quarterly Review* Winter 2009: 26–47. Web. February 26, 2013.

Ponte, Antonio José. *Corazón de skitalietz*. Cienfuegos, Cuba: Reina del Mar, 1998.

———. "Heart of Skitalietz." In *In the Cold of the Malecón and Other Stories*. Translated by Cola Franzen and Dick Cluster. San Francisco: City Lights Books, 2000.

Price, Magaret. "Defining Mental Disability." In *The Disability Studies Reader*, 4th ed. Edited by Lennard J. Davis. New York/London: Routledge, 2013, 292–299.

Quayson, Ato. *Aesthetic Nervousness: Disability and the Crisis of Representation*. New York: Columbia UP, 2007.

Todorov, Tzvetan. *The Fantastic: A Structural Approach to a Literary Genre*. Translated by Richard Howard. Ithaca: Cornell UP, 1975.

Turner, Victor Witter. "Social Dramas and Stories About Them." *Critical Inquiry* 7.1 (1980): 141–168. Web. December 8, 2007.

Willett, Jeffrey, and Mary Jo Deegan. "Liminality and Disability: Rites of Passage and Community in Hypermodern Society." *Disability Studies Quarterly* 21.3 (2001): 137–152. Web. February 26, 2013.

Part IV

# Imagining Other Worlds

Chapter 12

# The Disability Twist in Stranger Novels by Mario Bellatin and Carmen Boullosa

EMILY HIND

The difference between noting a bodily sensation and organizing those sensations as symptoms pertaining to a diagnosis aligns with the difference between meditating and narrating. In meditation, sensations that arise in the body and thoughts that pass through the mind receive judgment-free, passive observation. By contrast, narrative seeks out and assigns meaning to thoughts and sensations, and often works to group them into stories with plot arcs. Narrative tends to prefer diagnoses and cures—the opposite goal of the meditation that values impassivity and acceptance of things as they are. Disability scholar Lennard Davis anticipates the affinity between diagnosis and narrative habits when he describes the traditional novel as a journey through the artificially constructed abnormal state that concludes with an equally manipulative, reinstated ability or cure: "A normal situation becomes abnormal, and by the end of the novel, normality or some variant on it is restored" (*Bending Over Backwards* 98). The traditional novel, according to Davis, imagines certain qualities as "average" and claims this portrait of the "normal" as verisimilitude; in Davis's memorable wording for this formula, "real means average" (*Bending Over Backwards* 93). For readers interested in disability topics, the conflation of verisimilitude and the notion of the average causes problems not only because human complexity exceeds mathematical formula, but also because impairment tends to be excluded from the novelistic norm. Some ten years later, Davis updates his influential analysis and begins *The End of Normal* by arguing that even though language fashions have changed and the word "normal" has fallen from favor, a simple replacement has emerged for the offensive term: "*diversity* is the new *normality*" (1).[1] This new normalcy continues to define itself against impairment: "We want diversity in all things, but not insofar as medicalized bodies are concerned. It is in this realm that 'normal' still applies with force" (7). Giorgio Agamben's ideas regarding devalued bare life (*zoe*) and entitled specific life (*bios*) prompt Davis's "ultimate question" here regarding "whether diversity can ever encompass disability, which is another way of asking whether diversity can ever encompass abnormality or whether *bios* under neoliberalism can ever encompass *zoe*" (6). The radical difference between bare life and entitled life anticipates the finding in the present chapter that even experimental novelists fail to manage such inclusivity. Still, a literary scholar's best hope for resistance to the confusion of non-threatening diversity and the "real" might lie with experimental fiction that gestures toward meditation and not just diagnosis.

Mario Bellatin (Mexican born, Peruvian raised, now residing in Mexico City) and Carmen Boullosa (Mexican born and raised, currently residing in New York) craft what can be called "stranger" novels because the characters' wild impairments, a collection of unstable symptoms that pertain to an uncertain diagnosis, make the physical conditions weirder than the known courses of human illness; if readers insist on diagnosing these characters, they will soon realize that these strange figures cannot be confused with the "real." Against the truism that human longevity inevitably triggers disability—or, as Davis puts it for the benefit of the temporarily able-bodied audience, " 'them' is actually 'us' "—the physiques designed by Boullosa and Bellatin present impossible exoticism (*Bending Over Backwards* 4). Bellatin's *Biografía ilustrada de Mishima* (Mishima's Illustrated Biography) (2009) presents the experiences of a headless novelist and downplays any resulting impairment. In the context of the present essay, that sense of humor presents a sort of flaw, because the jokes allow Bellatin to remain faithful to the novelistic norm of the "average," now presented as amusing diversity, despite Bellatin's effort to break the narrative into meditative fragments. For her part, Boullosa repeats a scene of fantastic bodily mutation in three novels, *Cielos de la Tierra* (Heavens on Earth) (1997), *La novela perfecta* (The Perfect Novel) (2006), and *El complot de los Románticos* (The Romantic Plot) (2009). These scenes present a kind of free-form visual meditation that confounds the narrators, who gape, horrified, at what they consider abject impairment and the very embodiment of zoe. Despite the narrators' fear of these stranger abilities in each of the three novels, the reader can identify the meditative possibilities accessible in the unashamed bodily redesign, against the narrative approach that seeks diagnosis and cure.

If the experimental novels fall short of addressing Davis's worry that disability "undergirds our very idea of diversity," they do successfully refuse facile notions of "progress" (*The End of Normal* 8). Bellatin's meandering *Bio-*

*grafía ilustrada de Mishima* proves difficult to encapsulate in a plot summary because the novel does not "go" anywhere; it does not progress according to the standards of diagnosis. Bellatin installs this anti-progressive structure by avoiding hierarchical distinctions between principal and secondary levels of data. To name just one example of this confusing approach that declines to make some details "count" more than others, Bellatin ends a paragraph about a swimming ritual among monks with a seemingly extraneous detail: During the monks' trance, the yellow bus remained motionless in the yard where it had been parked. (15). The bus, under the rules of neutral observance privileged in meditation, forms a detail as important, or unimportant, as nearly any other data available in the text. To a lesser degree, the multiple frames and juxtaposed voices of Boullosa's *Cielos de la Tierra* work toward an indigestible novel, though the text still contains a semblance of a narrative arc that enables synopsis. In the same style, *La novela perfecta*—as anticipated by the parenthetical subtitle (*Un cuento largo*) (A Long Story)—features an intercalated short story and failed meta-plot for a novel, but still permits Vertiz, the protagonist, to undergo a familiar development arc: from suspicion, to acceptance, to rejection of the virtual technology behind the "perfect novel." Finally, with *El complot de los Románticos* Boullosa achieves a profusion of competing narrators and events that becomes so elaborate as to defy adequate plot summary. If Boullosa voices suspicion of progress, she sometimes locates her objection in the feared triumph of the image over the word. Unexpectedly perhaps, Bellatin's and Boullosa's divergent levels of open-mindedness toward stranger impairment correlates to their degree of openness to visual mediums. Boullosa's three texts explicitly dread the imagined victory of the image over intellectual coherence, and the narrators in these novels articulate a defense of the necessity of literature against the abject disability conjured by excessive reliance on the image. By contrast, Bellatin's *Biografía ilustrada de Mishima* concludes with fifty photographs, making the number of pictures roughly equal to the number of pages of written text, all couched in the context of ongoing jokes. The destabilizing, meditative approach of *Biografía ilustrada de Mishima* questions the slide between the real and the normal, and yet Bellatin's endgame seems merely to twist diversity into sameness in a banal gesture that fails to defy the concept of the "norm."

## Mario Bellatin and Biografía ilustrada de Mishima

For the reader unfamiliar with protagonist Yukio Mishima's historical biography (1925–1970), I should explain that the Japanese writer committed hara-kiri and then died of decapitation by sword-blade at the hand of a friend, Morita, who, both in factual history and in Bellatin's retelling of events, subsequently shot himself.[2] In the novel, death for the writer does not come in a "definitive" manner. In a chicken-or-the-egg paradox, Bellatin's text attributes Mishima's indefinite death to headlessness: "if [Mishima] had a head like everyone else he would be dead in the same way that the rest die: definitively" (47). The collection of reproduced photographs present the historical, black-and-white image of Yukio Mishima's severed head and a photo of Bellatin himself, captioned as an analyst who worked on Mishima's case. These captions manage to cite a reality known to the reader and challenge the veracity of that historical narrative with new information. Bellatin's intentionally clumsy stab at diagnosis jokes that Mishima seeks help in counseling, which justifies the photo of Bellatin, along with a female companion, as analysts. Hilariously for the reader attuned to the sensibility here, Mishima falls victim to a depression twenty days after his suicide, which he initially tries to treat with medication (52). The psychological counseling involves lying on a couch, in silence, while two analysts watch him. As Bellatin explains, tongue in cheek, the analysts consider this meditative exercise to wield "the eloquence of silence as a more than infallible method" (53). Bellatin's nod to meditative possibilities never quite moves into an exploration of the terrain of disability, as it is imagined to connote zoe in neoliberal diversity values, and therefore *Biografía ilustrada de Mishima* laughs at the tactics of diagnosis, even as it retains them.

This is not to say that Bellatin ignores the topic of impairment. Bellatin was born with only one hand and thus might agree with Davis's early support for the social model of disability that locates the dilemma of the disabled not with the individual, but in "the way that normalcy is constructed to create the 'problem' of the disabled person" (*Enforcing Normalcy* 24).[3] The "problem" of disability is only tenuously present in *Biografía ilustrada de Mishima*. When the reader learns that Mishima has penned many of Bellatin's famous titles, one implied joke teases that true disability is not located with the one-handed Bellatin or the headless Mishima, but in the reader's prejudice. In a related detail, the novel briefly recounts an allegorical farmyard experiment carried out by Mishima's uncle: a newly hatched chick with a ribbon tied to one leg is pecked to death in a matter of minutes by the intolerant chicks (41). Although the social model of disability would account for this death as a consequence of discrimination, the allegory does not hold for the rest of the novel. Because Bellatin's meditations defy the stability needed for allegorical interpretation, the sensitive reader cannot consistently apply allegorical explanations to decipher Mishima's experience as a headless writer. No single reliable understanding of Mishima's headless state appears in the text. Now viewed as inspiring gift, now as dangerous difference, now as sideshow attraction, now as banal medical issue, the exact nature of the character's "problem" as a decapitated writer is never dependably defined. This imaginary "problem" of decapitation allows Bellatin to flirt with meditation in addition to constantly changing the diagnosis. The lack of a narrative arc means that the meditation engages rapid-cycle fluctuations between diversity and sameness, which ultimately obey a realism/normalcy aesthetic.

A diversity-to-sameness twist that excludes actual disability—or "*that* kind of difference" according to Davis's careful italics in *The End of Normal*—hints that disability today becomes difficult to name. The critic ruminates, "Thus 'we are all different; therefore we are all the same' becomes 'we are all the same because we aren't *that* kind of different' " (*The End of Normal* 13–14). Davis struggles to articulate disability here, perhaps as a consequence of the silencing and invisibility that help to exclude the category he wants to recognize. Even if he, too, fails to name the excluded disability, Bellatin marvelously captures the twisting of diversity-into-sameness, and the longing of boring sameness to twist into admirable diversity. For instance, *Biografía ilustrada de Mishima* reviews an invented custom, in which the headless writer exchanges shoes with a female friend from college: "Almost without speaking to one another they practice a peculiar exchange of shoes" (10). This mysterious ritual intimates a kind of physical equality between the headless male and the female friend. In another example of diversity presented as more of the same, and sameness as somehow also representing a desirable diversity, when Mishima fails to convince a medical authority that his condition is owed to Thalidomide, the savvy nurse dismissively writes *Decapitated* on the paper that she gives him (38). This diagnosis prevents Mishima from fraudulently collecting a settlement that would allow him to buy a coveted type of prosthetic head, but the diagnosis does not otherwise affect him. Part of Bellatin's game here is to take what seems a chronic condition—for example, headlessness as disability—and treat it as a case of acute pain—for example, headlessness as diversity—that could be "remedied" with a prosthetic. After failing to acquire the desired prosthetic, Mishima perceives that the only true element in his life is that of absence: "The only true thing in life was a void. An empty space, impenetrable and infinite" (40). In case the reader manages to miss this key idea, it repeats: "The only real thing was a void" (53). Diversity bound into sameness leads, in the headless character's most perceptive moments of meditative insight, to the relief of nothingness. The implication that bios achieves enlightenment by sensing the void does not pose a particularly optimistic viewpoint from narrative standards, but it should delight the meditators. On this edge of nothingness bios and zoe might encounter one another, but *Biografía ilustrada de Mishima* does not develop Mishima's awareness of the void; he is otherwise occupied with measuring his diverse yet assimilated individuality in relation to the sameness of others around him.

Bellatin's protagonist does not necessarily cross a category boundary when his strange impairments are revealed, and this sameness can be described through the image of the Möbius strip. In the mid-1990s, Elizabeth Grosz's *Volatile Bodies* famously used a Möbius strip to reimagine the Cartesian duality of mind and body.[4] A Möbius model can be formed by taking a strip of paper, giving it a half twist, and taping together the resulting loop. The resulting surface that possesses only one side helps to imagine a boundaryless relationship between two states of health, here defined as diversity and sameness. If you trace the Möbius strip, your finger will touch what were two previously distinct sides of the paper without slipping off or crossing a boundary. However, as Grosz cautions, the Möbius model does not easily represent "modes of becoming, modes of transformation" (210). Her warning suggests that in Bellatin's game, sameness and diversity implicate one another from the start, and the loop itself and not the appearance of a journey converts diversity into acceptable equality or bios; bare life remains beyond the loop. Understandably, given his reluctance to engage with the abject difference of disability under neoliberal imaginings, Bellatin decorates the diversity-to-sameness strip with ironically nostalgic references to the false solution of the prosthetic. The road to sameness is studded with fake heads, the novel seems to counsel, mocking the very symbol of embodied wisdom. As the headless protagonist's efforts to hit upon the properly diverse prosthetic become more stylish, and thus ever more acceptably "diverse" under neoliberal dependence on perpetually renewed consumer expression, Mishima moves from wearing a rudimentary prosthetic head, which elicits negative reactions, to using a rhinestone-encrusted mask (45–46). Bellatin thus pushes impairment toward a fashion discussion, which rewards stylistic diversity, and works to ignore disability.

As mentioned, Mishima fails to acquire a "professional head" through the fraudulent scheme to sue for fetal Thalidomide damage, although he does collaborate with an artist who makes him a series of "head-pieces" (46). Disability critics David Mitchell and Sharon Snyder define the verb "prostheticize" as the effort "to institute a notion of the body with a regime of tolerable deviance" (*Narrative Prosthesis* 6–7). Bellatin's Mishima hints at familiarity with Mitchell and Snyder's analysis, as the character negotiates within the regime of the prosthetic and its struggle to dictate the normalcy codes. As predicted by Mitchell and Snyder's attribution of the quality of the prosthetic to all novels, *Biografía ilustrada de Mishima* cannot exit the loop that binds the diverse Mishima to the conformist Mishima. His urge to view absence as the only trustworthy element in the novel leads to a statement of tight contradiction regarding prosthetics: "Head and the creation of words. Mishima had perceived, especially in recent times, that there could not be one without the other. Or, more exactly, that one could not exist without the absence of the other" (47). In these consecutive sentences, Bellatin manages to accumulate ideas without constructing a reliably logical statement. If only, *Biografía ilustrada de Mishima* seems to wish, it were possible to eliminate diagnostic narrative and close the gap between mind and thought, between body and intellect, thereby creating a steady and spontaneous flow of experience-as-word-as-all, a point of sameness so total that it stands indivisible from nothingness. Sadly for Mishima and fortunately for writers, the division between mind and thought, word and experience, cannot be permanently soldered. Head and words, self-consciousness narrative and in-the-moment flow, continuously substitute the other, and their alternating presence implicates the unavoidable prosthetics of presence in representation. In the end *Biografía ilustrada de Mishima* is still narrated, even if it never "goes anywhere" novelistically.

In one last observation that prepares my reader to turn next to Boullosa's concerns about the image and technology as they threaten narrative, that is, as the digital and the posthuman threaten to fill the gap between "head and words," I should note that from the start Bellatin frames his novel as the gloss of a "film of reality." That is, the novel insinuates itself as a record of a series of "real" images, "a kind of film of reality" watched by an "us" defined as "the attendees" (10). This film opens with the very location from where the audience watches: "The first image to appear is the schoolyard where we are gathered" (10). The spontaneity and immediacy of such a film, reflective of the very reality that the audience experiences, perhaps means to challenge the process of narrative. Just as the desired film is hinted to form impenetrable sameness with the "reality" of the text, the supreme form of writing imagined in the novel seems to long for absolute unification with the written. Or, to put this ideal in terms of Diana Palaversich's seminal article, the essence of Bellatin's narrative aims to harness the "writable" and not the "readable" (37). Apparently for Bellatin, the question of how to write the desired literary text ends up seeking to eliminate the established binaries of the real and unreal, impairment and sameness, and the categories of writing and reading. This point is not as convoluted as it seems. *Biografía ilustrada de Mishima*, along with many of Bellatin's other novels, struggles with longing to connect the tool of writing with the "real" and thereby eliminate the aspect of "tool-ness" or the "prosthetic" in writing, or the distraction of narrative in meditation. One way for Bellatin to curtail the risk of pushing the novel too far and publishing an unreadable set of anti-norms is to gesture toward this possibility of pure writing, a creation that is never a supplement and therefore never a prosthetic. This pure writing as sameness, or the void, once again neatly sidesteps the question of the disability as bare life that lies just beyond the diversity loop, but then again, meditation does not claim to provide answers but merely relief from narrative.

True to Bellatin's perpetual, inexhaustible games with switching out the diagnostic arc in favor of spontaneous meditation and its idealized culmination in pure writing, the fictional academic who presents the "film of reality," identified this time as, "a kind of reflection of reality" comes to deny the reality of his subject (54). More specifically, the expert affirms Mishima's nonexistence: "The impeccable Japanese professor finished his intervention for that afternoon by affirming that Mishima has never really existed" (54). Not every novelist dares Bellatin's self-amused approach to the diversity twist that only seems to stop short when it hits upon the possibility that what *really* exists is nothing. This reality of nothingness, and the shifting, uncertain body of knowledge that leads the mind to perceive it, entails precisely the sort of uncertainty that terrifies Boullosa's narrators.

## Carmen Boullosa and the Stranger Novels

Boullosa's narrative voices differ from Bellatin's example because they wield moralistic judgments and tend to favor allegorical interpretations. These narrators belong in analysis informed by disability studies because they interrogate facile notions of progress, and for disability scholars, the connection between progress and normalcy is perpetually ripe for questioning. Historian Douglas Baynton locates the origin of the disability-rejecting concept of "normality" in its modern sense in the mid-nineteenth century, when it arose "in the context of a pervasive belief in progress" (36). Boullosa's texts tend to attribute the imagined, frightening new bodily abilities to thoughtless applications of technology, or a naïve belief in the linear march of progress. *La novela perfecta* illustrates this point. The "perfect novel" of the title turns out to be a virtual narrative machine that creates a "real" illusion through technology, in a vague parallel with Bellatin's "film of reality." As the informed reader can predict, given Boullosa's insistent defense of the literary word, the attempt by narrator Vertiz to harness the technology of the "perfect novel" and synchronize his imagination with the virtual image proves disastrous. Vertiz's creativity works along partially intuitive, meditative lines, and he needs to be able to write down ideas in order to arrange them later along a stricter narrative arc. Without the process of writing, and perhaps even better said, without the written negotiation that balances spontaneous fantasy and planned narration, Vertiz loses control over his art.

His flight of fancy expressed through first-draft-is-final technology ends up killing its scientific creator and forming an allegorical tableau of characters that captures the "essence of contemporary man": "Broken all, like disposable beings, repeated, forgotten that they are each a unique world, they ended up being slayed by that fabulous machinery, the vertigo of diamonds, the vertigo of money, the splendor of money" (150). Sameness, expressed here as having forgotten that everyone belongs to a unique world, nearly wins out. Boullosa hints that the void triggered by this sameness is not Bellatin's ideal, but an apocalypse. Though the chaos achieves a certain splendor before it winks out, the figures horrify Vertiz: "[. . .] they remained also filled with nonsense, insanity, repetition, violence, horror" (148). Boullosa's narrators need to believe in interpretative stability, and they express faith in the reliable presence of the prosthetics of writing with a fervor that Bellatin might label as naive. Because this vision of imagined mutilation, harboring the end of writing and the beginning of abysmal sameness, repeats in Boullosa's oeuvre, it seems worthwhile to cite at length from an example of the malfunction of narrative technology in *La novela perfecta*:

> No one realized who was the other, or the space each occupied, or the place; no one was anything to one group or to the other; no one knew who he was, nor whom she attacked; and as much as they penetrated each other, they also hit each other, they also kissed each other, without anything seeming to make any sense, and immediately the ones and the others began to. . . . How should I explain it? They dismembered themselves or the others, some ate the others or themselves within themselves, without any of those acts meaning anything either. (143)

The confusion produced with the use of vague pronouns and the absence of possessives indicates that Boullosa intends to build horror in these scenes by stripping out individualistic understandings of bodies and their borders. For narrator Vertiz, the body merging lacks morality, or in his words, an author: "I was not the author of that. I could not be the author of that. It was, above all, an image WITHOUT an author" (144). Vertiz requires diagnosis, a linear narrative arc, for meaning to emerge; when confronted with the meditative, nonprogressive, interdependence, Vertiz knows that his status as author, as diagnostician, critic, and moralistic observer, is threatened. Under conditions of free-for-all meditation, narrators are not needed.

Given Boullosa's staid interest in allegory, it perhaps comes as no surprise that even as her narrators reconsider the intellectual, environmental, and community damage caused by errant notions of progress, the narrators cling to an ideal of the "normal." Across Boullosa's stranger novels, the lonely narrators give the impression that they view themselves in terms of Rosemarie Garland-Thomson's concept of "normate" as "the constructed identity of those who, by way of the bodily configurations and cultural capital they assume, can step into a position of authority and wield the power it grants them" (8). The self-appointed, implicit demarcation of the normate appears with Lear of *Cielos de la Tierra*, Vertiz of *La novela perfecta*, and the principal narrator of *El complot de los Románticos*. These malcontents tend to lack children, living romantic partners, and promising careers. They are, thus, "diverse" from the mainstream and yet not abject; despite their discontented and hypercritical personalities, constantly primed to a bad mood and always alert to problems, they do not assess themselves as impaired, much less disabled or representative of bare life—*that* kind of difference applies to the posthuman or digital figures that horrify them. In addition to their privileged condition as bios, staked on their literary tastes if not skills, the narrators revel in their individuality as normates and emphatically recoil at scenes of unfamiliar bodily sameness or exchangeability.

To give another instance of this "normate" narrative, Boullosa's *Cielos de la Tierra* includes a posthuman race, the "Atlántidos," that decides to give themselves a language-destroying lobotomy. According to holdout narrator Lear, the language-free Atlántidos promptly exile themselves from stable chains of cause and effect, linear time, and expected spatial relations. Lear stays behind in the world of words, of narrative arcs, and of moralistic judgment, which allows her to diagnose her compatriots as hopelessly disabled. The postsurgical Atlántidos live in pure meditation, a mind without words, a state that Lear cannot view as freeing. Lear describes the Atlántidos' new abilities as gruesome, such as the scene in which the female character Carson removes, bloodlessly, one of her own arms; she opens herself up and sticks the arm into her torso, ultimately extending the fingers through her ear, nose, and mouth (352). Lear is repulsed by the grotesquely reformed body:

> The wonder and the horror would not allow me to keep my eyes closed. The opening left by the fringe of skin that now was hanging from her [Carson] in a frontal tail, exposed the arm that had entered through the hole, plus a countless number of things. Not of guts, but of *things*, things of different colors and shapes, things arranged in a rigorous order and economy of space within her body. (353)

Lear anchors the negative aspect of this uncertain diversity—that is, *that* kind of difference, or *disability* as bare life—in her companions' lack of shame over their new bodies. In fact, Lear seems less bothered by the bodily experimentations themselves than by the Atlántidos's insufficient embarrassment over their contortions, including wanton sexuality, which she describes in moralistic tones as "filthy acts" (353). To the Atlántidos' credit, it must be observed that the pro-lobotomy vote comes about because the Atlántidos cannot bear their state of perfect health. They seem poised for immortality, as long as they protect themselves from radiation, but they apparently cannot resist the desire for a "normalcy" plot. Just as Lennard Davis's formula predicts, the Atlántidos manufacture a situation of abnormality out of their perfection that needs solving, and so to eliminate the "problem" of lies and confusion, they eliminate language. Yet, this elected "cure" manages to kill the novel—a problem for the narrator. Lear finds her final solution in the abstract and places herself into a book: the "Heavens on Earth" of the title. To surmise from this meditation (a posthuman realm of perfect health) turned to plot (the lobotomy) turned toward meditation (the end of the novel), it would seem that no alternative to narrative exists *in the novel*: Lear's attempted construction of another "real" narrative platform constitutes merely another pass within the diversity loop, another embrace of carefully defined narrativized sameness, created by excluding disability, that incorporates two other narrators—Estela and Hernando—against the willing bypass of separated bios and zoe that her compatriots dare. Estela and Hernando are included in the embrace of narrativized sameness because—note the near paradox—they express uniqueness fashionable under a diversity discourse. Their difference is not *that* kind of difference but the winking sameness of acceptable diversity.

The sixteenth-century chair-bound narrator Hernando provides a case in point. Lear and the narrator from the 1990s, Mexican academic Estela, independently discover a text by elderly, largely immobile Hernando, who attracts the other narrators' platonic love. Hernando's impairment does not frighten Lear or Estela, probably because unlike the Atlántidos' postlobotomy state, the oppressed indigenous man's inability to walk or twist his head toward the sky does not threaten established relationships with narrative. Hernando's younger self, also described as metaphorically impaired, similarly fails to scare Estela or Lear. Despite Hernando's insistent image of having lost his hands, a symbol of the loss of his family's native culture in the colonial oppression of New Spain that leaves him with only a tongue through which to apprehend the world, he remains respectable in Boullosa's diagnostic manual (142–144). Hernando's literate isolation may underpin his appeal for Lear and Estela. This loneliness supplies a sort of "diversity chic" that defines a narrator's outlook as distinctive and yet within the limits of "normate-tivity."

As a final example of moralistic rejection of meditative body melding and mutation in Boullosa's novels, I cite *El complot de los Románticos* with its dead writers' conference held in Madrid. The organizer of this conference is also the main narrator of this experimental novel, and she blames the location for spurring the revived authors to turn too "alive" (211). That is, instead of writing or presenting papers as individuals on a reprieve from mortality in Madrid, the setting gets to them and they start "mixing it up." The result of this uncontrolled joie de vivre involves the catastrophic fusing of bodies:

> And the anomalous gymnastics turned sinister: the celebrated authors threw parts of themselves from themselves: a head launches itself to attack the foot of its own body; hands work loose, they turn into pinchers, they open chests, take out hearts, replace their locations; the legs walk without torsos; a shoulder wanders over there; the spinal column of every one of those present—except for we two mortals—became one column of vertigo, the feet were the hooves of imagination. Instead of grammar, there were muscles. It would be unthinkable, if we did not have the referent of comic books. In any case: horripid! So much so that even among the toughest of the mob, some felt moved. (249–250)

The scene does not require detailed interpretation because it fits with the previous citations of bodily confusion and mutation. Boullosa's narrator once again fears the ominous privileging of the image over the word, that is, "muscles" over "grammar," and the body part mêlée proves grotesque enough to put a permanent end to the yearly writers' conference. Apparently, the conference-curtailing threat has to do with the possibility that meditation and its retooled expectations for diagnosis, narrative arcs, and interpersonal relations threaten the very need for writers, whether dead or alive—and perhaps even for normates, those narrators who are not famous dead writers, but wish that they were fashionably exceptional enough to be like them.

Why don't Boullosa's narrators in *Cielos de la Tierra*, *La novela perfecta*, and *El complot de los Románticos* shake off the conventions of shaming diagnosis, break free from the compulsory judgment of the normate, and indulge the newly ungoverned and recombinant physique? The answer links Boullosa's intentionally limited experiment with that of Bellatin.

## Conclusion

Given the brisk pace of technological developments—from new pharmaceuticals to prosthetics and surgeries—Bellatin's decapitated novelist and Boullosa's detachable body parts may one day strike readers as not so far-fetched. The hypocrisy of the neoliberal diversity twist teaches with only pretend tolerance that unfamiliar bodily stylings are welcome. However, because Bellatin and Boullosa tinker with the structure of the novel, from *within* the structure of the novel, the very genre that according to Davis creates the problem of the realist average, their literary experimentations do obey certain constraints. If Bellatin and Boullosa cannot craft texts that exit the disability twist, this constraint may reflect the origin of novelistic protagonists as artificial abnormals made to "do the twist" and end up normal. The idea of bare life incorporated into the textual focus, into bios, to the extent that such a notion surfaces at all, in Bellatin's case seems to point toward a paradisiacal void of pure writing, and in Boullosa's novels seems to threaten the end of writing. Still, fiction matters to them both. In the final analysis, a literary critic finds herself hard pressed not agree. Whatever its limitations, narrative invites us to think again, even as it seems to want to think for us.

## Notes

1. The change in language sustains the original point of instituting the imaginary norm as reality; the novelistic formula means to ignore the fact that the "normal" is "not a static or peaceful, but a dynamic and polemical concept" (Canguilhem 239). Likewise, the inverse is true, and to cite one critic's wording, "Disability, as a category, is fundamentally unstable" (Hall 12).

2. Henry Scott Stokes's history explains that Morita did not get the job done and a fourth and final head-severing blow was delivered by the unruffled accomplice Furu-Koga, a messy detail not recovered in Bellatin's text (Stokes 31).

3. An impressive line of scholarship has cataloged Bellatin's fascination with strange bodies and seems to take inspiration in Bellatin's impairment. For example, in his Spanish-language prologue to a reprinted collection of Bellatin's novels, Ariel Schettini applies the English-language label "freak" and notes that Bellatin's odd figures use their physical difference as a means for integration into a community (9). Schettini lists some of Bellatin's stranger characters, such as the paralyzed man from *Perros héroes* [Hero Dogs] (2003), the one-handed writer from *Lecciones para una liebre muerta* [Lessons for a Dead Hare] (2005), and the long-nosed protagonist from *Shiki Nagaoka: una nariz de ficción* [Shiki Nagaoka: A Nose for Fiction] (2001).

This last title concerns a brilliant chapter in Susan Antebi's groundbreaking book on disability in Latin American fiction, and in a foundational article that first prepares the way for Antebi's and Schettini's thought, Diana Palaversich creatively juxtaposes Rosemarie Garland Thomson's review of freak shows and Bellatin's portrayed genetic human mutations in *Flores* (Flowers) (2000), the decomposing characters' bodies in *Salón de belleza* (Beauty Salon) (1994), and the odd bodily practices that obsess characters in both *Poeta ciego* (Blind Poet) (1998) and *La Escuela del dolor humano de Sechuán* (The School of Human Pain of Sichuan) (2001) (36). Palaversich observes that the experimentation with characters' physiques never denotes the abject in Bellatin's texts, and merely disturbs notions of unified identity. Because the aforementioned critics have not yet taken up *Biografía ilustrada de Mishima*, I chose that title for my analysis.

4. Kristin Lindgren cites Grosz's use of the Möbius strip in *Volatile Bodies* (1994) in order to articulate the notion in autobiography of illness, aka pathography, that imagines a postillness self "not as a distinct, bounded entity entirely separate from the old self but as a fluid configuration in which elements of old and new, self and other, inside and outside, exist concurrently" (148). Joy Cypher and Deb Martin use the Möbius strip to model the goal of critical thinking in the disability studies classroom. They praise the flux and lack of endpoint in the Möbius strip, which for their purposes came to be "not a thing but rather an undulating activity" (Cypher and Martin).

## Works Cited


Antebi, Susan. *Carnal Inscriptions: Spanish American Narratives of Corporeal Difference and Disability.* New York: Palgrave Macmillan, 2009.

Baynton, Douglas C. "Disability and the Justification of Inequality in American History." In *The New Disability History: American Perspectives.* Edited by Paul K. Longmore and Lauri Umansky. New York and London: New York UP, 2001, 33–57.

Bellatin, Mario. *Biografía ilustrada de Mishima.* Buenos Aires: Entropía, 2009.

Boullosa, Carmen. *Cielos de la Tierra.* México: Alfaguara, 1997.

———. *La novela perfecta. Un cuento largo.* México: Alfaguara, 2006.

———. *El complot de los Románticos.* México: Siruela, 2009.

Canguilhem, Georges. In *The Normal and the Pathological.* 1966. Translated by Carolyn R. Fawcett. Introduction by Michel Foucault. New York: Zone Books, 1989.

Cypher, Joy and Deb Martin. "The Mobius Strip: Team Teachers Reflecting on Disability Studies and Critical Thinking." *Disability Studies Quarterly* 28.4 (2008): n.p. Web. May 16, 2013.

Davis, Lennard J. *Enforcing Normalcy: Disability, Deafness, and the Body.* London and New York: Verso, 1995.

———. *Bending Over Backwards: Disability, Dismodernism and Other Difficult Positions.* Foreword by Michael Bérubé. New York and London: New York UP, 2002.

———. *The End of Normal: Identity in a Biocultural Era.* Ann Arbor: U of Michigan P, 2013.

Garland-Thomson, Rosemarie. *Extraordinary Bodies: Figuring Physical Disability in American Culture and Literature.* New York: Columbia UP, 1997.

Grosz, Elizabeth. *Volatile Bodies: Toward a Corporeal Feminism.* Bloomington: Indiana UP, 1994.

Hall, Alice. *Disability and Modern Fiction: Faulkner, Morrison, Coetzee and the Nobel Prize for Literature.* New York: Palgrave Macmillan, 2012.

Hayden, Deborah. *Pox: Genius, Madness, and the Mysteries of Syphilis.* New York: Basic Books, 2003.

Lindgren, Kristin. "Bodies in Trouble: Identity, Embodiment, and Disability." In *Gendering Disability.* Edited by Bonnie G. Smith and Beth Hutchison. New Brunswick, NJ: Rutgers UP, 2004. 145–165.

Mitchell, David T., and Sharon L. Snyder. *Narrative Prosthesis: Disability and the Dependencies of Discourse.* Ann Arbor: U of Michigan P, 2000.

———. *Cultural Locations of Disability.* Chicago and London: U of Chicago P, 2006.

Oliver, Michael. *Understanding Disability: From Theory to Practice.* 2nd ed. New York: Palgrave Macmillan, 2009.

Palaversich, Diana. "Apuntes para una lectura de Mario Bellatin." *Chasqui.* 32.1 (2003): 25–38.

Schettini, Ariel. "Prólogo. En el Castillo de Barbazul: El caso de Mario Bellatin." *Tres novelas: Salón de belleza, Jacobo el mutante, Bola negra.* Mérida, Venezuela: El otro el mismo, 2005. 7–18.

Shakespeare, Tom. *Disability Rights and Wrongs.* London and New York: Routledge, 2006.

Stokes, Henry Scott. *The Life and Death of Yukio Mishima.* Revised edition. New York: Farrar, Straus and Giroux, 1995.

Thompson, Clive. "The Rules of Panic: Why Some Technologies Seem Benign and Others Scare the Bejesus Out of Us." *Wired* 20. November 11, 2012: 70.

Chapter 13

# The Blur of Imagination

## Asperger's Syndrome and *One Hundred Years of Solitude*

Juan Manuel Espinosa

The idea for this chapter began with an image, that of a lonely man sitting at his desk in front of old documents, enthralled by the deciphering of their hidden meanings, all the while the world is tearing itself apart. That is the final scene of Gabriel García Márquez's *One Hundred Years of Solitude* (*Cien años de soledad*, 1967) in which Aureliano Babilonia, the last living descendant of the Buendía family, deciphers Melquíades's parchments long after several generations of Buendías had tried and failed to do so. When he does, the parchments reveal to him and to the novel's readers that he is reading what has been in fact happening in real life (Rodríguez Monegal 486). This is an image of painful loneliness, not simply because of the contingent circumstances that surround the character—Macondo will soon be swallowed by a hurricane—but because, just as Babilonia understands the story that explains his world, his family and himself, said world is being destroyed. The moment of recognition of an order of the world is the same moment in which the hurricane destroys that world and its order. It is a weird ending. The real world inside the book loops into the parchments, and because it is the end of the book itself, it seems to hint that there is some kind of ending of the real world as well.

Fast-forward forty years and we find Aureliano Babilonias everywhere, in books, films, and other registers of popular culture: an awkward person with difficulties in relating to others, who has a limited set of interests but cultivates them with extreme intensity, a person who could continue reading even if the world were to be blown away. In popular parlance today, this outsider character has several names: the *geek*, the *freak*, the *nerd*, the *outcast*. All the versions of this character suffer the same painful loneliness: as soon as they understand the order of the world, the world seems to change.

If these traits were previously attributed to and understood as idiosyncrasies at best or defects at worst in a person's character, with the medicalization of culture (Conrad 3–19) we have now attached a formal diagnosis to this new cultural icon. If we were to overlap these characteristics into a Venn-Diagram we would find, at their meeting point, the current cultural image of a person with Asperger's syndrome (AS): a person who seems to be always looking for the meaning of the world in the social cues of others, for a rule-based understanding of their own surroundings, for a place in a world that is constantly changing. As we see below, Asperger's has become a trait with high cultural value today.

The cultural reception of the medical diagnosis constitutes a very broad and rough interpretation, one which we find in all types of cultural artifacts. However, even if inaccurate, the relation to imagination that this diagnosis has within culture is what I place on center stage, as it is what connects the cultural valences of AS to *One Hundred Years of Solitude*. In this chapter, I am not proposing to apply symptoms of Asperger's diagnosis to fictional characters and to their reactions to narrative events. Rather, I think through the role of imagination as constructed by two different concepts: Asperger's syndrome and Magical Realism. In both phenomena I believe imagination—what it means and how it works on fiction and on the ways we understand each other—is transformed in unexpected ways. It is this transformation that forces us to understand Magical Realism as a particular genre and enjoy its flourishes, but also, regrettably, it makes us separate nontypical ways of understanding the world and diagnose them as "conditions." Magical realism has infused literature beyond its particular point of origin, be that *One Hundred Years of Solitude* or its predecessors and it has shaped how we read today. Asperger's syndrome is no longer exclusively a medical condition to be treated, but rather it has been transformed into an identity to be embraced, and a character trait used in fiction, movies and cultural discourse. Nevertheless, these new uses come at the price of misunderstanding, particularly because the medicalization of culture has progressively become the only way we deal with mental differences.

In this chapter, instead of medicalizing Asperger's syndrome, I attempt to explain it as a particular way of mentally organizing—imagining—the world, and I draw a connection to a way of reading *One Hundred Years of Solitude*. I do this by briefly addressing the history of the concept of imagination: how it transformed from the faculty that allows us to apprehend the reality around us, into a cherished ability to escape the limits of that reality, and how this new iteration has been applied in medicine and culture, turning its absence into a symptom for the former, and into a character trait for the latter. Then I describe Asperger's syndrome, paying particular attention to the ways imagination works—in AS people and, crucially, in their diagnosis. Finally, I read the first page of García Márquez's novel in an Asperger's-like key, that is, while paying particular attention to the moments when readers bear witness to the creation of an imaginative world that does not follow preestablished categories, and when the text forces readers to release those received ideas and patterns and create a new image of that "new" world. If there is something to be learned from reading the page this way, it is to allow us to understand the real-life process of creating a new image of a new world that people with AS do continuously, not as a disorder or mental condition, but as a genre in the repertoire of world-organization that humans are capable of carrying out.

## Imaginations

In his *Critique of Pure Reason* (1781/1787), when Immanuel Kant refers to imagination, he uses the term as it was most commonly employed at the time, as an ability every mind has of integrating multiple sensory data when perceiving them. The following passage captures this sense of the faculty of imagination.

> Because every appearance contains a manifold, so that different perceptions are in themselves encountered in the mind sporadically and individually, these perceptions need be given a combination that in sense itself they cannot have. Hence there is in us an active power to synthesize this manifold. This power we call imagination: and the act that it performs directly on perceptions I call apprehension. For the imagination is to bring the manifold of intuition into an image. (*CPR* 167 [A 120])

After Kant, however, with the rise of Romanticism, another meaning—which had existed parallel to the first one—came to the forefront: the mind's ability to be creative, to produce analogies, to be fanciful, to create images not based on—or independent from—reality. Both may be active mental powers, but while Kant's understanding of imagination is a necessary capacity for all human beings, the Romantic imagination is only attributed to certain gifted people. This is *fancy*, the realm where imagination stops being a faculty of the mind and starts being a social, cultural, or artistic quality that provides an escape from one's immediate surroundings. Kant's broader sense of imagination has receded to the background, since then reappearing only sporadically, and it is my belief that in order to understand Magical Realism and Asperger's syndrome, and to change how we confront these two phenomena, we need to bring Kant's meaning back into view.

The change from the Kantian definition to the understanding of imagination as mere fancy is not an innocent one. As Lorraine Daston has shown in "Fear and Loathing of Imagination in the Arts":

> This early nineteenth-century confrontation of individualistic, brashly subjective art with collective, staunchly objective science was not simply the collision of some timeless faith in the imagination with an equally timeless faith in facts. Rather, it signaled a mutation in the meanings both of imagination and of facts that still shapes the moral economy of science. (17)

Daston shows how imagination at first was seen as controllable by reason, by facts, and by a clear communication between scientists—the rise of objectivity as an array of commitments to a set of instruments, procedures and standards (23). But later on, this cautionary view began to give way to a loathing of imagination. Quoting again from Daston:

> The power of the imagination had long awakened fear among scientists—and theologians, poets, artists, and doctors, to boot—because it could make up a world of its own that was livelier, lovelier, or more logical than the real world. In extreme cases the imagination could conquer the body as well as the mind, leading not only to madness but also to violent somatic crises. But Enlightenment theorists of the imagination had been confident in the right and competence of reason to discipline the imagination. (27)

The Kantian aspect of imagination was coalesced into fancy, the faculty of drifting away from facts. The fear and loathing of imagination in the sciences has navigated into the realm of culture, and although there is no such thing as a fear and loathing of imagination pure and simple in the arts, there is an everyday treatment of imaginary objects and texts according to heavily regulated protocols and surrounded by an array of cautionary tales. These tales are based precisely on the idea that some genres, motifs or ideas are based "on reality" (realism and naturalism, for example) and others are an escape from it (fantasy and speculative fiction and all its subgenres).[1] In this dyad, realism carries all the weight of seriousness, relevance and intellectual and cultural authority, while fantasy is at best relegated to child's play (or to children's literature). Fantasy is the genre of entertainment where imagination is given free reign, while realism is the genre that can deal with truths and facts precisely because imagination is kept in check.

When readers first encountered Gabriel García Márquez's novel *One Hundred Years of Solitude*, something that did not exist before appeared in their consciousness, something that thanks to the media was popularized under the term *magical realism*.[2] What appeared before the reading public was not simply a literary genre; it was a different way of organizing a manifold of perceptions, a different way of imagining the world. What was new in this novel, and what a magical realist text and Asperger's syndrome have in common is that the readers—and non-Asperger's individuals—are forced into understanding imagination in Kant's sense. That is, they are confronted with a singular way of organizing perceptions that is different from our culture's shared imaginative practices.

The historical reason for this meeting point between a syndrome and a narrative genre, is that the drive for objectivity and communicability in the sciences was also at the core of nineteenth-century and twentieth-century philological and literary history projects—and therefore the way we traditionally ascribe order to literary genres. The need to separate fact from fiction and the scientific from the artistic rehashed the old idea of a dualistic notion of the world divided into the everyday world and the world of ideas that can be traced back to Plato. The borders between these two terms have been constantly put into question, deconstructed and reviewed in both Continental and Anglophone philosophical traditions—albeit in different ways—and in literary studies, but in this analysis I am interested in the moment when a reader experiences that dyad not in terms of separation, but in the blurring and mixing of worlds. Magical Realism is a nowhere land, or better yet, a land that embraces the dyad of reality and the imaginary, and where there is no hesitation regarding the difference between them.

Right at the moment when the novel ends by turning in on itself, readers are left with the realization that the world has changed. In the last sentence of the final chapter they understand that the text has bled into reality; the fiction has surreptitiously infused itself into the pillars of what is for everybody "real," blemishing the clean-cut separation between reality and imagination. This is the impasse of imagination that we find both in the novel and in the interpretation of AS traits. Readers today, in their constant need to understand a world that changes before it is completely comprehended, have grabbed onto the magical realist blurring of fantasy and reality; at the same time they feel represented by characters whose traits bring the loneliness of a lack of a communicable imagination to the fore. From this point of view, it is in this impasse and blurring of different versions of imagination that we can locate the reasons why readers and viewers find a novel like *One Hundred Years of Solitude* and the portrayal of the lived experiences of people with AS so enticing: it is their chance to see imagination (in Kant's sense) at work, creating individual noncommunicable worlds, while at the same time empathizing with the solitude and alienation that comes out of that process of imagining a world (a more Romantic reaction).

## Asperger's Syndrome

Asperger's syndrome is classified as one of five pervasive developmental disorders, "a group of disorders characterized by delays in the development of socialization and communication skills" (National Institute of Neurological Disorders and Stroke [NINDS]). The main symptoms that need to be present to diagnose someone as in the pervasive developmental disorders spectrum are problems with language, difficulty relating to people and events; and, in the case of Asperger's, a limited but very intense interest in a particular topic. Due to stark differences in diagnostic criteria, the prevalence estimates of Asperger's disorder in the population vary greatly, but according to Ehlers and Gilberg it can be said that 2.6 persons per thousand have this condition. It is not, then, a very common diagnosis.

Nonetheless, the cultural prevalence of Asperger's would seem to tell a different story. In the science fiction TV series *Alphas*, a character with Asperger's was able to visualize all electromagnetic signals. In TV sitcoms, we only need to think of *The Big Bang Theory*, where we find Sheldon Cooper, a character with Asperger-like traits, or Abed Nadir in *Community*, who had a strong proclivity to seeing and understanding everything around him as if it were a TV show. In nonfiction, Oliver Sacks, probably the most visible figure in the fraught process of popularization of medical cases, helped undermine long-established prejudices against mental disorders while also smoothing out the path to the medicalization of social and cultural phenomena.[3] While Sacks does not focus his attention exclusively on AS, a whole array of other writers have published bestsellers on the topic. Irish psychiatrist Michael Fitzgerald has written several books that try to make the case for Asperger's as the origin of creativity in many famous figures throughout history. Persons diagnosed with the syndrome have also penned their own books about their life experiences (Grandin, Tammet, and Elder Robison), and movies and documentaries have started to appear with increasing frequency. In terms of fiction the most notable examples are Mark Haddon's *Curious Incident of the Dog in the Night-time*, and in Mexico, Sabina Berman's *Me, Who Dove into the Heart of the World.* [*La mujer que buceó dentro del corazón del mundo*].[4]

The diagnostic criteria of the AAA (Adult Asperger Assessment) require three or more symptoms of qualitative impairment in verbal or nonverbal communication (lack of emotional reciprocity, difficulties understanding social situations, apparently inflexible adherence to specific nonfunctional routines and rituals, repetitive motor mannerism are some of them) and at least one symptom of what are considered to be impairments of imagination:[5]

> 1. Lack of varied, spontaneous make-believe play appropriate to developmental level.
> 2. Inability to tell, write or generate spontaneous, unscripted or unplagiarised fiction.
> 3. Either lack of interest in fiction (written, or drama) appropriate to developmental level or interest in fiction is restricted to its possible basis in fact (e.g. science fiction, history, technical aspects of film). (Attwood 50)

As many of the forum postings in online support pages for persons within the PDD spectrum and their families show, there is a crucial misunderstanding regarding imagination.[6] When the AAA fixes lack of "make-believe" play "appropriate to developmental level" as a symptom and understands fiction as "spontaneous, unscripted and unplagiarised," and its proper reception as not "restricted to its possible basis in fact," it is leaving behind the general faculty of imagination described by Kant and reaching towards the concept of fancy, prevalent thanks to Romantic notions of the self as autonomous producer of fantasy. There is no such thing as an impossibility or impairment of imagination if it is understood as the faculty of synthesizing multiple sensory perceptions into mental images of the world. These mental images do not need to be flights of fancy to be creative; they are creative in the sense of being a personal or exclusive rearrangement of an individual's perceptions of the world. Therefore, we could say that the difference between AS and neurotypical imaginations relies on how communicable this uncommon rearrangement in fact is. In the case of a person with Asperger's, this rearrangement could be understood as not following the preestablished codes or categories that allow for the sharing or communicability of the rules of such an imaginative world. However, it does not mean this type of imagination is not creative, but rather simply that it cannot be easily classified according to conventional communicable categories, one of which, used in the AAA, is the division between reality and fantasy.

It seems ironic then that the sciences, characterized by Daston by an alleged "fear and loathing of imagination," define a disorder according to a lack of imagination. Imagination then has suffered another transformation. If once, according to Kant, it was a general faculty to make sense of the manifold of appearances, and then under the Romantics, it was a quality that only some brilliant people have, today *the lack* of this second and more exclusive definition is being used as a symptom of a disorder.

This is why a simple reading in a certain key can help us find a different path to understanding AS: not as a disorder but as a variation in the repertoire of how humans mentally organize the world around them. If we do not define AS as a mental deficit but as a genre in the multiple ways of imagining how the world works, then we will not be limited to understanding AS in diagnostic terms, but as a variation in human experience.

How can we imagine inhabiting that construct? The following reading may suggest a way to do so.

## *One Hundred Years of Solitude*

García Márquez's novel starts with one of the most recognized and memorized sentences in world literature today: "Many years later, as he faced the firing squad, Colonel Aureliano Buendía was to remember that distant afternoon when his father took him to discover ice" (1). Much has been said about its apparent simplicity, and about how it hides a strange difficulty in ascertaining the position from which the narrator is telling the story: Is he talking to us after the Colonel's death, or years before, through that strange grammatical construction "había de recordar"—roughly translated as "was to remember"?[7] Furthermore, the childhood remembrance immediately throws us back into the first years of Macondo, showing us the Colonel's parents and town founders José Arcadio Buendía and Úrsula Iguarán. Only once again in the opening chapter will we readers be informed of anything else about the Colonel—although we will begin to know a little about his childhood—while the chapter will end by recovering that initial image of seeing ice for the first time.

Others have seen in that same first sentence a quick and powerful move by the author to transport readers to a time—far gone by now for many of them—when refrigerators were not just uncommon but completely unknown, and to a place—very different also from the usual cosmopolitan sites of 1967's reading public—where winter did not exist, or if it did it was never cold enough to freeze water. In such a remote time and place, many years later, a firing squad would nevertheless appear. This means that within a single lifetime a town has gone from discovering ice to being faced with guns, military organizations, and political institutions—after all, Aureliano is a colonel. Within a single lifetime, the sentence is also telling us, this town has gone from existing in a mythical place and time to becoming a participant in history and in the historical accident we call "war."

Readers understand the plot of the first chapter even if they do not know exactly what kind of fictional universe they have entered, because they are able to deploy theories and interpretations, create emotional and mnemonic links, without ever feeling that the novel is pushing against their expectations. The novel seems to let readers riff their own interpretations about the categories under which they should classify the narrative, without telling them they are not right. There are no communicable patterns or standards of what imagination and facts should be, as there are in science (Daston 27).

Let us return to the end of the first sentence to see how this blurring of categories comes to be: Here, the readers' musings regarding Aureliano's psychology—why is that particular memory so important for him—immediately go off-board upon coming across the following sentence: "At that time Macondo was a village of twenty adobe houses, built on the bank of a river of clear water that ran along a bed of polished stones, which were white and enormous, like prehistoric eggs" (1). It starts as a simple, properly realist and descriptive sentence, with all the gritty stuff needed to classify it as such: the materials the houses are made of and the town's location along a riverbed. It would remain a simple descriptive sentence if it were not for that last simile: the riverbed's huge white rocks like prehistoric eggs. The narrator then knows more than the characters: he knows about evolution and prehistoric time—while for Aureliano, seeing ice for the first time was a world-changing moment and a long-lasting memory. The mythical time and place that were evoked in the first sentence start to dissipate when the narrator brings forth a wisp of scientific discourse just by using the word "prehistoric," even if "prehistoric eggs" is a flight of fancy indeed.

However, the scientific discourse that would have made so much sense in a nineteenth- or early twentieth-century naturalist novel with its minute descriptions and empirically based explanations, is in turn quickly trumped by the next sentence: "The world was so recent that many things lacked names, and in order to indicate them it was necessary to point" (1). With this hyperbole the narrator seems to be mocking his readers: a narrator who knows about prehistoric times cannot immediately state that the world is recent, and even less, that humans can communicate without names for objects. That uncertainty regarding the exact position in time from which the narrator is speaking, the same effect the first sentence produced by means of grammar, the narrator is now producing in readers thanks to the coalescence of cultural discourses that usually do not meet, or if they do it is only to contradict or argue against each other: the scientific discourse and the mythical or religious one. Nevertheless, something seems to be tying them together for the moment.

In this land of nowhere and at this uncertain point in history, an event familiar to every reader takes place: the arrival of something different from what we commonly see, the arrival of the New. Be it the arrival of the circus, the fair, a ship, the press talking about the city's underbelly, the release of a summer blockbuster, a new technological device or the introduction of the next iPhone, all of these instances are brought from an "outside" into our familiar space and mindset. In the case of the novel, those who introduce the new are the quintessential outsiders for almost any European or American reader: gypsies. "Every year during the month of March a family of ragged gypsies would set up their tents near the village, and with a great uproar of pipes and kettledrums they would display new inventions. First they brought the magnet" (1). Here, just when readers, because of the contradiction of discourses in the narrator's voice, could start to distance themselves from this world—it could easily seem to be not real enough, too much inside the sandbox of fantasy—the arrival of the gypsies is portrayed in such generic terms that it works in readers' minds as a mnemonic wildcard, connecting itself with any particular memory of seeing something new in a strange place.

According to the traditional understanding of what magical realism means, people in Macondo do not experience or recognize a strict separation between what is customary and normal and what is new and marvelous. This blurring of the separation is accomplished by the blemishing of cultural, geographic or historical ideas we readers use to organize our world, rules we have agreed on or have had imposed onto us. Every time gypsies arrive to town in this chapter the narrator describes their marvels with facets of both premodern alchemical ideas and modern scientific discourses. At the end of the chapter, when the travelers bring the ice, a new moment of blurring between myth and science appears, as they declare ice to be the "most startling discovery of the sages of Memphis" (16). An alchemical train of thought may bring us to the conclusion that they are referring to Memphis, the ancient capital city of Egypt, but at the same time they could easily be referring to Memphis, Tennessee, or any other North American city whose name appeared, in small letters, on the name tag of every new machine arriving early in the twentieth century to small Caribbean towns through U.S. expansion. "What do ancient cities like Memphis or Syracuse have to do with technological innovation?" is the question flabbergasted readers, cued by a corpus of common knowledge, would ask themselves: the common assumption is that cities of the Ancient World should not have any relevance in the arrival of a technological wonder to a small tropical town. By mixing references to arcane traditions and ancient cities along with perfectly explainable scientific phenomena, the text is stripping away the monopoly that science has had on wonder since the beginning of modern times and creating a semblance of a place that is ancient and modern at the same time. The reconfiguration of discourses and organizing categories is one of the crucial aspects that have attracted readers to *One Hundred Years of Solitude* and to Magical Realism.

While this effect is marvelous for readers, it should also remind us of the solitude of understanding the world differently. The sense of wonder that people bring to the written page is left there when they close the book, and when it comes to dealing with people who accomplish the very same procedures on a daily basis, they automatically return to a medicalized understanding of phenomena. When categories of knowledge and patterns of imagination are constructed but not shared, that is when solitude is experienced—a solitude not due to an excess of imagination (as is the case for some of the novel's characters) or a lack of it (as for people with AS according to the AAA), but due to an imagination that is not communicated to others. This solitude will continue to be experienced due to the common misunderstanding of the always singular, often difficult-to-share images of the world in each AS person's mind. Beyond more precise diagnostic practices, then, we need to recover the Kantian, non-Romantic notion of imagination and regard imagination as a fundamental human characteristic that is exercised in many different ways. Close engagement with texts such as *One Hundred Years of Solitude* may provide an opening to these insights.

In his 1982 Nobel acceptance speech, García Márquez addressed Spanish America's troubled relationship with imagination and history, and how the region has been traditionally misunderstood by the West:

> Poets and beggars, musicians and prophets, warriors and scoundrels, all creatures of that unbridled reality, we have had to ask but little of imagination, for our crucial problem has been a lack of conventional means to render our lives believable. This, my friends, is the crux of our solitude.
>
> And if these difficulties, whose essence we share, hinder us, it is understandable that the rational talents on this side of

> the world, exalted in the contemplation of their own cultures, should have found themselves without valid means to interpret us. It is only natural that they insist on measuring us with the yardstick that they use for themselves, forgetting that the ravages of life are not the same for all, and that the quest of our own identity is just as arduous and bloody for us as it was for them. The interpretation of our reality through patterns not our own, serves only to make us ever more unknown, ever less free, ever more solitary.

If we were to replace in our minds "Spanish America" with the AS experience of the world for a moment (that is, a combination of individual imagination, medical diagnostic practices, and the cultural construction of AS in literature, film and other media), the abandoning of the Kantian sense of imagination reveals its consequences. Therefore, we need to recover the rich complexity of the epistemological concept of imagination, if we are to try to comprehend the AS lived experience of world-imaging (and of epistemological solitude, according to García Márquez). Only if we push the limits of our definitions of what imagination means will we be able to include these cases of blurrings of imagination into our ethical and political lives. Then, my suggestion is simple but extremely difficult at the same time: read Asperger's syndrome like a magical realist fiction, letting AS imaginations marvel us and teach us how varied and wonderfully complex the organization of the world may be.

## Notes

1. Although it has changed in recent decades, grown-up literature was realist literature, a useful genre because it dealt with real-life problems. In a certain sense, the definition—and the lack of prestige—of imaginative and/or children's literature depends on the traditional division made between childhood and adulthood, wherein the adult has to deal with problems they face in real-life, instead of retreating "like children" into imaginary worlds.

2. Magical realism as a term already existed in visual arts with Frantz Roh, in Spanish-American literature with J.L. Borges, A. Carpentier, and A. Uslar Pietri, and in Spanish-American literary criticism by Ángel Flores and Luis Leal (Cf. Zamora and Faris 1–19). My purpose here is not to go against the grain of literary history, but to shed light on a moment of the history of a literary text. It is García Márquez's book, and others that came after, that bring to most readers' mind the idea of Magical Realism, not Roh's work or Flores's criticism.

3. He has also been seen as taking advantage of the cases for his own career (Shakespeare 137), and being in a troublesome, nowhere position where the ethical codes of anthropology and medicine do not apply (Couser 7).

4. According to a Wikipedia entry, the appearance of characters in films, movies, video games, and comics who have AS and other degrees of the PDD spectrum grows every year ("List"). The list may not be complete, and if complete it is difficult to determine the objectivity of its contributors, but its very existence is a telling sign in itself.

5. Developed by Simon Baron-Cohen at the Autism Research Centre at the University of Cambridge (www.autismresearchcentre.com/arc_tests).

6. Autismsupportnetwork.com, Wrongplanet.net, Aspiesforfreedom.com are the most active.

7. Early on in the United States by McMurray (1969), and since then usually covered in monographs like Wood.

## Works Cited

Attwood, Tony. *The Complete Guide to Asperger's Syndrome*. London: Jessica Kingsley. Kindle Edition. 2006.

Autism-help.org. "Autism Spectrum Disorders Fact Sheet." *Autism-help.org*. n.p. Web. February 25, 2013.

Baron-Cohen, Simon. *Mindblindness: An Essay on Autism and Theory of Mind*. Cambridge, MA: MIT Press, 1995.

Berman, Sabina. *La mujer que buceó dentro del corazón del mundo*. Barcelona. Destino, 2012.

———. *Me, Who Dove into the Heart of the World*. Translated by Lisa Dillman Picador. New York: Holt, 2012.

Conrad, Peter. *The Medicalization of Society: On the Transformation of Human Conditions into Treatable Disorders*. Baltimore: Johns Hopkins UP, 2008.

Couser, G. Thomas. *The Cases of Oliver Sacks: The Ethics of Neuroanthropology*. Bloomington: Poynter Center, Indiana University, 2001.

Daston, Lorraine. "Fear & Loathing of the Imagination in Science." *Daedalus* 134.4 (2005): 16–30.

Ehlers, S., and Gillberg, C. "The Epidemiology of Asperger Syndrome." *Journal of Child Psychology and Psychiatry* 34.8 (1993): 1327–1350. Reprinted with Permission on OASIS @ MAAP. n.p. Web. www.aspergersyndrome.org/Articles/The-Epidemiology-of-Asperger-Syndrome—A-Total-Pop.aspx

Fitzgerald, Michael. *Autism and Creativity: Is There a Link between Autism in Men and Exceptional Ability?* New York: Brunner-Routledge, 2004.

———. *The Genesis of Artistic Creativity: Asperger's Syndrome and the Arts*. London: Jessica Kingsley, 2005.

García Márquez, Gabriel. *One Hundred Years of Solitude*. Translated by Gregory Rabassa. New York: Harper Perennial Modern Classics, 2006.

———. "Gabriel García Márquez-Nobel Lecture: The Solitude of Latin America." *Nobelprize.org*. n.p. Web. February 25, 2013.

Grandin, Temple. *Thinking in Pictures: And Other Reports from My Life with Autism*. New York: Doubleday, 1995.

———. *The Way I See It: A Personal Look at Autism & Asperger's*. Arlington, TX: Future Horizons, 2008.

Grandin, Temple, and Margaret Scariano. *Emergence: Labeled Autistic*. New York: Warner Books, 1996.

Haddon, Mark. *The Curious Incident of the Dog in the Night-Time*. New York: Doubleday, 2003.

"Imagination, n." *OED* Online. Oxford UP. n.p. Web. May 27, 2013 www.oed.com/view/Entry/91643?redirectedFrom=imagination

Kant, Immanuel. *Critique of Pure Reason*. Translated by Werner S. Pluha. Indianapolis: Hackett, 1996.

"List of fictional characters on the autism spectrum." *Wikipedia, The Free Encyclopedia*. Wikimedia Foundation. n.p. Web. February 25, 2013.

McMurray, George. "Reality and Myth in García Márquez' *Cien años de soledad*." *The Bulletin of the Rocky Mountain Modern Language Association*. 23.4 (1969): 175–181.

NINDS (National Institute of Neurological Disorders and Stroke). "NINDS Pervasive Developmental Disorders Information Page." ninds.nih.gov. n.p. Web. February 25, 2013.

Robison, John E. *Look Me in the Eye: My Life with Asperger's*. New York: Crown, 2007.

Rodman, Karen E. *Asperger's Syndrome and Adults—Is Anyone Listening?: Essays and Poems by Partners, Parents, and Family Members of Adults with Asperger Syndrome*. London: Jessica Kingsley, 2003.

Rodríguez Monegal, Emir. " 'One Hundred Years of Solitude': The Last Three Pages." *Books Abroad* 47.3 (1973): 485–489. Web. May 26, 2013.

Shakespeare, Tom. "An Anthropologist On Mars (Book)." *Disability & Society* 11.1 (1996): 137–139. SocINDEX. Web. May 27, 2013.

Tammet, Daniel. *Born on a Blue Day: Inside the Extraordinary Mind of an Autistic Savant: A Memoir*. New York: Free Press, 2007.

———. *Embracing the Wide Sky: A Tour Across the Horizons of the Mind*. New York: Free Press, 2009.

Wood, Michael. *Gabriel García Márquez: One Hundred Years of Solitude*. Cambridge: Cambridge UP, 1990.

Zamora, Lois P., and Wendy B. Faris. *Magical Realism: Theory, History, Community*. Durham, NC: Duke UP, 1995.

# Epilogue

## #YoSoy

Robert McRuer

*Libre Acceso: Latin American Literature and Film through Disability Studies* is not only an apt title for this important volume: the concept of "libre acceso" also points to the Latin American hopes and aspirations that have captured the attention of the world over the past few years. In this brief epilogue, I weave the critically disabled project of this volume—which after all concludes with a section "Imagining Other Worlds"—into those Latin American/global hopes and aspirations.

The title of my epilogue evokes the hashtag made famous on Twitter by the Mexican student movement that emerged in 2012: #YoSoy132 (I am 132). On May 11, 2012, Enrique Peña Nieto, the future president of the country and then-presidential candidate for the Partido Revolucionario Institucional (PRI), spoke to a group of students at the Ibero-American University in Mexico City. He was questioned by some of the students about civil unrest and charges of police brutality that occurred in San Salvador Atenco in 2006, when—as governor of the state of Mexico—Peña Nieto called in police to shut down a protest by local flower vendors and their supporters. The protestors had barricaded the highway leading from Atenco into a local market where the vendors had been prohibited from selling their wares. Peña Nieto called in the police to break up the protest; in the ensuing clash, two protestors were killed. Peña Nieto defended his 2006 actions as governor, but the Ibero students were not satisfied. They sharply critiqued his campaign in particular and state violence in general, and later uploaded a video of their confrontation with the candidate to YouTube.

When the major Mexican news outlets covered the events at Ibero, they reported, contrary to the facts, that the vocal critics of Peña Nieto were not actually enrolled students of the university. Legitimate students were, in other words, unrecognized and delegitimized by dominant media. In response, 131 students published another video on YouTube identifying themselves with their Ibero-American University identification cards. The video was circulated across the city, country, and world, eliciting the hashtag #YoSoy132. The statement "I am 132" indicated support for the students as well as for a burgeoning movement against police brutality, corruption, and institutionalized political power. Although in 2012 the PRI had been out of power for more than a decade, it was still perceived by the students, along with its primary rival (the Partido Acción Nacional, or PAN, which had held power since 2000), as both entrenched and corrupt. Perhaps most importantly, #YoSoy132 marked collective resistance to the ways in which the dominant media had colluded with political power structures that are—in the view of the students and their supporters—undemocratic and brutal. #YoSoy132 imagined other worlds and other representations. It also called for recognition that was necessarily both individual and transindividual. "I am" the hashtag shouted, demanding recognition and condemning willful misrecognition. But "I am" simultaneously and paradoxically meant "we are." Like students in Chile from 2011 on demanding free and accessible education for everyone, or protestors across Brazil in 2013 calling for hospitals and schools rather than multimillion dollar stadiums, the Mexican student movement insisted that "we" have another, collective, vision of openness, access, democratic inclusion, justice, and freedom.

#YoSoy132 was not, at least on the surface, a disability action, but *Libre Acceso*, this volume, similarly pivots between the call for individual recognition (and a concomitant refusal of ongoing, systemic misrecognition) and the expansive affirmation of a collective (and here, openly and generatively disabled) existence. It is, I would argue, not merely coincidental that this volume, even as it examines almost a century of cultural production, emerges from a specific historical moment when varied agents across the region are demanding and working to materialize freer, more accessible futures. Indeed, this volume posits, those imagined futures are necessarily disabled, in that they can and must take into account the full diversity of bodies and minds that compose the social both in Latin America and globally. The volume works through what Juan Manuel Espinosa calls in his chapter "an impasse of the imagination that we have not yet explored thoroughly enough." "We need," Espinosa insists, "to expand our notion of what imagination means and to use this expanded idea when trying to understand others' worldviews." We also need, as Nicola Gavioli's chapter on the implicit violences of documentary filmmaking makes clear, to call out (as the Mexican student movement did in 2012) misrepresentations or willful misrecognitions.

Thus, the volume essentially says, "Yo soy," meaning with that implicit assertion, all at once, I am, we are, and we can imagine something else, something beyond the here and now. The editors in fact structure this pivot—from individual identification or self-realization to collective reinvention—into the volume's organization. Contributions by Lina Meruane, Kevin Goldstein, and Beth Jörgensen open *Libre Acceso*, considering the varied ways in which specific authors (including Jorge Luis Borges, Meruane herself, Gabriela Brimmer, Ekiwah Adler-Beléndez) think with and through individual experiences of blindness or cerebral palsy. Attending to the work of those "who produce art from a situation of disability," Jörgensen insists in her chapter, can expand "our understanding of the complexities and the possibilities of negotiating geographies of exclusion and access in Latin America." Her consideration of both the life writing and the activism of the Mexicans Brimmer and Adler-Beléndez leads into the second major part of the book.

Following these opening chapters, essays by several contributors theorize the collective, considering what Susan Antebi calls in her chapter "an affectively and historically loaded, yet potentially open-ended moment of exchange, and hence a productively disabled intercorporeality." Valerie M. Souza and Melissa Schindler, in chapters that specifically examine cultural production in Brazil, focus on how this disabled intercorporeality is necessarily racialized, on how (in Schindler's words) "the discourses of race and disability are co-constitutive." Victoria L. Garrett, similarly, in her overview of the New Latin American Cinema of the 1960s and 1970s, locates "injurability and resulting physical alterity" as "inseparable from racial, aged, ideological, and socio-economic marginality." *Libre Acceso* the volume, and "libre acceso" more generally, thus depend on acknowledging and articulating both individualized disabled experiences and collective and varied experiences of intercorporeality.

Some of the chapters in *Libre Acceso* speak to tensions between the individual and collective or, even more provocatively, interrogate the ways in which certain forms of recognition (particularly within the context of neoliberal capitalism and globalization) are bound up with misrecognition, dispossession, and displacement. In Latin America, which continues to sustain some of the highest levels of inequality in the world, what anthropologist João Biehl calls "zones of social abandonment"—"where living beings go when they are no longer considered people" (2)—coexist with, and in many ways depend on, other zones where difference (including, at times, disabled difference) is acknowledged, recognized, and incorporated in limited ways. Biehl writes about both Brazil and impairment/disability, openly considering, for example, "how life-enhancing mobilizations for preventing and treating AIDS could take place at the same time that the public act of allowing death proliferated" (4). The public act of allowing death is evident for Biehl in the zone of social abandonment that is the specific focus of his study (a Porto Alegre asylum called Vita). Many Brazilians, however, had similar thoughts about a gap between state-sanctioned rhetoric and lived reality in 2013. They took to the streets and demanded, beneath the banner (and hashtag) of #OGiganteAcordou ("the giant has awoken"), that the state not simply cater to the whims of transnational capital as it prepared for the 2014 World Cup and 2016 Olympic Games, but rather take into account the needs (and intercorporeality) of all its citizens. Brazilians were protesting the fact that total expenditures preparing for the upcoming games could top $3 billion and that such expenditures would benefit only the few while millions of others faced inadequate care and support and lacked basic social services. When the football star Ronaldo Luís Nazário de Lima—popularly known as "il Fenômeno"—crassly suggested that "you host a World Cup with stadiums, not hospitals," one father of a child with disabilities posted his own retort on YouTube, saying that his daughter did not walk, see, or speak and that it was for citizens such as her that protestors were taking to the streets ("Em video").

Biehl's analysis resonates with the complex and contradictory ways in which embodiment and impairment materialize across Latin America. The day before International Disabled People's Day and the day after his December 1, 2012, inauguration, at the presidential residence of Los Pinos in Chapultepec Park in Mexico City, Peña Nieto—in his first official act as president—awarded the Premio Nacional de Deportes to (among others) Gustavo Sánchez, a Paralympic swimmer who won two gold medals, one silver, and one bronze at the 2012 London Games: "Este es el momento de México y vamos a hacerlo realidad. Quiero una nación sana, y fuerte, y ustedes, los deportistas son el mejor ejemplo a seguir" ("Entregan"). ("This is Mexico's moment and we are going to make it reality. I want a nation healthy and strong and you, the athletes, are the best example to follow.") Mexico's moment (a moment on December 2, 2012, of disabled recognition and incorporation), however, was inevitably haunted by what had come before and what the students had called out: corruption, state violence, and the willful misrecognition of embodied students, citizens, and activists.

Victoria Dickman-Burnett's chapter in this volume effectively conveys this double move of incorporation and dispossession. Dickman-Burnett attends to and questions Roberto Bolaño's representation in *2666* of, on one side, the spectacle of an individual artist, Edwin Johns, who severed his hand as an act of performance art and, on another side, the dozens and dozens of anonymous, maimed, and mutilated bodies of women left in fields and alleys and trash dumps in Santa Teresa, the novel's fictional version of Ciudad Juárez: "The intersection of globalization and general capitalistic excess has created a world where an entire class of people, mostly female, does not matter, and faces the marginalizing forces of global capitalism as it colonizes Santa Teresa." Many of those who do not matter in the borderlands, or who work in the *maquiladoras*, or who have been murdered in Ciudad Juárez, are or were also disabled, even if their impairments have not been recognized as disabilities by the state in the same way as, say, Gustavo Sánchez's. "Unusually high" rates of depression, for example, have been noted among women working and living in the borderlands (Brenner et al. 286). As Laura Kanost makes clear in her own contribution to *Libre Acceso*, "Mental illness is especially critical to the development of Latin American disability studies because of the prevalence of these experiences in the region and the way that they intertwine physical, social, and political factors." Indeed, I would venture to say that a Latin American disability studies, in part because of the ways in which Latin American literature and film have long engaged these issues, is primed to lead the field in a turn that it is now taking away from a central or representative focus on physical impairments and to a more thorough consideration of other impairments, including mental illness and mental disability. As Ryan Prout's chapter on Alzheimer's and María Novaro's 2010 film *Las buenas hierbas* implies, this reorientation of the field can and should come with a sharp critique of current geopolitics (in Prout's analysis, of cultural imperialism and a globalized biomedicine).

Latin America has given the world, however, from the first World Social Forum held in 2001 in Porto Alegre, Brazil, the idea that "Another World Is Possible." And *Libre Acceso* indeed concludes with an exploration of alternative forms, modes of being-in-common, and caring for and attending to each other. Even as Emily Hind's contribution in the final section makes clear that the forces of normativity in cultural forms, particularly the novel, are strong, it also demonstrates that Latin American novelists such as Mario Bellatin and Carmen Boullosa continue to reach for "boundary-defying" forms and structures. This boundary-defying volume rewrites both Latin American studies and disability studies in its exploration of new representations and its novel approaches to old representations. Both interdisciplinary fields have arguably misrecognized each other in the past few decades, to judge by how much cross-fertilization remains to be done. Yet, over and over again, *Libre Acceso* essentially presents readers with disabled figures insisting "Yo soy"—I am, we are, and we can imagine something different.

## Works Cited

Biehl, João. *Vita: Life in a Zone of Social Abandonment.* Berkeley: U of California P, 2005.

Brenner, Joel et al. "Neoliberal Trade and Investment and the Health of *Maquiladora* Workers on the U.S.-Mexico Border." In *Dying for Growth: Global Inequality and the Health of the Poor.* Edited by Jim Yong Kim et al. Monroe, ME: Common Courage Press, 2000, 261–290.

"Em video, pai dá resposta comovente à polêmica declaração de Ronaldo 'Fenômeno.'" *Hoje em Dia* June 6, 2013. Web. January 4, 2014.

"Entregan PND en Los Pinos." *Plano Deportivo* December 2, 2012. Web. January 4, 2014.

# Contributors

**Susan Antebi** is associate professor of Spanish and director of the Latin American Studies Program at the University of Toronto. She works in the areas of contemporary and twentieth-century Mexican cultural production and disability studies, and is the author of *Carnal Inscriptions: Spanish American Narratives of Corporeal Difference and Disability* (2009), and co-editor of the volume, *Digital Media, Cultural Production and Speculative Capitalism* (2011). Her current book in progress seeks to contextualize disability and the project of disability studies as integral to reading Mexican cultural and public health history, with emphasis on eugenic discourses of the post-Revolutionary period.

**Victoria Dickman-Burnett** is a PhD student in education and community-based action research at the University of Cincinnati. Her research interests include theory-driven activism and writing and action research

**Juan Manuel Espinosa** is chair of Seminario Andrés Bello, Instituto Caro y Cuervo, Bogotá. He focuses on Caribbean and Latin American intellectual and cultural histories, specifically on how sense perception gets reconfigured in these regions as they come in contact with aesthetic and epistemological theories.

**Victoria L. Garrett** is teaching assistant professor of Spanish and director of Latin American Studies at West Virginia University. She is co-author of *The Improbable Conquest: Sixteenth-Century Letters from the Río de la Plata* (2015), and she is completing a monograph on the performance of everyday life in early twentieth-century Argentine popular theater. Her articles on Latin American literature and cinema have appeared in *Arizona Journal of Hispanic Cultural Studies, Hispania,* and *Romance Quarterly.*

**Nicola Gavioli** is assistant professor of Portuguese at the Florida International University in Miami, Florida. He holds a PhD in Hispanic Languages and Literatures with an emphasis in Portuguese and Brazilian studies from the University of California Santa Barbara. Among his research interests: Portuguese and Brazilian novels; ethics, human rights and literature, and witness literature. On these topics he has published articles in academic journals in the United States and in Brazil.

**Kevin Goldstein** is a doctoral candidate in comparative literature at New York University. His research interests include the literature of the Americas, disability studies, oral poetics and mnemonics, and cognitive approaches to literature. His dissertation concerns the influence of late-onset blindness on the work of several American writers, including Jorge Luis Borges, María Josefa Mujía, and João Cabral de Melo Neto.

**Emily Hind** is associate professor of Spanish at the University of Florida, Gainesville. She specializes in Mexican studies. Her publications include: *Femmenism and the Mexican Woman Intellectual from Sor Juana to Poniatowska: Boob Lit* (2010), *Entrevistas con quince autoras mexicanas* (2003), and a second book of interviews titled *De Abenshushan a Xoconostle* (2013) featuring Mexican writers born in the 1970s. Authors treated in her recent articles include Sabina Berman, Bernardo Esquinca, Guadalupe Loaeza, Fabio Morábito, Cristina Rivera Garza, Guadalupe Amor, Carlos Fuentes, and Asunción Izquierdo Albiñana.

**Beth E. Jörgensen** is professor of Spanish at the University of Rochester. Her primary research interests include the work of Mexican women writers, the genre of the chronicle, and disability studies in Mexico. In addition to journal articles, Jörgensen is the author of *The Writing of Elena Poniatowska: Engaging Dialogues* (1994) and *Documents in Crisis: Nonfiction Literatures in 20th-Century Mexico* (2011), which was awarded the LASA Mexico Section Book Prize in the Humanities for 2010–11. She is co-editor with Ignacio Corona of *The Contemporary Mexican Chronicle: Theoretical Perspectives on the Liminal Genre* (2002).

**Laura Kanost** is associate professor of Spanish at Kansas State University. Her studies of constructions of gender and disability in Latin American literature have appeared in journals such as *Hispanic Review*, *Frontiers*, and *Hispania*. She is co-author with Elvira Sánchez-Blake of a forthcoming (2015) volume on representations of madness in narratives by contemporary Latin American women writers.

**Robert McRuer** is professor of English and chair of the Department of English at George Washington University, where he teaches critical theory, disability studies, and queer theory. He is the author of *Crip Theory: Cultural Signs of Queerness and Disability* (2006), *The Queer Renaissance: Contemporary American Literature and the Reinvention of Lesbian and Gay Identities* (NYU, 1997), and *Crip Times: Disability, Globalization, and Resistance* (forthcoming). He is co-editor of several volumes, including (with Anna Mollow) *Sex and Disability* (2012) and (with Merri Lisa Johnson) two special issues of the *Journal of Literary and Cultural Disability Studies* on the theme of "Cripistemologies."

**Lina Meruane** is a Latin American fiction writer and scholar with a PhD from New York University. Her fiction has been awarded prestigious grants, international prizes, and has been translated into several languages. Her scholarly book, first published in Spanish, was translated by Palgrave MacMillan as *Viral Voyages, Tracing Aids in Latin America* (2014). Meruane currently teaches at the Global Liberal Studies Program at New York University.

**Ryan Prout** is senior lecturer in Spanish at Cardiff University's School of Modern Languages. His publications include a monograph on Juan Goytisolo, a co-edited volume titled *Seeing in Spanish: From Don Quixote to Daddy Yankee—22 Essays on Hispanic Visual Cultures* (2011), and a forthcoming book on neuro-diversity in Spanish film and comics. He is a member of the advisory board for *Film Matters* and contributes reviews and festival reports to *Film International.*

**Melissa Schindler** is a doctoral candidate in English at the State University of New York, Buffalo. She has been a Peace Corps volunteer in Mozambique and a Fulbright scholar in Brazil. Her dissertation compares literatures of the African Diaspora in Sri Lanka, Mozambique, and Brazil.

**Valéria M. Souza** holds a PhD in Luso-Afro-Brazilian Studies & Theory from the University of Massachusetts Dartmouth. She is currently a lecturer of Portuguese at Washington University in St. Louis. She has published scholarly articles with Routledge, *Brasil/Brazil* and *Portuguese Literary & Cultural Studies* and is co-editor, with Victor K. Mendes, of *Garrett's Travels Revisited.* Her doctoral dissertation examines representations and the aesthetics of disability in Brazilian author João Guimarães Rosa's novel *Grande Sertão: Veredas.*

# Index